IDEOLOGY
AND
AMERICAN EXPERIENCE

Essays on Theory and Practice
in the United States

The Washington Institute for Values in Public Policy

The Washington Institute sponsors research that helps provide the information and fresh insights necessary for formulating policy in a democratic society. Founded in 1982, the Institute is an independent, non-profit educational and research organization which examines current and upcoming issues with particular attention to ethical implications.

ADDITIONAL TITLES

IDEOLOGY
AND
AMERICAN EXPERIENCE

Essays on Theory and Practice
in the United States

Edited by
John K. Roth and Robert C. Whittemore

A Washington Institute Book

Published in the United States by
The Washington Institute Press
1667 K Street, NW
Suite 200
Washington, DC 20006

A Washington Institute Press book

Cover design by Anne Baird

Library of Congress Cataloging-in-Publication data:

Ideology and American Experience

   Includes bibliographies and index.
   1. National characteristics, American. 2. United
States—Politics and government—Philosophy. 3. United
States—Economic conditions—Philosophy. 4. United
States—Foreign relations—Philosophy. 5. Ideology.
I. Roth, John K. II. Whittemore, Robert C. (Robert
Clifton), 1921-
E169.12.I34 1986   320.5'0973   86-13151
ISBN 0-88702-015-1
ISBN 0-88702-019-4 (pbk.)

Contents

INTRODUCTION: ONE, AND YET MANY
John K. Roth and Robert C. Whittemore   3

PART I   Ideology and American Philosophy

I. THE PHILOSOPHICAL ANTECEDENTS
OF AMERICAN IDEOLOGY
Robert C. Whittemore   13

II. IDEOLOGY, OBJECTIVITY, AND
POLITICAL THEORY
Douglas B. Rasmussen   45

III. THE REPUBLICAN IDEOLOGY
Andrew J. Reck   73

PART II   Ideology and the American Economy

IV. SELF-INTEREST AND AMERICAN IDEOLOGY
Douglas J. Den Uyl   99

V. PROPERTY RIGHTS AND THE
DECENT SOCIETY
Tibor R. Machan   121

76929

VI. IDEOLOGY AND THE AMERICAN ECONOMY
   Gordon C. Bjork   145

PART III   Ideology and America's Place in the World

VII. IDEOLOGY AND UNITED STATES
     FOREIGN POLICY
     P. Edward Haley   183

VIII. IS THERE AN AMERICAN IDEOLOGY?
      Morton A. Kaplan   211

IX. IDEOLOGY AND THE AMERICAN FUTURE:
    REFLECTIONS TOWARD PUBLIC PHILOSOPHY
    John K. Roth   229

    NOTES ON THE CONTRIBUTORS   253

    INDEX   257

INTRODUCTION

One, and Yet Many

JOHN K. ROTH and ROBERT C. WHITTEMORE

Ralph Ellison's classic, *Invisible Man*, tells the story of its unnamed narrator, a black man who seeks to understand what it means to be human and American at once. This odyssey takes him from the rural South to the heart of Harlem. It fills him with anticipation and hope, but also with disillusionment and despair. As clarity and confusion collide, ambivalence marks his quest to locate a sensible identity for himself and his nation. The outcome, however, is affirmative, and in the novel's Epilogue, Ellison sums up what his protagonist discovered. One of those themes serves well to introduce what follows in *Ideology and American Experience*.

"America," the Epilogue's voice observes, "is woven of many strands; I would recognize them and let it so remain . . . Our fate is to become one, and yet many—This is not prophecy, but description."[1] The essays published here exhibit that pattern, and the reason traces back to their origin. Inspired by Richard L. Rubenstein, President of The Washington Institute for Values in Public Policy, a task force of nine American scholars— philosophers, political scientists, economists—worked throughout 1984-85. Meeting in Phoenix, Arizona, in Washington, D.C., and in other places, this group—diverse in outlook but one in its shared concerns—discussed and wrote about a broad and crucial public policy question: In a world fraught with uncertainty and danger, what should American identity be? Our findings fill the pages ahead.

Global uncertainty and danger, we agreed, ultimately derive from the fact that people and states hold conflicting views about the nature and proper aims of human life. In addition, we sensed that Americans are more confident about the views they oppose in this regard than about the affirmative claims they want to make. Internationally, that tendency keeps the United States needlessly on the defensive, particularly against Marxist philosophies that have a much more centralized vision of reality than our nation's pluralistic ways encourage. Could we Americans do better in stating what we are for, as well as what we are against? That was one basic question that motivated our inquiry. It drove us to confront hard issues about *ideology*.

In general, ideology refers to the sociopolitical beliefs and aims characteristic of a nation or culture. Moreover, it is commonplace to say that ideological conflict divides the late twentieth-century world. True as they are, however, both of those propositions lead into a thicket of thorny problems. For example, if we think of fascism and communism as ideologies, do capitalism and even democracy belong in that category, too? If there is a Soviet ideology, is there also one that is American? And if not, should there be? Close by those parts of the thicket are others containing problems that are perhaps even more fundamental: What is the relation between ideology and truth? How does ideology differ from philosophy, if it does? What, in short, is the best way to construe ideology? And how might the answers to those questions require Americans to reconsider the character, purpose, and future of our national existence?

Such questions unified our inquiry because clear thinking about them is vital for wise public policy decisions. We found, however, that many strands persisted in our answers. Some of the differences remain. They cannot be resolved in this Introduction because they pertain to fundamentals such as the meaning of ideology itself. But that irreducible diversity contains more than itself. Within it there is agreement on crucial fundamentals and insight that can help us Americans to state more effectively our basic beliefs and the reasons for them. In the words of *Invisible Man*, thought's diversity can help "to affirm the principle on which the country was built."[2] Although the same affirmations are not all made in the same way by the contributors to this book, precisely in the mixture is to be found "the principle" that is worth affirming. Three of its facets correspond to the three sets of papers that comprise the book's major parts.

Part I, "Ideology and American Philosophy," reveals that Robert C. Whittemore, Douglas B. Rasmussen, and Andrew J. Reck do not interpret ideology in the same way, a pattern that characterizes Parts II and III as well. But as Whittemore calls for an examination of our social and epistemological suppositions, and as Rasmussen urges us not to fall prey to a skeptical relativism, there is an underwriting of Reck's thesis that "the principle" entails commitment to the "the essential ingredients of a republic as a government": law, freedom, recognition of shared civic interests, popular sovereignty, and pluralism, too.

Part II, "Ideology and the American Economy," concentrates on self-interest, property rights, and the changes that in three centuries have taken American economic life beyond the paths of agrarian colonialism to the fast lanes of technological enterprise in a global marketplace of unprecedented complexity. New conditions impel reconsideration of the assumptions on which the United States was founded, but the three essays by Douglas J. Den Uyl, Tibor R. Machan, and Gordon C. Bjork show that the American "principle" still rightly rests, in the latter's words, "on extensive private property and individual freedom to use one's property in a self-interested way."

Such beliefs lead naturally to Part III, "Ideology and America's Place in the World," for the issue of individual rights and how to use property brings the United States into a host of difficult international dilemmas that also require us to think again about individual and collective American identity. While P. Edward Haley, Morton A. Kaplan, and John K. Roth approach those considerations quite differently, they also have a shared vision about features of "the principle" that deserve remembering.

Haley refers to an American outlook that is "a compound of a belief in inalienable individual rights, representative democracy, limited and decentralized government, civilian dominance of the military, and the separation of powers." This outlook, he adds, "favors the preservation of liberty rather than governmental efficiency."

Kaplan speaks of an American belief system. He stresses, however, that it is not so much systematic as pragmatic. That is, Americans have to keep finding, self-critically, how to discern the best mix between two fundamental strands: "a high emphasis on individuality and human autonomy" on the one hand; and "a concept of public duty in support of the common weal" on the other.

Roth, in turn, urges a revival of American public philosophy, which would encourage debate on the issues raised by our American outlook or belief system, concentrating in particular on a view "which reminds us that the highest forms of social realization depend not only on the *sanctity* of the individual person's life but also on the *cooperative interdependence* of pluralistic selves." Whatever they choose to call it, these authors hold in common the conviction that a basic part of "the principle" is simply the willingness to reason together self-critically in a thoroughgoing fashion.

In sum, the essays that follow contain different definitions of terms and arguments that analyze problems from diverse angles. Their variety, however, does contain a cohering perspective: The principle worth advancing is that we Americans should ensure the strength of our republic so that it honors individual rights, including those pertaining to private property, while encouraging self-critical debate that seeks vigilantly the just balance among personal autonomy, public duty, and international responsibility. In other words, whether or not there is an American ideology, the heritage and future of the United States—and indeed the well-being of the world beyond our borders—depend largely on locating the best ways to sustain and share the affirmation of Ellison's *Invisible Man*: "Our fate is to become one, and yet many—This is not prophecy but description."

NOTES

1. Ralph Ellison, *Invisible Man* (New York: Vintage Books, 1972), p. 564. The novel was originally published in 1952.
2. Ibid., p. 561.

PART I

IDEOLOGY
AND AMERICAN
PHILOSOPHY

I

The Philosophical Antecedents
of American Ideology

—

ROBERT C. WHITTEMORE

The word "ideology" itself is of foreign origin and (with most of those who use it) is suggestive of a casuistry alien to the American way. Political pundits and social scientists who should know better almost invariably employ the term in a pejorative sense. In the etymonic sense, however, "ideology" simply denotes any systematic organization of ideas, and as such its pedigree is traceable back to the theory of eternal and unchangeable Forms expounded by Socrates in Books VI and VII of Plato's *Republic*. For Plato, these Forms, or ideas, conceived as a hierarchically ordered realm apart from and other than the visible things that imitate or recollect them, are the Real, all else being dismissible as mere appearance. To know is, therefore, to grasp discursively or intuitively the essential purport or denotation of ideas. Which being so, it follows, according to Plato, that whatever we claim to know only on the basis of our sense experience is at best belief, ordinarily opinion, and at worst illusion.[1] This Platonic Idealism, modified by Aristotle (the form is inseparable from the visible thing), restated by Plotinus (the many is a procession from and a reversion to the One), deified by Augustine (the Form of forms, the Good, is God), endures to the present day as a basic component in the cosmology of Whitehead (the elemental constituents of the universe are actual entities and eternal objects or forms). All of which is simply to say that from the strictly etymological standpoint, ideology, metaphysics, rationalism, and speculation are cognate, if not correlative, terms. Speaking somewhat more generally, Edward Shils will have it that "an ideology is the product of man's need for imposing intellectual order on the world."[2]

From Bacon to Napoleon

It is customary for historians of ideas to date the beginning of the modern era in philosophy from the publication of Descartes' *Discourse on Method* in 1637, but considered from the perspective of ideology, that honor belongs rather to Sir Francis Bacon.[3] The fragments of chapters entitled *Valerius Terminus*[4] antedate the *Discourse* by 34 years. In this early work, published in 1603, he sounds the major themes later elaborated in baroque detail in *The Two Books of Francis Bacon on the Proficience and Advancement of Learning, Divine and Human*,[5] and in his magnum opus, *Novum Organum*, namely, the limitation of knowledge to the experience of sensible and material things, the new method (observe, describe, enumerate) for the discovery of truth, the *idola* impeding human understanding, and the error inherent in the search for final causes and eternal forms. "For if any man can," he writes, "by the strength of his anticipations, find out forms, I will magnify him with the foremost,"[6] since such a one, he believes, would be himself divine. Even those who, like Socrates, have sought knowledge for itself, "and not for benefit, or ostentation, or any practicable enablement in the course of their life, have nevertheless propounded to themselves a wrong mark, namely, satisfaction, which men call truth, and not operation."[7]

If we would, then, operate to a useful end, according to Bacon, we must free ourselves from all false notions of things and from every erroneous way of looking at nature. To be specific, we must free our understandings from the idols that cloud our judgment and mislead our endeavors. These he sees as being four in kind.[8] First, there are the idols of the tribe, the propensity, that is, of mankind to suppose that there exists in nature a greater order and regularity than observation warrants. For Bacon, these idols include the Platonic insistence on ascribing reality to pure abstractions or figments of the mind. Second, there are the idols of the cave, i.e., those errors and fallacies arising from the biases of individuals. He would have us hold in suspicion whatever our minds seize and dwell upon with particular satisfaction. The third class of idols are those of the marketplace, defined by Bacon as errors growing out of the misuse of words. Herein he anticipates by three centuries the analytic and pragmatic schools of thought. For Bacon also the meaning of a term is its use; the true is that which works, that which becomes true in operation. The last class of idols distinguished are those of the theater, that is, false modes of thought derivative from suspect methods of demonstration. Bacon sees three such modes: (a) the sophistical, the exemplar of which is the Aristotelian scheme of categories; (b) the empirical, leaping to general conclusions on the basis of limited evidence; and (c) the superstitious, by which he understands the corruptions of philosophy by poetical and theological fantasies. These several idols being smashed, the way becomes clear for the inauguration of the new method.

The new method itself, practiced and advocated for thirteen generations by the doyens of British and American empiricism, is today taken for granted. Philosophers and scientists alike presuppose the Baconian operations of observation, description, and enumeration. Whitehead speaks for all in noting that "the elucidation of immediate experience is the sole justification for any thought; and the starting-point for thought is the analytic observation of components of this experience."[9] But he is quick to add that the method of rigid empiricism if consistently pursued must leave not only philosophy but science where it found them, and that because Bacon has forgotten one vitally important element of investigation. "What Bacon omitted was the play of a free imagination, controlled by the requirements of coherence and logic."[10] For Whitehead, it is not the least of the merits of John Locke[11] that he recognizes this missing ingredient, thereby anticipating by two centuries one main feature of process thought. To his view, "the enduring importance of Locke's work comes from the candour, clarity, and adequacy with which he stated the evidence, uninfluenced by the bias of metaphysical theory."[12] This is why, in both the eighteenth-century school of ideology and its nineteenth-century critics, the pervasive methodology and influence is not that of Bacon but of Locke.

In the Baconian spirit, he assays in the four books comprising *An Essay Concerning Human Understanding*:[13]

> To inquire into the original, certainty, and extent of *human knowledge*, together with the grounds and degrees of *belief*, *opinion*, and *assent*;—I shall not at present meddle with the physical consideration of the mind . . . or by what motions of our spirits or alterations of our bodies we come to have any *sensation* by our organs. . . . These are speculations. . . . I shall decline, as lying out of my way. . . . It shall suffice to my present purpose, to consider the discerning faculties of a man, as they are employed about the objects which they have to do with.[14]

These "objects," in Locke's lexicon, are ideas. How is it, then, the mind comes to be furnished with them? That is, for Locke, the primordial question, and it is not, he thinks, answered adequately or at all by assuming as the Platonists and their theological progeny are wont to do, that we come into this world with certain innate principles and primary notions already imprinted on our minds and stamped upon our souls. For were that true, all men might with equal facility claim to possess knowledge, and the want of it in children and idiots, not to mention the utter lack of agreement among men with respect to the substance of these notions and principles, suffices to destroy that claim.

But if there are no innate ideas, then we are left with the supposition that in its origin the mind is like unto an "empty cabinet" or a sheet of blank white paper. How, then, does it come to possess ideas? "To this I answer," says Locke, "in one word, from EXPERIENCE. In that all our knowledge is founded; and from that it ultimately derives itself. Our observation employed either, about external sensible objects, or about the internal operations of our minds perceived and reflected on by ourselves is that which supplies our understandings with all the *materials* of thinking. These two are the fountains of knowledge, from whence all the ideas we have, or can naturally have, do spring."[15] First, our senses convey into the mind the perception of things external. Subsequently, the soul comes to reflect upon and consider the ideas we have of those things, comparing, combining, compounding the simple into the complex in myriad manners. In this way is the complete inventory of all of our ideas without exception derived. "These two, I say, *viz*, external material things, as the objects of SENSATION, and the operations of our own minds within, as the objects of REFLECTION, are to me the only originals from whence all our ideas take their beginnings."[16]

If this is so, what meaning, if any, can there be to abstract ideas, that is, ideas abstracted from time and place as common names or terms applicable to every member of a species or genus, or to ideas indifferent to place and time such as the ideas of a pure mathematics? And what of those ideas professedly immaterial such as the idea of soul or the conception of God? How, given Locke's assumption, do we come by these notions? Moreover, by what criteria do we establish that an idea is true or false or meaningless? Locke's answers to these and other cognate questions take up most of Book IV of the *Essay*, and were our specific concern with the merits of Lockean sensationalism rather than, as it is, with its *influence* on the rise of ideology, it would be incumbent upon us to assess the adequacy of his answers in some detail. But ideology, for all that it presupposes a theory of knowledge and, as we shall see, deserves in the final analysis to be judged on the basis of the cogency of that theory, is not yet identical with it, nor is it, in the philosophy of Locke, so far even manifest.

Nevertheless, Locke's influence on the ideologies of the modern West has been pervasive, and that not only with respect to the subsequent course of British empiricist thought. The argument of his *Two Treatises on Government* is echoed in the American Declaration of Independence and in the American Constitution's provision for the separation of church and state.[17] *Some Thoughts Concerning Education* is modern in its emphasis on education for living as opposed to rote learning. His three *Letters Concerning Toleration* vindicate freedom of opinion in matters of religion. In colonial America his epistemology dictated the case for a consistent Calvinism; in France, no less than in Great Britain, his sensationalism is seminal.

According to Locke, we can know of the existence of things and persons other than ourselves only by sensation: "No particular man can know the existence of any other being, but only when, by actual operating upon him, it makes itself perceived by him. . . . Concerning the existence of finite spirits, as well as several other things, we must content ourselves with the evidence of faith."[18] To the mind of Locke's foremost French interpreter, however, the evidence of faith is no evidence at all, nor, Condillac argues in his *Traité des sensations*,[19] is the evidence of our minds, as the objects of reflection, in any better case; and that because there can be no such thing as a second independent source of ideas if once we have allowed that sensation is all. If we study our senses separately, carefully distinguishing which of our ideas we owe to each sense, and noting just how it is that the senses reinforce each other, the result will reveal that all human knowledge is transformed sensation only, that, indeed, the so-called faculty of reflection itself is simply sensation hypostatized. And as it is with reflection, so also, Condillac thinks, is the case with memory and the passions; these too are nothing but sensation transformed.

This sensationalist principle, strictly applied, provides a rationale for discarding not only the metaphysics of the past, but also that vision of society founded upon the verities of the Christian faith and the inequality before God of the several estates or classes of mankind. If sensation is all, then all men are equal in the possibility of knowledge, and if in knowledge why not in everything else? In eighteenth-century France, the seed of sensationalism, transformed by Condillac into sensualism, fostered the social skepticism of Voltaire,[20] the democratic romanticism of Rousseau,[21] and the hylozoistic materialism of Diderot.[22] These pillars of the French Enlightenment, together with others like-minded of lesser philosophical status,[23] articulated the arguments which in the closing

decade of the century inspired a disparate group of theorists[24] to believe
in the possibility of a new social and political order grounded upon a
new empirical science of ideas. One of their number, Destutt de Tracy,[25]
proposed as the most appropriate name for the new science, the new
word "ideology"—"appropriate" because to de Tracy's view, the word,
being original, did not hint of anything doubtful or unknown, nor did
it bring to mind the discredited notion of cause; "appropriate" because
"ideology" is the literal translation of "science of ideas."

As Emmet Kennedy has made clear in his recent and definitive study
of de Tracy, the term as envisioned by "the last of *les philosophes*" was
never intended to designate simply the theory of ideas as opposed to
their practical application. On the contrary, ideology was to be "positive,
useful, and susceptible of rigorous exactitude."[26] Like Bacon, de Tracy's
conception embraced the notion of a purely naturalistic unity of sciences
as a system of science. Unfortunately, that was not to be, not in his time
nor yet in our own. Nor has "ideology" retained the neutral denotation envisaged at its coining. The social and political reforms proposed
by the school of ideology, culminating in the republican constitution
of 18 Brumaire (November, 1799), engaged the vigorous opposition of
Bonaparte, who saw in them a direct challenge to his assumption of
consular powers. To discredit his ideological opponents he resorted to
ridicule. The ideologist's disparagement of metaphysics was now visited
on ideology. In the vocabulary of Napoleon, *les idéologistes* became
ideologues, that is, sectarians and subversives as opposed to factionally
neutral social scientists.[27] This pejorative usage, initiated by the Cor-
sican and his coterie, afterwards reinforced in the polemics of Marx and
his posterity, still taints the term. In our time, de Tracy's vision of a
neutral system of ideas scientifically validated has given way to the notion of ideology as visionary, partisan speculation. Modern definitions
vary rather widely. Every writer on the subject has one of his own to
offer. But there is hardly one among them, or indeed any contemporary
advocate of political and social action, willing to confess to the name.
The sociologists have an aphorism that says it all: "I have a social
philosophy; you have political opinions; he has an ideology."

Early American Developments

The antipathy of Napoleon to that ideology which he conceived of
as tending to undermine his aspirations to empire, effectively ended the

hopes of de Tracy and his colleagues to effectuate the reform of the social and political institutions of France through the agency of the new science of ideas. But if not in France, perhaps in the new American republic? Might not the President of the United States *and* of the American Philosophical Society be precisely the man needed to inaugurate the envisaged new age? Jefferson was known to them from his various missions to France on behalf of American independence. Franklin was an old acquaintance, and the Marquis de Lafayette, their intermediary, was both friend and sympathizer with the program of ideology. In 1806 de Tracy dispatched the manuscript of his *Eléments d'idéologie* to Jefferson with a letter explaining that political circumstances in France forbade its appearance there and seeking the President's good offices on behalf of an English translation and American publication. Jefferson, nothing loth, sent it to his friend Duane, the Philadelphia publisher, who arranged for a translation and returned it to Jefferson, who in turn revised some passages and wrote a brief introduction. Although he never professed a commitment to ideology, he did share de Tracy's passionate attachment to republicanism and so far sympathized with the latter's views on economic philosophy as to undertake a decade later the translation of de Tracy's *Traité d' economie politique*. Alas, even Jefferson's influence could not suffice to awaken Americans to the virtues of ideology. No one was converted, or, if they were, they kept silent about it. One lone voice was raised. Elihu Palmer prophesied a renovation in the moral situation of man conditional upon his acceptance of the principles of "civil science,"[28] but no one took heed. Of course, it is arguable that the philosophy of Locke, ingredient in the consistent Calvinism of Jonathan Edwards and Timothy Dwight and in the Preamble to the Declaration, was *de facto* an ideology in de Tracy's sense, if not in that of Napoleon; but none then identified it as such, and none opposed it until John C. Calhoun, the "cast-iron southerner" arose in the Senate to propound his theory of the concurrent majority and the ideology of States Rights.

Doctrine and theory alike, in Calhoun's view, find their ultimate justification in the Declaration and the Constitution. So far, then, the underlying philosophy is, as before, that of Locke, albeit Calhoun reasons to a conclusion, the right of the several states to secede from the federal union, that Locke might have hesitated to support, at least based on the reason given for justifying that secession, namely, slavery. Granting that the authors of the Constitution intended to create a federal union, that is, a union of sovereign states united through a central agency, it

follows from this intention, according to Calhoun, that the right of each
of the several states to safeguard its own particular sovereignty is reserved
to the individual state. This right presupposes that of nullification, the
right, that is, of each state to repudiate any federal statute it deems inimical to its own best interests. Nullification in turn presumes the right
of secession, i.e., the right of the state to withdraw from the federal partnership. Secession, as Calhoun understands it, is justified whenever the
very life of the state is threatened, as it was by the proposal to abolish
slavery. The South in general and South Carolina in particular simply
could not abandon an institution on which the economic life of the
community was utterly dependent. The North, for its part, even as it
recognized the economic necessity of slavery, found it morally intolerable.
As in all such impasse situations, so too in this one; economic necessity found moral justification. Thus the necessary evil becomes in Calhoun's
public pronouncements after 1836 the positive good. The basic premise
by which this conclusion is attained is the natural inferiority of the Negro
race. The authority for this premise Calhoun thinks to have found in
the *Politics* of Aristotle. With Aristotle, he believes that some men are
slaves by nature, just as other men are naturally free. For the shibboleth
that all men are born equal he has only scorn. "Taking the proposition
literally (it is in that sense it is understood) there is not a word of truth
in it. . . . Men are not born. Infants are born. . . . They are not born
free. While infants they are incapable of freedom. . . . Nor is it less false
that they are born "equal." They are not so in any sense in which it
can be regarded. . . . "[29] The Declaration asserts that all men are *created*
equal, but this, Calhoun argues, is no less erroneous. It is, therefore,

> . . . a great and dangerous error to suppose that all people are equally entitled
> to liberty. It is a reward to be earned, not a blessing to be gratuitously lavished
> on all alike—a reward reserved for the intelligent, the patriotic, the virtuous and
> deserving—and not a boon to be bestowed on a people too ignorant, degraded
> and vicious, to be capable either of appreciation or of enjoying it.[30]

The rhetoric is objectionable. The point of view is pernicious. Many,
I suspect, would willingly dismiss Calhoun's arguments as gratuitous
political opinion. Calhoun himself, invoking the massive authority of
Aristotle,[31] would, of a certainty, characterize his position as philosophical. I submit, however, that it is neither philosophical nor yet opinion-
ated pilpul, but, rather, ideological in the sense defined by Edward Shils.
According to Shils, the central features of an ideology (as distinguished

from outlooks, creeds, thought-systems, movements, and intellectual programs) are (a) a high degree of explicitness and authoritative promulgation centered about one or more preeminent values or ideals diverging from or alien to the prevailing social order, and (b) a passionate concern to bring to pass the realization of these values or ideals. *All* ideologies, as Shils conceives them, arise in conditions of crisis and "entail an aggressive alienation from the existing society: they recommend the transformation of the lives of their exponents in accordance with specific principles; they insist on consistency and thoroughgoingness in their exponent's application of principles; and they recommend either their adherents' complete dominion over the societies in which they live or their total self-protective withdrawal from these societies."[32] Measured by these criteria, it would seem that the social philosophy of Calhoun is very properly characterized as ideological. In the polemics of John C. Calhoun we find the first systematic variant of a nascent American conservative ideology.

From Hegel to Marx

In the Preface to his *Philosophy of Right*,[33] published in 1821, Hegel is careful to remind his reader of the obvious, i.e., that every philosophy, including this one, is necessarily a product of its own times, conditioned by the regnant morality and cultural shibboleths common to the age and to the society in which it appears. "It is," he writes,

> just as absurd to fancy that a philosophy can transcend its contemporary world as it is to fancy that an individual can overleap his own age. . . . If his theory really goes beyond the world as it is and builds an ideal one as it ought to be, that world exists indeed, but only in his opinions, an unsubstantial element where anything you please may, in fancy, be built.[34]

In light of the transformation wrought in Hegelianism by those who undertook to correct its principles to the point of contradicting them, it is essential to keep Hegel's reminder firmly to the forefront in what follows, the more so as these critics of Hegel, collectively known as the Young Hegelians,[35] were one and all convinced that their own several visions of reality were, unlike those of their teacher, presuppositionless and culturally unconditioned.

They were all very young men imbued, like Destutt de Tracy and his fellow ideologists, with a zeal to remake the world, specifically the theologically and politically conservative German world whose intellectual champion was Professor Hegel. Their advance beyond Hegel was in the first instance a relentless critique of religion in general and the Christian religion in particular. They started from real religion and actual theology. No less than the Old Hegelians, they took for granted the authority of divinity, but where the former were prepared to accept the Hegelian interpretation of Christian dogma as the truth of Spirit, the Young Hegelians saw in it only myth and illusion. Man, argues Feuerbach, creates God in his own image, then falls to his knees in worship of his own creation. The young Marx is equally blunt: "Man, who has found only his own reflection in the fantastic reality of heaven, where he sought a supernatural being, will no longer be disposed to find only the semblance of himself, only a non-human being, here where he seeks and must seek his true reality."[36] "In direct contrast to German philosophy (i.e., Hegelianism) which descends from heaven to earth, here we ascend from earth to heaven."[37]

Yet even as he associates himself with the Young Hegelian critique of religion, Marx sees the "parochial narrowness" of their position.[38] With Hegel they take all thought to be but the product of consciousness. Consequently, their critique is limited to the demand that consciousness be transformed out of its Hegelian mode into one more specifically humanistic, atheistic, or even egoistic. Herein, Marx believes, they remain inherently bourgeois: "Their bleating merely imitates in a philosophic form the conceptions of the German middle class."[39]

> The most recent of them have found the correct expression for their activity when they declare they are only fighting against *"phrases."* They forget, however, that to these phrases they themselves are only opposing other phrases, and that they are in no way combating the real existing world when they are merely combating the phrases of this world.[40]

In their preoccupation with "phrases" to the exclusion of German reality, they share in the religious illusion of the epoch and make that the driving force of history. Following the fashion of Destutt de Tracy and his coterie, they have abandoned the realm of real history to constitute themselves a school of German ideology, a school and a term that, in the lexicon of Marx, becomes a putdown.

If Marx is right, if consciousness can never be anything else but conscious *existence*, if the existence of real, active men is nothing other than their *actual life-process*, then, obviously, any philosophy which presumes to reduce reality to a form of consciousness is deserving of contempt. For as Marx notes, "life is not determined by consciousness, but consciousness by life."[41] Kierkegaard, in his *Concluding Unscientific Postscript*, written in the same year as *The German Ideology*, makes the same point, and in both books it is simply assumed that Hegel is ignorant of this fundamental existential truth. To label his work and that of his posterity as ideology is, therefore, to identify it as false consciousness, false to the degree that it ignores or denies the existent as such. Thus at a blow "morality, religion, metaphysics, all the rest of ideology and their corresponding forms of consciousness"[42] become of no account—if Marx is right.

That Marx is right, at least as far as concerns his understanding of the basic presupposition underlying speculation,[43] is highly doubtful. The existentialist critique of Hegel has not survived the careful inspection of recent scholarship. Kierkegaard to the contrary, an existential system is not impossible.[44] Not Kierkegaard, nor even Marx, but their great master, Hegel, is, according to Richard Kroner, "the inaugurator of existential philosophy."[45] Paul Ramsey concurs: "Before it became a logic, the philosophy of Hegel was an existentialism; even as logic, it is," he insists, "a logic of movement."[46] What Hegel called speculation, and Marx dismisses as ideology or false consciousness, has in our time emerged as the philosophical analogue of the world view of modern physics, and as such the superior claimant to that truth "which is empirically verifiable and bound to material premises."[47]

It remains to note Marx's alternative conception of ideology as class apologetics. As earlier, in Part One of *The German Ideology*, he has professed to find in the writings of the Young Hegelians the epitome of ideology as false consciousness, so in Part Three he claims to see in English political economy the epitome of ideology as apologia. The vituperation before visited on Feuerbach and Stirner, now falls upon Bentham, Burke, and Malthus. The assumption throughout is that no social philosophy other than that of Marx and his disciples is or can be class-neutral. As before, it is a proposition of dubious validity.

Social Darwinism and William Graham Sumner

In his lifetime Marx gained no significant American converts. Such concern for the plight of the proletariat as was manifest in the decades preceding the Civil War found expression not in any clash of social classes but in utopianism. Brook Farm, Fruitlands, New Harmony, Nashoba—all owed their origin to the dream of a free society of free men and women, freely sharing their goods, their work, and, to the eternal scandal of respectable society, themselves one with another without respect to sex or race. These and other less radical experiments in communal living flourished briefly and died away leaving no enduring ideology behind to mark their passage. It was not until after the war, and the popularization of the theory and metaphysics of evolution in the writings of Herbert Spencer and his American disciple John Fiske, that a new social philosophy emerged, a philosophy whose root idea was to exert an abiding ideological influence.

Social Darwinism, as it came to be called, had its origin in Darwin's and Spencer's conviction that what was true of nature as a whole could not be false of nature's social part. If they were right, then the factors controlling the life of man in society, their followers thought, must be identical with those governing every evolutionary process. The struggle for existence, culminating in the survival of the fittest, was, then, as true of society as of the jungle. If only the fittest deserved to survive, obviously those who lost out in the competitive struggle had no cause for complaint. Exploitation was nature's way, and *laissez-faire* capitalism its social manner of expression. Anything, therefore, that interfered with the free development of economic competition was not only unnatural but immoral, since it must inevitably end in the preservation of the unfit. More than this, it must end by destroying liberty, for liberty, as the Social Darwinist conceives it, is simply the freedom to do one's best to triumph in the struggle for existence. To refuse to any man his right to win is, he believes, tantamount to denying the cardinal condition making for social progress. The idea that social progress is identifiable with social equality is rejected completely. It is unknown in nature and never illustrated in history. The fact of the matter, observes William Graham Sumner,[48] "is that when laws and customs are made with a view to equality they crush out progress."[49] It is, he thinks, high time that socialists and reformers face up to the challenge of facts. That competition is a law of nature is a fact.

> If we do not like it, and if we try to amend it, there is only one way in which we can do it. We can take from the better and give to the worse. . . . We shall thus lessen the inequalities. We shall favor the survival of the unfittest, and we shall accomplish this by destroying liberty.[50]

To demonstrate the truth of this conviction was Sumner's one grand aim, and the zeal with which he pursued it through a dozen books and numerous articles made him the natural leader of those who found in Social Darwinism their philosophical justification and in free-enterprise capitalism their ideology.

The Marxists hold out the promise of a golden future when capitalism will have been swept away, but, Sumner notes, how this is to be accomplished without the instrumentality of capital they do not say. "In attacking capital they are simply attacking the foundations of civilization, and every socialistic scheme which has ever been proposed, so far as it has lessened the motives to saving or the security of capital, is anti-social and anti-civilizing."[51] In sum, "the maxim or injunction, to which a study of capital leads us is, Get Capital."[52] This, according to Sumner, is the first and great social commandment, and the second is like unto it: Use capital to better your position in the struggle for existence.

It has been said that this is monstrous doctrine; that Christian charity no less than democratic morality demands that we should help one another to the end that the race itself might socially advance. The truth is, says Sumner, that we owe to each other only such help as consists in helping others to help themselves. As we have no duty to mind other people's business, so they have no right to share ours. "There is a beautiful notion afloat in our literature and in the minds of our people that men are born to certain 'natural rights.' If that were true, there would be something on earth which was got for nothing, and this world would not be the place it is at all. The fact is," he concludes, "that there can be no rights against Nature, except to get out of her whatever we can, which is only the fact of the struggle for existence stated over again."[53] "Nature's forces know no pity. Just so in sociology. The forces know no pity."[54]

The forces are facts, and facts, not motives, purposes, or ideals, are the subject matter of the science of society. Herein, Sumner maintains, lies the fundamental distinction between socialism and sociology. The socialist is free to consider society as he would wish that it were; the unproven panacea is his stock in trade. The socialist can and does irresponsibly refuse the challenge of facts; if necessary he will kill society to cure it. No such option is open to the sociologist. "The sound student of sociology can hold out to mankind, as individuals or as a race, only one hope of better and happier living. That hope," as Sumner sees it, "lies in an enhancement of the industrial virtues (industry, frugality, prudence, and temperance) and of the moral forces which thence arise."[55] Fortunately for society, there are those who daily cultivate these virtues in quiet anonymity. Since they invariably mind their own business they are forgotten by all save the tax collector. Yet on the backs of these forgotten men the burden of society rests; for it is they who produce the national wealth which the reformers and politicians so lightly give away; it is they who are the life and substance of society. All of us have known the man Sumner describes.

> He works, he votes, generally he prays—but he always pays—yes, above all, he pays. . . . He keeps production going on. He contributes to the strength of parties. . . . He is strongly patriotic. . . . He may grumble some to his wife or family, but he does not frequent the grocery or talk politics at the tavern. Consequently, he is forgotten. He is a commonplace man. He excites no admiration. He is not in any way a hero. . . . nor a burden. . . . nor an object out of which social capital may be made. . . . nor one over whom sentimental economists and statesmen can parade their fine sentiments. Therefore he is forgotten. All the burdens fall on him, or on her, for it is time to remember that the Forgotten Man is not seldom a woman.[56]

Long years after Sumner's death, Franklin Delano Roosevelt would misappropriate his phrase to characterize the one third of a nation then "ill-fed, ill-housed, and ill-clothed," but Roosevelt's "forgotten man" only served to focus attention away from the men and women who really were, and are still, forgotten, the two-thirds who, in Sumner's bitter words, are "weighed down with the cost and burden of the scheme for making everybody happy."

Still, the poor and weak, the misfit and the unfit, are always with us. Does society owe anything at all to such as these? No, answers Sumner:

> It is totally false that one who has done [his share] is bound to bear the care and charge of those who are wretched because they have not done so. The silly popular notion is that the beggars live at the expense of the rich, but the truth is that those who eat and produce not, live at the expense of those who labor and produce.[57]

Let those who can, then, work; and those who will not work, let them remember that "this is a world in which the rule is, 'Root, hog, or die.' "[58]

There is, of course, much more to Sumner than this. He was a curmudgeon to be sure, but he also was and remains the most lucid and logical exponent of free trade and free enterprise that America has yet produced. His importance in the history of American ideology is attested by the fact that three-quarters of a century after his death, most of his work remains in print providing live ammunition for conservative ideologues.

The Social Theory of Lester Frank Ward

It is a peculiarity of Americans that they tend to overvalue philosophies and ideologies of foreign origin even as they are prone to disparage the achievements of native thinkers. This is certainly true as respects the work of Sumner, who has remained a prophet without much honor in his own country, and it is even more true as regards the reputation of Lester Frank Ward.[59] "The American Aristotle," his biographer has called him, and the title is not undeserved, for Ward too was a master of those who know. During his forty years as a civil servant he did important work in statistics, botany, paleobotany, and geology. Throughout these years he was also writing the pioneering tomes which were to seal his claim to be the founder of the sociology of knowledge.

Like his contemporary, Sumner, he was more appreciated abroad than at home. Ludwig Gumplowicz, the famous Austrian sociologist, accounted him a giant among scholars. Spencer corresponded with him for twenty years; he was honored by the French, and the Russians burned the first volume of his *Dynamic Sociology*. Conversely, America was hardly aware of his existence. Neglected in his lifetime by all save a handful of professors and professional scientists, in death he has been consigned to an undeserved oblivion.

To see why is at once to understand the narrow conservatism of the American mind. To begin with, Ward was a nonconformist. His ideas fitted into no established patterns of thought. His sociocracy sounded to American ears too much like socialism; his attacks on the social evils of capitalism struck staunch conservatives as subversive. Nor did he show forth the reassuring character of a Christian believer. In his youth he had been such, but as his mastery of science grew, his faith fell away, as did the Christian claim to uniqueness when viewed in the cold light of the sociology of evolution. In sum, he was, as the title of the periodical he edited during the early seventies proclaimed, an iconoclast, and Americans, even professorial Americans, have never taken kindly to the breed.

His crime in the eyes of the professors was simple yet sufficient: he belonged to no one discipline. To the physical scientists he was too much the sociologist; the sociologists thought him too philosophical; as for the philosophers, misled by the titles of his books, they never thought of him at all. And yet, the world view of Lester Frank Ward may well be, when all is said, the most important philosophical synthesis yet produced by an American.

Ward was a professional scientist. To his way of thinking the sole business of science was the elucidation of the real, and the real, including man, is, for Ward, matter. "Besides matter itself, only the relations of matter can be conceived to exist."[60] Matter moves. This is the fundamental fact on which every sound world view builds. Energy seizes upon matter and expresses itself as motion. To the question, "Why?" no answer is possible. Matter in motion, says Ward, is simply what it appears to be. The task of the scientist is rather to explain the "how."

Matter moves, and gradually the material molecules contract into the inorganic aggregations which constitute the subject matters of astronomy, physics, chemistry, and geology. It develops in complexity, and eventually into those organic aggregations which are the topics of biology, anthropology, and psychology. When it becomes protoplasm, life begins. "The great truth that now comes squarely home to us is that *life is a property of matter*. It is simply the result of the movements going on among the molecules composing a mass of protoplasm. It is a phenomenon presented by this most highly complex form of matter, and which is never absent from it."[61]

That such frank materialism was bound to offend the sensibilities of the tender-minded, Ward well knew. With these, however, he was not especially concerned. The several hundred pages in *Dynamic Sociology* and others of his writings devoted to the scientific justification of his conclusion were not so much designed to persuade the average reader as they were to lay a firm foundation for the refutation of the Spencerian understanding of evolution presupposed by Social Darwinism. If the case for sociocracy was to be successfully made against the rugged individualism and *laissez faire* proclaimed by Sumner and his followers, the scientific facts had to be made clear. One fact in particular had Spencer and his American disciples misunderstood, which failure, as Ward saw it, invalidated the whole of Social Darwinism. What they had failed to grasp was the nature and significance of the human mind in social evolution.

From matter, mind arises. Mind is a state of matter. Only recognize this, Ward argues, and the so-called "mystery of mind" dissolves. For Spencer and Sumner notwithstanding, the mind is not a mysterious something of whose kinships we must be forever ignorant. On the contrary, its laws are as discoverable as those of matter. In fact, "they are the laws of matter in its most highly developed form."[62] Just how and when mind evolved out of living matter (protoplasm), Ward does not profess to know. He is, however, certain that its evolution is a matter of feeling. What men untrained in the biology of the mind call reason is, then, simply the end product of the evolution of feeling. Not intellect but feeling is, then, the dynamic basis of society. A true philosophy of man and society will, therefore, begin with the recognition of feeling as the force that explains them both.

According to the Social Darwinists, the forces that animate and motivate society are essentially those governing and activating all of nature, namely, those vital forces that biology discovers. Which being so, the law of society, no less than that of the jungle, is the survival of the fittest or, economically speaking, *laissez faire*. This conclusion, whose implications Sumner had made plain in his *Social Classes*, the reformer in Ward would not allow him to abide, any more than the scientist in him would permit him to admit that sociology was not a science. There had to be a way around the Spencerian theory of society, and as it turned out there was. The key to the solution of the problem Ward saw in the fact of nature's total indifference to feeling and pleasure. The end of nature is function, i.e., life. Whether or not the organism enjoys or suffers its life is no part of nature's aim. It functions to proliferate life; its end is purely biological. From the standpoint of the higher organisms including man, however, exactly the opposite holds true. For man, function is simply a means to feeling. The end of every higher organism, including man, is the satisfaction of its desires. It seeks not merely to live but to enjoy. To this end mind is born. Through the dynamic agency of desire the vital forces are transmuted into psychic forces. Given, then, that the social forces are psychic forces, we may conclude, says Ward, that the science properly foundational to sociology is not, as the Social Darwinists preach, biology, but rather psychology. It matters not that psychology rests in its turn upon biology. Once admit that the natural forces inspiring social activity are psychic rather than vital, and the scientific case for *laissez faire* collapses.

For the fact is, Ward insists, that men are not powerless pawns driven by forces over which they have no control. On the contrary, all that man has accomplished in the course of civilization is owing entirely to his refusal to let nature take its senseless course. Society, properly understood, is the product of mind functioning dynamically to secure the satisfaction of its desires, and directively to insure that these desires are such as conduce to social progress. In our time, the writings of Bergson, Whitehead, and Bradley have done much to justify Ward's theory of mind as feeling generating intellect. Had he lived to read their various vindications of his ideas, Ward would have been greatly pleased if not overly impressed. For his vision was and is greater than that of his successors. He realized clearly what no American thinker save perhaps John Dewey has seemed to realize at all, that society must evolve as mind evolves, as ideologies evolve and the social forces fall under the control of reason. We are, as he was fond of saying, socially still stone-age savages compared to what it lies within our social power to become.

How is this millennium to be brought to pass? Ward's answer is education. "Give society education . . . and all things else will be added."[63] What matters is that every citizen should have *information* of those great scientific truths on which the future of society depends. This alone, he argues, is deserving of dissemination. That culture which commonly passes for knowledge among cultivated men is, he feels, a luxury society can well do without. The task is, by education in science, to transform the environment so as to bring within the range of all that knowledge which is at present the monopoly of the fortunate few. To the objection that it is manifestly impossible to educate every man up to even the present level of the intelligentsia, Ward's answer is that this is not what he is proposing. Not the details but the basic principles of science are what the ignorant need to master. Granted that not every man or woman is capable of appreciating the subtler nuances of Darwinian theory, still, virtually all are capable of grasping the essential idea of evolution. Since government alone has at present the resources and authority to ensure that these basic principles reach those who need to know, it follows that education must be public; since the ignorant cannot be expected to immediately appreciate the boon that is being conferred upon them, it must be compulsory and universal. This faith in education as "the great panacea," Ward never lost. From his first book to his last, his hope for a better society rides with the democratization of knowledge. "To the developed intellect nature is as clay in the potter's hands. . . . It is what man makes it, and rational man always seeks to make it better. The true doctrine therefore is *meliorism*—the perpetual bettering of man's estate."[64] Its end is sociocracy—man's estate brought under scientific control by the collective mind of society itself.

The formula for sociocracy is society acting for itself. As the individual acts now in his own best interests, so society in the sociocratic state will imagine itself as an individual, and becoming fully *conscious* of those interests it [will] pursue them with the same indomitable *will* with which the individual pursues his interests. . . . In a word, society [will] do under the same circumstances just what an intelligent individual would do. It would further, in all possible ways, its own interests.[65]

This sounds like socialism, and many, some among them Ward's disciples, have so interpreted it. Ward himself, however, denied the identification. The difference between socialism and sociocracy as he understood it, is precisely that between a collectivism artificially imposed and one naturally evolved. Whereas the socialist would abolish all artificial inequalities by legislative fiat, the sociocrat is content to arrive at equality via the gradual process of social evolution. He sees, as the socialist does not, that the end is not to be had without the means, that society can no more be reformed from the top down than a house can be begun with the roof. "It is," he writes,

high time for socialists to perceive that, as a rule, they are working at the roof instead of at the foundation of the structure they desire to erect. Not that much of the material which they are now elaborating will not "come in play" when society is ready to use it, but that their time would be better spent in working out the basal principles which will render social reform possible.[66]

In short, take care of the means (education), and the end (collectivism) will take care of itself.

As a practicing scientist and an eminently practical man, Ward knew better than to try to pin down the shape of the future. Just how sociocracy will come to pass, or when, he did not venture to predict. Most probably it will emerge out of democracy, since democracy as it ought to be would, to Ward's view, already be sociocracy. For democracy, understood as government of, by, and for *all* the people, plainly implies collectivism. Thus from here to sociocracy, if Ward is right, it is only a matter of time. Which being so, if Ward is right he who would espouse democracy ought to abandon free enterprise since this latter is manifestly incompatible with any consistent collectivism. That Ward is right, the conservative attitude towards democracy bears witness. For conservatives, forced to a choice between free enterprise and democracy, have invariably opted to abandon the latter. For Hamilton, Calhoun, and Sumner alike, the truth is that our form of government is not a democracy but a republic. Moreover, if free enterprise is, as many conservatives assume, in principle synonymous with patriotism, then democracy, like every other form of collectivism, ought to be rejected as un-American.

Whether or not democracy is un-American is a question we cannot here undertake to decide. Certainly Ward did not think so. Unlike many Americans today, he was not prepared to concede that any scientific theory of society must be, by definition, Marxist. Indeed, for Ward, the hallmark of any science, social or physical, is precisely its independence of any ideology. In that, he is surely mistaken, since like Marx he simply assumes that his own sociocratic science of society is beyond ideology. But that, as we have seen, is true if and only if ideology is properly a pejorative term, and that remains to be shown.

Ideology and Utopia

In our times, the ideological influence of Sumner and Ward has been pervasive, if generally unacknowledged. The theoretical foundations of Franklin Roosevelt's New Deal are laid in Ward's volumes on pure and applied sociology,[67] while the 1980 and 1984 Republican party platforms faithfully echo Sumner's emphasis on the merits of free enterprise. Between these antipodal ideologies, excepting only the absonant lunatic left and the really radical right, every significant expression of American ideology in the twentieth century finds its place. There have appeared in our century two accounts of ideology which bear particularly upon our subject. These are, first, Karl Mannheim's exposition as given in his seminal study, *Ideology and Utopia* (1929–31)[68] and, of more recent vintage, Daniel Bell's chapters on the exhaustion of utopia in his *The End of Ideology* (1960).[69]

According to Mannheim, the analysis of the term "ideology" discloses two distinct and historically separable meanings of the term, namely, the particular and the total. Particular ideology functions on a purely psychological level; its referent is always the individual, its outcome the personalization of reality. Total ideology, on the other hand, presupposes the development of a philosophy of consciousness; its initial referent is the *Volksgeist* and afterwards class consciousness. Both types entail the distortion and falsification of the historical reality and, adds Mannheim, Marxism furnishes no exception to this rule.[70] When we pass from the distortion or concealment of a past or present reality to a state of mind incongruous with and transcendent of that reality, we have reached the utopian mentality. As for what is ideological and what utopian in the mentality of any particular time or epoch, that, Mannheim confesses, is not always easy to say. However,

> If we look into the past, it seems possible to find a fairly adequate criterion of what is to be regarded as ideological and what as utopian. The criterion is their realization. Ideas which later turned out to have been only distorted representations of a past or potential social order were ideological, while those which were adequately realized in the succeeding social order were relative utopias.[71]

The progress of society is charted in the passage from the "deluding" influence of ideology to the approximation in real life of utopias once regarded as completely transcendent of historical reality. The future of society is opaque, but for Mannheim it is a truism that "no interpretation of history can exist except in so far as it is guided by interest and purposeful striving."[72] The socialist-communist utopia remains in the making, as indeed does capitalism, and Mannheim does not venture to predict which one will finally conquer, preferring to occupy himself in the balance of his work with the theoretical and descriptive generalities of a nascent sociology of knowledge.

Daniel Bell, writing a generation later and from an American perspective, is more forthright. The old ideologies, he thinks, are played out, the old utopias betrayed. The age of idealistic, humanistic, socialistic ideology is at an end. In its place Bell foresees the rise of a new ideology of industrialization, nationalism, and economic development fostered, not by intellectuals, but by a new breed of political leaders. "For the newly risen countries, the debate," as he sees it,

> is not over the merits of Communism—the content of that doctrine has long been forgotten by friends and foes alike. The question is an older one: whether new societies can grow by building democratic institutions and allowing people to make choices—and sacrifices—voluntarily, or whether the new elites . . . will impose totalitarian means to transform their countries.[73]

At this writing, a quarter-century further down the road to utopia, the question still awaits a definitive answer.

Beyond Ideology?

From Napoleon to Daniel Bell the denotation of the term "ideology" has been distorted by a composite group of contumelious connotations. "Visionary," "arbitrary," "impractical," "pernicious," "incoherent," "mythic," and "false" are the epithets commonly applied. The pejorative usage of Marx has been preserved in the works of Marxists and anti-

Marxists alike. And yet, if for Marx and his echoes, ideology is false consciousness and/or an apology for bourgeois values, it would seem to follow that a synoptic and coherent ideology grounded on an epistemology compatible with the world view of contemporary cosmology is arguably true. For its detractors to the contrary, there is nothing intrinsically invidious about ideology as such. The term properly understood carries no emotive baggage. Any ideology is *per se*, simply an expression of principled interest. The principle may be good, bad, or indifferent. In any case, it deserves and requires to be judged on its merits. Also, it must never be forgotten that there is no exempt science of society. Every sociologist is, willy-nilly, an ideologist; every social philosophy is, *eo ipso*, an ideology in the etymonic sense of the term.

Which being so, it ought to be clear that not all ideologies are morally or even epistemologically equal. Marxism, for example, presupposing as it does an outworn and simplistic materialism allied to a naive epistemological realism, is, by contemporary scientific criteria, an anachronism. And the same may be concluded of any ideology resting upon an unexamined or discredited theory of knowledge and reality. Consequently, it behooves any ideology, American or foreign, aspirant to general social approval, to look to its epistemological and cosmological presuppositions, for as Collingwood has taught us, by their absolute presuppositions shall ye know them.

Unfortunately, social theory in our time is not much given to examining its presuppositions, preferring after Marx to believe that it is presuppositionless and that it is always the other fellow who suffers from false consciousness and misplaced bias. Consequently, it is relatively easy for those who think thus to deny that there is any such thing as an American ideology, and given Shils' characterization of the term, they are justified in their denial. Withal, that characterization is not necessarily prescriptive, nor is the fact that the generality of Americans are not united in commitment to a singular visionary ideal proof that we are not a nation of ideologues. The truth is that we are a people beset by a plethora of competing ideologies, most of them implicit rather than explicit, but ideologies for all of that. Our schools are captive to an anti-intellectualism masquerading as progressive education; our sports are mortgaged to the ideal that winning is everything; our economy is hostage at once to the theory of social activism and the supply-side gospel. Few indeed are the politicians who are free to disregard the spiritual strictures of the "moral majority,'' and there is hardly one among us who can for long remain indifferent to the variable winds of doctrine. In brief, for Americans, no less than for other nations, ideology is inescapable, and it remains that our only real option is our freedom to choose for better or worse.[74]

NOTES

1. Plato, *Republic*, VI, 507b–511c, VII, 514a–532b; *Parmenides*, 129a–135c; *Sophist*, 246b–254c.

2. Edward Shils, "Ideology: The Concept and Function of Ideology," in *International Encyclopedia of the Social Sciences*, ed. David L. Sills (New York: The Macmillan Company & The Free Press, 1968), 7:66-76. Hereafter cited as Shils. "The need for an ideology," he adds, "is an intensification of the need for a cognitive and moral map of the universe, which in a less intense and more intermittent form is a fundamental, although unequally distributed, disposition of man."

3. Francis Bacon, youngest son of Sir Nicholas Bacon, Privy Councillor during the reign of Elizabeth I, was born at London in 1561. Very little is known of his life prior to his matriculation at Trinity College (Cambridge) in 1574. Subsequently, he studied law at Gray's Inn, qualified as a barrister, and in 1584 was elected to Parliament. He held various offices during the reigns of Elizabeth and her successor, James I. For his services to the latter, he was knighted and in 1618 promoted to the office of Lord Chancellor. In that same year he was made Baron Verulam and in 1621 created Viscount St. Albans. Unfortunately, he was not immune to the temptations of high office. Accused of accepting bribes, he was convicted, heavily fined, briefly imprisoned in the Tower, and finally pardoned. His last years were spent on intellectual pursuits in retirement. He died of pneumonia at London in 1626. See James Spedding, *An Account of the Life and Times of Francis Bacon*, 2 vols. (Boston: Houghton, Mifflin, 1880).

4. Basil Montague, ed., *Valerius Terminus of the Interpretation of Nature in The Works of Francis Bacon*, 2 vols. (Philadelphia: Parry and McMillan, 1856), 1: 85–96. The references following are to the pages of this edition.

5. First published in 1605. Book I, revised and expanded, was reissued in 1623 under the title, *De Dignitate et Augmentis Scientiarum*. The second book, *Novum Organum Scientiarum*, also greatly enlarged, appeared in 1620.

6. *Valerius Terminus*, p. 90.

7. Ibid., p. 87.

8. *Novum Organum*, in *The Works of Francis Bacon*, 15 vols., ed. and comp. James Spedding, Robert Leslie Ellis, and Douglas Denon Heath (New York: Hurd and Houghton, 1864–66), 8:76–98.

9. Alfred North Whitehead, *Process and Reality*, corrected edition, ed. David Ray Griffin and Donald W. Sherburne (New York: The Free Press, 1978), p. 4.

10. Ibid., p. 5.

11. John Locke, eldest child of John Locke, a small landowner and attorney of Wrington in Somersetshire, was born in 1632. The family were Puritans, the father briefly a captain in the Parliamentary Army, and it was owing to the influence of his colonel that young John was educated at Westminster School and afterwards at Christchurch College, Oxford, a relationship which he was to maintain for thirty years. He tried tutoring Greek, served on a

diplomatic mission, and was inclined to take holy orders, but eventually decided on the study of medicine, albeit failing to take a degree. The turning point in his life was his meeting in 1666 with Lord Ashley, later first Earl of Shaftesbury. Locke was to serve Shaftesbury as confidential secretary and physician for fifteen years until political events forced both into exile in Holland. He now began to write and to produce the works which made him notorious in his own time and famous in posterity. His great work, the *Essay on the Human Understanding*, appeared in 1690 shortly after his return to England in the entourage of King William and Queen Mary. His last years were spent in writing and polemics. He died at the country house at Oates in Essex in 1704.

12. Whitehead, p. 145.

13. John Locke, *An Essay Concerning Human Understanding*, 2 vols., ed. and comp. with a prolegomena by Alexander Campbell Frazer (Oxford: Clarendon Press, 1894). All references following are to this edition.

14. Ibid., 1:26–27.

15. Ibid., 1:122.

16. Ibid., 1:124.

17. See Bernard Bailyn, *The Ideological Origins of the American Revolution* (Cambridge: Belknap Press, 1967), Ch. 3.

18. Ibid., pp. 325, 337.

19. Étienne Bonnot de Condillac was born at Grenoble in 1715. As a young man he took holy orders, becoming l'Abbe de Mureau, but his vocation was nominal only, his comfortable family circumstances enabling him to spend most of his life in secular speculations. His earliest significant work, *Essai sur l'Origine des Connaissances Humaines* (1746) hews closely to Locke. His *Traité des Systemes* (1749) is a criticism of rationalism in the spirit of his English mentor. However, by the time he came to write his *Traité des Sensations* (1754) he had emancipated himself from Locke and laid the foundation for a behavioristic psychology. His other works, on logic, language, and government, are of lesser significance for our times. Albeit he was a sensationalist, Condillac was no materialist. With Berkeley he believed that "we never get outside our selves—it is always our own thoughts we perceive." His last years were spent in retirement at his country estate near Beaugency. He died there in 1780.

20. François Marie Arouet de Voltaire (1694–1778), French philosopher, dramatist, historian, satirist, and man of letters, doyen of the French Enlightenment, and, arguably, the greatest man of his era.

21. Jean-Jacques Rousseau (1712–1778), French philosopher, social theorist, romantic, and advocate of democracy.

22. Denis Diderot (1713–1784), French encyclopedist, critic, playwright, novelist, and satirist.

23. Julien Offray de La Mettrie (1709–1751), Charles Bonnet (1720–1793), Paul von Holbach (1723–1789), Claude Adrien Helvétius (1715–1771).

24. Collectively denominated *Les Idéologues*. The most complete account

of their numbers, teaching, and influence is that of François Picavet, *Les Idéologues, Essai sur l'histoire des idées de des theories scientifiques, philosophiques, religeuses, etc. en France depuis 1789* (Paris: Félix Alcan, 1891). The most definitive recent history of the movement is Sergio Moravi's *Il tramento dell' Illuminismo* (Bari, 1968). See also, Jay W. Stein, *The Mind and the Sword* (New York, 1961).

25. Antoine Louis Claude Destutt, Comte de Tracy, aristocrat, sometime cavalry officer, later senator, subsequently member of the Institut National, the Academie Francaise, the Chamber of Peers, and the Institut Royal, was born in 1754. His childhood hero was Voltaire, his mentors Condillac and Cabanis. Franklin was his friend and Jefferson a valued correspondent. He lived to witness and participate in all the great events of his time from the rise of republicanism to the revival of empire. He died in the fullness of years and honors in 1836. The story of his life, works, and influence is well-told by Emmet Kennedy, *A Philosophe in the Age of Revolution: Destutt De Tracy and the Origins of "Ideology"* (Philadelphia: The American Philosophical Society, 1978).

26. Tracy, *Memoire sur la faculté de penser*. Quoted in Kennedy, p. 47.

27. Napoleon's antipathy to ideology was reinforced when in 1812 while at Smolensk he was informed of a conspiracy to overthrow the government and replace it with a fifteen-member cabinet of *idéologues*. Although Senator Tracy and his colleagues were not personally involved in the plot, Napoleon, seeking a scapegoat for his Russian debacle, blamed the failure of his campaign on ideology. Addressing his Council of State on his return to Paris, he insisted that, "we must lay the blame for the ills that our fair France has suffered on ideology, that shadowy metaphysics which subtly searches for first causes . . . rather than making use of laws known to the human heart and of the lessons of history." Quoted in Kennedy, p. 215.

28. Elihu Palmer, *An Inquiry Relative to the Moral and Political Improvement of the Human Species* (New York, 1797), p. 26.

29. *The Works of John C. Calhoun*. 6 vols., ed. Richard K. Cralle (Charleston, 1851–1857), 4:507–8. Cited as *Works*.

30. Calhoun, *Works*, 1:55.

31. A detailed account of the philosophy of Calhoun documenting his indebtedness to Aristotle, is given in August O. Spain, *The Political Theory of John C. Calhoun* (New York: Bookman Associates, 1951).

32. Shils, p. 68.

33. George Wilhelm Friedrich Hegel, *Naturrecht und Staatswissenschaft im Grundrisse and Grundlinien der Philosophie des Rechts*. English translation by T.M. Knox, *Hegel's Philosophy of Right* (Oxford: Clarendon Press, 1942).

34. Ibid., p. 11.

35. So-called in contradistinction to those "Old Hegelians" for whom the works of Hegel remain the final word in philosophy. Those generally accounted

as members of the "Young Hegelian" movement are: David Friedrich Strauss (1808–1874), author of the iconoclastic *Life of Jesus*; August von Cieszkowski (1814–1894), revisionist world-historian; Ludwig Feuerbach (1804–1872), author of *The Essence of Christianity*, a work doing for religion in general what Strauss's book did for Jesus; Bruno Bauer (1809–1882), the leader of the pack; Arnold Ruge (1802–1880), the champion of humanism; Edgar Bauer (1820–1886), anarchist; Friedrich Engels (1820–1895), Marx's collaborator; Karl Marx (1818–1883); Max Stirner (1806–1856), the poet of the ego; Moses Hess (1812–1875), the father of German socialism; and Karl Schmidt (1819–1864), critic of everything. Bruno Bauer and Stirner in particular suffered the wrath and scorn of Marx, being castigated as "ideologists."

36. Karl Marx, *A Contribution to the Critique of Hegel's 'Philosophy of Right'* in *The Young Hegelians, An Anthology*, ed. Lawrence S. Stepelevich (Cambridge: The University Press, 1983), p. 310.

37. Karl Marx and Friedrich Engels, *The German Ideology*, ed. C. J. Arthur (New York: International Publishers, 1970), 1:47. Subsequent citations, except as noted, are to this edition, hereafter cited as *German Ideology*.

38. *German Ideology*, p. 40. According to Marx, "the entire body of German philosophical criticism from Strauss to Stirner is confined to criticism of *religious* conceptions. The critics started from real religion and actual theology. . . . The dominance of religion was taken for granted. . . . The Young Hegelians are in agreement with the Old Hegelians in their belief in the rule of religion, of concepts, of a universal principle in the existing world. Only, the one party attacks this dominion as usurpation, while the other extols it as legitimate." Ibid., pp. 40–41.

39. Ibid., Preface.

40. Ibid., p. 41.

41. Ibid., p. 47.

42. Ibid.

43. In his seminal essay of 1801 on the difference between Fichte's and Schelling's system of philosophy, Hegel draws a distinction between Reflection, i.e., the view that the object of which I am conscious is independent of my consciousness of it, and Speculation, that is, the point of view which denies not the externality but the independence of the object of consciousness. The principle of Speculation is the identity of subject and object, and for Hegel, Speculation alone is worthy of the name Philosophy. See G.W.F. Hegel, *The Difference between Fichte's and Schelling's System of Philosophy*, ed. and trans. H.S. Harris and Walter Cerf (Albany: State University of New York Press, 1977), pp. 80, 89–93.

44. For the argument, see R.C. Whittemore, "Pro Hegel, Contra Kierkegaard," *The Journal of Religious Thought*, 13 (Spring-Summer, 1956): 131–44.

45. Richard Kroner, Introduction to Hegel's *Early Theological Writings*

(Chicago: University of Chicago Press, 1948), p. 46.

46. Paul Ramsey, "Existenz and the Existence of God," *Journal of Religion* 28 (1948): 160.

47. *German Ideology*, p. 47.

48. Yale's greatest teacher was born at Paterson, New Jersey, in 1840. His parents were English immigrants, the father a machinist who eventually settled his family in Hartford. William worked to scrape up the money to enter Yale in 1859, and then worked his way through college. In 1863 he was drafted into the Union Army but escaped service when a wealthy classmate paid his exemption. This same friend advanced him funds for graduate study in Europe and at Oxford. He thought to become an Anglican priest, was ordained, and in 1869 accepted a call to Morristown, N.J. However, he soon found that he was temperamentally unsuited to the pastoral life, and when Yale offered him a professorship in 1873 he eagerly accepted. Henceforth his life would be devoted to Yale and to the New Haven community. He died in New York City in 1910.

49. *Essays of William Graham Sumner*, 2 vols, ed. Albert Keller and Maurice Davie (New Haven: Yale University Press, 1934), 2:314. Hereafter cited as *Essays*.

50. Ibid., p. 95.

51. Ibid., p. 109.

52. William Graham Sumner, *What Social Classes Owe to Each Other* (New York: Harper, 1903), p. 78. Hereafter cited as *Social Classes*.

53. Ibid., pp. 134–35.

54. Ibid., p. 154.

55. *Essays*, 2:121–22.

56. *Essays*, 1:493–94.

57. Ibid., p. 478.

58. Ibid., 2:127. How Sumner impressed this principle on one of his students is told by William Lyon Phelps: "Professor, don't you believe in any government aid to industries? No! it's root, hog, or die. Yes, but hasn't the hog a right to root? There are no rights. The world owes nobody a living. . . . Well, suppose some professor of political economy came along and took your job away from you. Wouldn't you be sore? Any other professor is welcome to try. If he gets my job, it is my fault. My business is to teach the subject so well that no one can take the job away from me." And no one ever did.

59. The tenth and last child of Justus Ward, an itinerant mechanic, and Silence Rolph Ward, a clergyman's daughter, Lester Frank Ward was born at Joliet, Illinois, on June 18, 1841. His childhood and youth were periods of hardship. He worked as a laborer by day and at night by candlelight. He was twenty before he scraped together funds sufficient to attend his first real school. In 1862 he married and shortly thereafter enlisted as a private in the Union Army. Seriously wounded at Chancellorsville, he was invalided out and gravitated

to Washington. He sought and eventually secured a clerkship in the U.S. Geological Survey, rising after thirty years' service to the rank of paleontologist. In the interval, he somehow found time to earn three degrees in law and science. In 1883 he published his first great work in philosophical sociology, and in the years that followed, four more big books and several dozen articles and essays. In 1906, upon his retirement from government service, he accepted an invitation from Brown University to become its first full-time professor of sociology. He died in 1913.

60. Lester Frank Ward, *Dynamic Sociology*, 2 vols. (New York: Appleton, 1883), 1:222.

61. Lester Frank Ward, *Glimpses of the Cosmos*, 6 vols. (New York: Putnam's, 1913), 5:320.

62. Ibid., 5:95.

63. Lester Frank Ward, "Solution of the Great Social Problem," quoted in Samuel Chugerman, *Lester F. Ward, The American Aristotle* (Durham: Duke University Press, 1939), p. 465.

64. Lester Frank Ward, *Outlines of Sociology* (New York: Macmillan, 1921), p. 26. *Meliorism*, on Ward's definition, is "humanitarianism *minus* all sentiment." *Dynamic Sociology*, 2:468.

65. Lester Frank Ward, *The Psychic Factors of Civilization* (Boston: Ginn & Co., 1892), pp. 324, 327.

66. *Dynamic Sociology*, 2:597.

67. Lester Frank Ward, *Pure Sociology: A Treatise on the Origin and Nature of Society* (New York: Macmillan, 1903) and *Applied Sociology: A Treatise on the Conscious Improvement of Society by Society* (Boston: Ginn & Co., 1906).

68. Karl Mannheim, *Ideologie und Utopie* (Bonn: F. Cohen, 1929). English translation by Louis Wirth, *Ideology and Utopia* (New York: Harcourt, Brace, 1936). Hereafter cited as IU.

69. Daniel Bell, *The End of Ideology* (Glencoe, Illinois: Free Press, 1960), Part III and Epilogue. Hereafter cited as EI.

70. IU, p. 69.

71. Ibid., p. 184.

72. Ibid., p. 234.

73. EI, p. 374.

74. In addition to works mentioned or cited, the following have been consulted in the preparation of this paper.

Apter, David E.   *Ideology and Discontent* (Glencoe, Illinois: Free Press, 1964).

Carlsnaes, Walter,   *The Concept of Ideology and Political Analysis,* (Westport, Connecticut: Greenwood Press, 1981).

Drucker, H.M.	*The Political Uses of Ideology* (London: Macmillan, 1974).
Feuer, Lewis S.	*Ideology and the Ideologists* (New York: Harper & Row, 1975).
Kaplan, Morton A.	*On Historical and Political Knowing* (Chicago: University of Chicago Press, 1971).
Lichtheim, George,	*Marxism* (New York: Frederick Praeger, 1961).
MacIntyre, Alasdair,	*Against the Self Images of the Age* (London: Gerald Duckworth, 1971).
Seliger, Martin,	*Ideology and Politics* (New York: Free Press, 1976).
Seliger, Martin,	*The Marxist Conception of Ideology* (Cambridge: Cambridge University Press, 1977).

II

Ideology, Objectivity, and Political Theory

—

DOUGLAS B. RASMUSSEN

If relativism signifies contempt for fixed categories and men who claim to be the bearers of objective, immortal truth . . . then there is nothing more relativistic than Fascist attitudes and activity. . . . From the fact that all ideologies are of equal value, that all ideologies are mere fictions, the modern relativist infers that everybody has the right to create for himself his own ideology and to attempt to enforce it with all the energy of which he is capable.

———

Benito Mussolini

The political tradition of the United States as expressed in the Declaration of Independence claims that individual human beings have the natural rights to life, liberty, and the pursuit of happiness. According to this political document, the purpose of government is to preserve and protect these rights, and these rights constitute the normative criteria by which governments are to be evaluated. The Declaration of Independence, then, not only claims that there is a difference between *de facto* and legitimate political power, it enunciates the normative principles in terms of which such a differentiation is to be made. The claims of the Declaration of Independence stand in sharp contrast, not only politically but also epistemologically, to those of Mussolini. Yet, are the claims of the Declaration of Independence anything more than the expression of an ideology? The answer to this question depends, of course, on what is meant by *ideology*, and this will be examined shortly. There is, however, an even larger question here: Can a political theory that differentiates between *de facto* and legitimate political power be objective—that is, can it be true and not merely a matter of opinion? Whether the claims of the Declaration of Independence are anything more than the expression of a dominant political opinion of its time is an issue that involves questions of an extremely difficult nature: Is moral knowledge possible? Do persons have any natural rights, and if so, in what do they consist?

The urgency of finding an answer to these questions cannot be avoided by noting that Mussolini's "inference" to a right to create and enforce his values is a *non sequitur*; for the very same error is present in those thinkers today who claim that since no one knows what is right or wrong, no one should attempt to impose his values on others. The error in logic is the same: if there are no moral truths, then neither policies of fascism nor policies of tolerance follow. One cannot claim to know what ought or ought not to be done, and despite how contemporary thinkers might twist and turn, the problem of moral knowledge and objectivity in general remains. The fundamental questions of philosophy demand attention if we are to have any hope that public policy decisions will ever be more than expressions of the most dominant and powerful interests of the time. The issue is as old as philosophy itself: Does might make right? Or is there a right to which might can be subordinated?

The author of the Declaration of Independence had little doubt regarding the truth of the normative claims expressed therein. Indeed, belief in an objective moral order was pervasive among American revolutionary thinkers. It characterized the literature and logic of the American Revolution.[1] It almost goes without saying that such is not the situation we face today. Belief in an objective moral order does not pervade today's intellectual scene, and any attempt to treat the claims of the Declaration of Independence as normative truths would most certainly be regarded by many as naive. Are there ethical truths and are the claims of the Declaration of Independence included among them? Answers to these difficult questions must be provided if the Declaration of Independence is to be considered a document that is relevant for our times. Answers to these difficult questions cannot be provided here, but some observations can be offered about the philosophical preconditions necessary for the success of any argument on behalf of the natural rights claims made in the Declaration of Independence. These observations will involve differentiating philosophy from ideology. It is, then, to a consideration of ideology that we should now turn.

Ideology and Philosophy

The word *idéologie*, as introduced by Destutt de Tracy in 1796, refers to a program of reductive semantic analysis which aims to study the formation of ideas, their expression and combination in language and logic, and their application in economic, moral, and legal arenas. Destutt de Tracy regarded ideas as direct and self-contained objects of the human mind. His "science of ideas" sought to replace classical logic, and he maintained that if one learned how to analyze one's ideas, then one could learn which ideas were grounded in sensation and which were groundless. Ideas were to be examined in a manner no different from how one would study the properties of minerals, plants, or animals. Ideology was part of zoology. Ideas were to be observed, analyzed, and classified and then explained through their psychological and anthropological origins.

During Napoleonic times "ideology" took on a depreciative meaning, namely, the use of ideas to justify a course of action that was really based on other motivations. Later in the nineteenth century, Marx adopted the Napoleonic use of "ideology" when using the term to refer to social myths or "opiates" that are foisted on men in the interest of the oppressive ruling class. In *German Ideology* Marx and Engels closely identified ideology with philosophy, especially philosophies that were regarded as inimical to the "scientific" revolutionary philosophy that Marx advanced. In this sense, ideology included not only epistemology and politics but also metaphysics, religion, ethics, and "any 'form of consciousness' which expresses the basic attitudes or commitments of a social class."[2] Marx, of course, did not consider his "scientific" philosophy to be merely an ideology of the revolutionary working classes. He claimed to have discovered the real as opposed to the apparent significance of ideological claims. Thus, there was still a difference between a philosophy that functioned as a social myth and a philosophy that told us what was true.

Throughout the nineteenth century and even into our own, there developed a greater and greater tendency to identify ideology and philosophy.[3] Conceiving of philosophy as an ideology did not necessarily mean that philosophy took on the pejorative meaning that "ideology" had acquired during the Napoleonic era, but it did mean that the examination of the tools and methods of human knowing, implied by Destutt de Tracy's call for a "science of ideas," would come to fruition. Indeed, Kant's "transcendental turn" had already occurred. Destutt de Tracy, of course, had argued for a radical empirical analysis of the human mind, and though his particular program of reductive semantic analysis did not win acceptance, his general concern for a science of ideas did. As doubt increased regarding the ability of the human mind to know the nature of an extra-mental reality, many nineteenth-century philosophers came to recognize that their fundamental task, whether as ethicists, political theorists, metaphysicians, theologians, or epistemologists, was to investigate the very standards that philosophers used to evaluate philosophical theories. In particular, the concept of objectivity became the object of examination and analysis. As Henry D. Aiken has observed regarding philosophers in the nineteenth century:

> Some of them, at least, came to increasingly recognize that objectivity is not so much a fact about the universe as it is a matter of common standards of judgment and criticism. Objectivity, in short, is now conceived as inter-subjectivity. Inter-subjective norms are not agreed to by the members of a society because they are objective, but, in effect, become objective because they are jointly accepted.[4]

Philosophy thus became ideology in the etymological sense of that term—an account (*logos*) or science of ideas—and this account did not try to discover objective standards and principles inherent in "the nature of things." Rather, it looked elsewhere for the source of such standards and principles.

Kant thought that he had discovered the source of such standards and principles. He claimed that the forms of intuition and the categories of human understanding were presupposed by the very possibility of something's being an object for our awareness. Kant regarded the forms of intuition and the categories of the understanding as fixed and universal features of human knowing. They provided the common element in knowing that allowed inter-subjectivity to be the foundation for objectivity. Yet, the discovery of non-Euclidean geometry and the development of physics along non-Newtonian lines, as well as intrinsic difficulties in transcendental idealism,[5] undermined the belief that fixed and universal standards had been discovered. It did not seem plausible to assume that Kant had discovered, once and for all, the *a priori* principles by which all rational beings must think.

Without trying to recount all of nineteenth- and twentieth-century philosophy,[6] it is not stretching things too far to say that much of philosophy after Kant can be interpreted as an attempt to find a basis for the norms that determine objectivity. From Fichte's "Ego" to Hegel's historical consciousness of the Absolute, from Marx's dialectical materialism to Nietzsche's genealogy of morals, from the early Wittgenstein's *a priori* structure and limits of language to the later Wittgenstein's language games, there have been diverse attempts to provide a basis for and/or explanation of how we go about determining objectivity. Further, there does not any longer seem to be much concern that the standards or norms which determine objectivity be fixed or even universal. This last point, however, requires elaboration and is best illustrated by examining some contemporary views of knowledge.

Some Contemporary Views of Knowledge

Consider the following statements by Willard Van Orman Quine:

> For my part I do, qua lay physicist, believe in physical objects and not Homer's gods; and I consider it a scientific error to believe otherwise. But in point of epistemological footing the physical objects and the gods differ only in degree and not in kind. Both sorts of entities enter our conception only as cultural posits. The myth of physical objects is epistemologically superior to most in that it has proved more efficacious than other myths as a device for working a manageable structure into the flux of experience.[7]

And:

> The relativistic thesis to which we have come is this, to repeat: it makes no sense to say what the objects of a theory are, beyond saying how to interpret or reinterpret that theory in another.[8]

Everything which is said to exist, then, is a posit, a myth, from the standpoint of theory creation and, at the same time, a reality from the standpoint of a developed theory.[9] According to Quine, it makes no sense to try to say what something really is, because in order talk about the world we must impose the conceptual scheme peculiar to our language on it; we cannot detach ourselves from one conceptual scheme or another and compare that scheme to an unconceptualized reality. We can, of course, change our conceptual schemes, but the standard governing such changes is pragmatic, not correspondence of that scheme to reality.[10]

The information provided by our senses is, according to Quine, not only inconclusive regarding what posit to make (what myth to accept), but always so.

> We have no reason to suppose that man's surface irritations even unto eternity admit of any one systematization that is scientifically better or simpler than all possible others. . . . Scientific method is the way to truth, but it affords in principle no unique definition of truth.[11]

The language of the theory goes beyond the observation sentences. Sense perception is neither the basis for theory creation—as Popper argued—nor capable of showing a theory to be false; for it is always possible to make *ad hoc* adjustments in a theory. Thus, with the hypothetico-deductive method in full force, when a predicted event implied by the theory fails to materialize, there are some choices to be made regarding what to do with the theory. Given that any theory is in principle underdetermined by sense experience,[12] there is considerable latitude in the range of possible hypotheses that can be made. Quine, however, does not consider this a situation that is entirely without restraints. As he sees it, there are six virtues that plausible theories have: conservatism, modesty, simplicity, generality, refutability, and precision,[13] and the theory that ought to be accepted is the one which best measures up to the six virtues.   It is not necessary to detail Quine's understanding of these virtues, nor do we need to consider their application; for the issue to be faced is simply this: Why should we accept these six virtues of plausibility? One might be inclined to say that theories which manifest these virtues provide us with the best presently available account of the real, but it is hard to see how Quine could answer in this way. If we can only talk about reality as we conceive it, never as it is, if all reference is intra-theoretical, never extra-theoretical, then what entitles Quine to say that these virtues are guides to the best presently available account of reality? After all, there is no first philosophy for Quine, and epistemology is only science self-applied—that is, "a chapter of psychology and hence of natural science"[14]—and cannot be used to evaluate scientific method without begging the question.

Perhaps a defender of Quine would reply that questioning the virtues of plausibility betrays an uncritical acceptance of thing-in-itself talk.[15] Yet, the problem is not that the critic of Quine has adopted a Kantian approach to knowledge; rather, it is that Quine has adopted a Kantian approach! Milton Munitz describes Quine's approach to knowledge as "a severely modified form of Kantianism."[16] Even when Quine denies that he is patronizing something by calling it a posit (or a myth), he still understands its existence to be a function of theory.

> Everything to which we concede existence is a posit from the standpoint of a description of the theory-building process, and simultaneously *real from the standpoint of the theory that is being built.* Nor let us look down on the standpoint of the theory as make-believe: for we can never do better than occupy the standpoint of some theory or other, the best we can muster at the time.[17] (Emphasis added.)

What is, then, the difference between posits and reality? It seems that the only difference between posits (myths) and reality is the difference between something which is regarded as existing when we are creating a theory and something which is regarded as existing by the theory that is being created. Quine refuses to accept any ontological distinction between posits and reality. As Roger Trigg notes:

> Posits can be real, and indeed in positing certain entities we are saying that they are real. The reason we would deny reality to Homeric gods is not that they are

posits, but that they are not *our* posits. According to Quine, reality is, in effect, what we believe exists. In terms of our present conceptual scheme, he thinks that this means looking to scientists to tell us what reality is like.[18]

Quine is a mitigated Kantian in the sense that he has given up on even talking about reality as it is but nonetheless holds that what things are is a product of one's conceptual scheme. Thus, the problem remains: How is Quine's version of the scientific method to be justified? What supports his belief that the scientific method is the way to truth?

Quine's approach to knowledge is a pragmatic one. He does not want to explain a theory's truth in terms of correspondence. How do we determine which theory is "efficacious" or "pragmatic?" Sense perception will not work. If we appeal to the six virtues of plausibility, we again face the question as to why we should accept them, and asserting that scientific method is the way to truth only begs the question. Admittedly, most scientists accept such virtues and do indeed judge different theories by reference to them. Yet, if the consequences of accepting a scientific theory based on these virtues threaten other values one holds dear, why should one accept the scientific theory? Paul Feyerabend claims that "science has no greater authority than any other form of life."[19] Thus, if the theory of evolution should threaten one's religious and moral values, why should one accept this theory? Non-acceptance will no doubt cause one to be branded "non-scientific" or "fundamentalist." Yet, what argument is there on behalf of adopting the scientific method? As Feyerabend states:

> The lesson is plain: there does not exist a single argument that could be used to support the exceptional role which science plays in society. Science has done many things, but so have other ideologies. Science often proceeds systematically, but so do other ideologies (just consult the records of the many doctrinal debates that took place in the Church) and, besides, there are no overriding rules which are adhered to under any circumstances; there is no "scientific methodology" that can be used to separate science from the rest. *Science is just one of the many ideologies that propel society and it should be treated as such* (this statement applies even to the most progressive and most dialectical sections of science).[20]

It should be noted that Feyerabend does not consider science an ideology in the pejorative sense of the term. Rather, science is a system of ideas about how people should proceed to attain certain goals—namely, people should create and adopt theories that measure up to the virtues of plausibility. People who are committed to these goals (people who share a similar faith?) are called scientists.

However, science is only one of the possible ideologies that a person may adopt, and even then, it is possible to change the character of science. According to Feyerabend, science should become more human, less objective. He notes:

> It seems to me that an enterprise whose human character can be seen by all is preferable to one that looks "objective." . . . Such a development, far from being undesirable, changes science from a stern and demanding mistress into an attractive and yielding courtesan who tries to anticipate every wish of her lover.[21]

Indeed, we may construct a world in which science plays much less of a role or even no role whatever.

> We may wish to construct a world in which it [science] plays no role whatever (such a world I would suggest, would be more pleasant that the world we live in today).[22]

What basis Feyerabend has for saying that a world in which science has no role might be preferable to one in which science has a role is dubious, and yet what can be said for the claim that a world in which science has a role is preferable to one in which science has no role? The problem is analogous to John Stuart Mill's attempt to derive the desirable from the desired. What justifies the norms that provide the basis for objectivity appears to be determined by one's commitments to certain goals, and scientific method seems to be nothing more than a system of ideas—an ideology—that one uses to attain desired goals. Yet, there seems to be no fixed or universal standard by which to determine what one should desire—what commitments one should have.

The problem of finding a basis for objectivity is not easy when it is held that one cannot know what things really are and that talk of an independently existing reality is spurious. Some philosophers, however, might be willing to accept the claim that in the sciences objectivity cannot be determined independently of a conceptual scheme and that science is merely one type of conceptual scheme (one type of ideology). Such philosophers believe that philosophy can somehow stand above the problems that science faces.[23] Yet, such an attitude would certainly seem to be a case of whistling in the dark. The very idea that philosophy is in the last analysis the discipline from which an answer might be found regarding the basis of objectivity has been severely questioned throughout this century; and Richard Rorty's recent work, *Philosophy and the Mirror of Nature*, takes dead aim at the belief that philosophy can even be understood as a process of inquiry, let alone capable of finding standards of objectivity. Rorty denies that intentionality is the criterion of the mental[24] and, in effect, that there is an ontological difference between subject and object. Intentionality is a functional phenomenon only, and any account of human knowledge that can be offered will be, at most, a description of human behavior.[25] Accordingly, philosophy does not have to discover truths. Rather, the function of philosophy is to keep the conversation going, to engage in a kind of useful kibitzing. The reason why Wittgenstein and Heidegger are not understood, and regarded as ridiculous, Rorty claims, is because they were "edifying" philosophers. They said something—they participated in a conversation—but they did not have views about how things are. According to Rorty, keeping the conversation going is all that philosophy can and should strive to do.

If Rorty is correct, there is no special knowledge the philosopher can offer about anything. There can be no such thing as epistemology, and hence no such thing as discovering the standards for objectivity. When it comes to ethical, legal, and social and political matters, there is nothing unique that philosophers can contribute. The only reason[26] to continue to engage in philosophy is to prevent some current way of thinking from becoming dominant, to prevent man from "deluding himself with the notion that he knows himself, or anything else, except under optional descriptions."[27] The questions remain: Why should one be concerned with preventing a current way of thinking from becoming dominant? What's so terribly wrong with being deluded? And how do we differentiate being deluded from just having a radically different point of view?

Ideology and the Sociology of Knowledge

Rorty, of course, might not be right, but this is not the place to take up that issue. The point of the foregoing examination of some contemporary views of knowledge was to illustrate how the norms or standards used to determine objectivity are no longer regarded as fixed or universal. Rather, they are understood as belonging to conceptual schemes— schemes that can be replaced depending on the goal one desires to pursue. Further, beyond the fact that a conceptual scheme or system of beliefs can be used to attain goals to which one is committed, there does not seem to be any justification for choosing one conceptual scheme or system of beliefs over another. According to these contemporary views of knowledge, it is hard to see how knowledge could be understood as anything other than a well-developed system of beliefs that one uses to attain goals to which one is committed. What constitutes a knowledge claim, as opposed to mere opinion, is thus determined by one's system of beliefs—that is, by one's ideology.

If what constitutes a knowledge claim is ultimately determined by one's system of beliefs, and if a system of beliefs is nothing more than an instrument to be used to attain desired goals, then what basis could there be for distinguishing between a study that investigated the psychological, sociological, and anthropological sources for one's commitments or desires and a study that attempted to find a justification for them? After all, anything that is claimed to justify or establish the truth of one's commitments could only do so from the standpoint of some system of beliefs or conceptual scheme; and as we have already seen, the truth of a system of beliefs or conceptual scheme is not determined by any correspondence with a self-subsistent reality but rather presupposes that one is committed to the values that that system or scheme can attain. There is, further, no reason to assume that the values a system of beliefs or conceptual scheme can attain are either fixed or universally accepted. Thus, there is no basis for distinguishing questions of origin from questions of validity or truth. They are all mixed together. As R. Young notes:

> The traditional distinction between genetic and analytic accounts in philosophy and science should be softened so as to mesh in with the weaker use of that distinction in interpersonal and social interpretations. Similarly *the whole distinction between the content and validity of an idea and its context should also be considerably softened. Nothing is ultimately contextual: all is constitutive.*[28] (Emphasis added.)

Confusing questions of origin with questions of validity and truth is no longer possible. The "genetic fallacy" is no longer a fallacy, and the set of disciplines—sometimes called the "sociology of knowledge"— that study the origins and causes of the fundamental commitments people make is not merely the study of what passes for knowledge. It is the study of knowledge. The sociology of knowledge thus replaces epistemology in its traditional role.

With the proposed replacement of epistemology by the sociology of knowledge we have come full circle and returned to a feature of Destutt de Tracy's conception of ideology. Ideas, systems of belief, conceptual schemes are ideologies. They are to be observed, analyzed, and studied by the psychological, sociological, anthropological, and biological sciences. Nevertheless, it is doubtful if Destutt de Tracy would have taken his science of ideas as far as some have taken the sociology of knowledge. He certainly would have differentiated between a belief's origins and its justification. The sociology of knowledge cannot allow this distinction. There can be no question of an ideology's validity or truth, or at least no question independent of some ideological standpoint. All attempts to answer such a question must be done through human consciousness and, as Young observes, "consciousness is a socio-political and ideological mediator."[29] It seems that even the suggestion that philosophy and ideology can be contrasted is no longer viable.

Any system of thought that claims to understand the forces in society that give rise to the values and, ultimately, the ideologies used to promote them is extremely important, and this, no doubt, explains much of the attraction that Marxist thought has for the sociology of knowledge.[30] There are, however, grave self-referential difficulties faced by any system of thought that claims to know real as opposed to apparent sources of people's beliefs. Namely, how is it possible for this system of thought, say Marxism, to be capable of knowing the real as opposed to apparent forces behind the development of ideologies? Why is it not the case that this account of the forces that cause ideologies to form is merely one conceptual scheme among others that can be used to describe what happens? Why is this account of the process to be preferred to another? And if reasons can be given as to why, for example, the Marxist account is to be preferred over the non-Marxist account, has not a basis for the "genetic fallacy" been provided and with that a basis for objectivity discovered?[31] These questions, however, cannot be dealt with here. Rather, it is sufficient for our purposes merely to note that, given the contemporary views of knowledge that have been examined, ideologies reign supreme, and there just does not appear to be any way of getting around it.

Political Theory, Objectivity, and Some Observations

The problem of objectivity is a doubly difficult one for a normative enterprise, because it is not only necessary to find a basis for the factual claims that are made, it is also necessary to find a basis for the normative claims. Of course, if the foregoing views of knowledge are correct, the problem is no longer "How do we find values in a world of facts?" but rather, "How do we find facts in a world of values?" The situation is therefore a very difficult one for anyone who believes that normative claims can be a matter of knowledge, and that the basis for these normative claims is rooted in human nature. Basil Mitchell describes this type of normative theory well:

> If we place morality in the context of human needs and insist that moral judgments require to be supported by reasons, and that these reasons must relate to some

intelligible and defensible conception of human well-being, it becomes clear that an adequate understanding of morality is no longer attainable in total independence of our beliefs about the nature and destiny of man.[32]

Yet, are these beliefs about the nature and destiny of man anything more than the results of an optional description—a description with no more truth and validity to it than some other? If the philosophical arguments on behalf of the natural rights proclaimed in the Declaration of Independence are to have any chance of success, certain things must be done in order to differentiate philosophy from ideology and thus show how any claim to know the nature of man is more than an "optional description." What follows, then, are some observations regarding what needs to be done.

1. When speaking of ideology, the study of ideas, do philosophers mean the study of ideas themselves or what they are about? Aiken has observed that "one is never quite certain when they [nineteenth-century philosophers] are talking about the mode of thought, and when they are talking about its object."[33] There is a fundamental difference between the mode or act of awareness and the object of awareness; and the study of ideas, propositions, conceptual schemes, systems of belief or language is not the same as the study of what they are about, that is, their objects. Yet, the failure to keep this fundamental difference in mind permeates the non-pejorative use of "ideology." When philosophers talk of ideologies, they are seldom, if ever, concerned with modes or acts of awareness themselves. However, since they choose to speak of ideologies, they are not merely talking about the objects of these modes or acts of awareness. Ideas, propositions, conceptual schemes, systems of belief or language are treated as direct, self-contained objects of human awareness that are to be analyzed or unpacked. They are not treated as modes or acts of awareness that are reflectively examined. It is as if what is being studied are the ideas, etc., themselves but without their being thereby made an object of some act of awareness. Yet, to treat modes or acts of awareness as direct, self-contained objects of human awareness is to confuse modes or acts of awareness with objects of awareness. It is to treat what is fundamentally an activity and a means by which knowledge is acquired as if it were a thing and what our knowledge was directly of. This is a mistake.

Inherent in the non-pejorative use of "ideology" is a conflation of the use of the various modes or acts of awareness with their mention.[34] When "Persons have a right to live their own lives" is said to be an example of bourgeois ideology, this example is not regarded as a claim about what people in fact, independent of this point of view, have a right to; and yet this example is not regarded as pertaining to the ideas, propositions, conceptual schemes, systems of belief or language that are used by bourgeois ideology. Yet, if "Persons have a right to live their own lives" is neither used to make a claim about what is in fact the case nor to make a claim about the "ideas," etc., used by bourgeois ideology to make this claim, then what is it supposed to be about? If we say, "What the bourgeoisie believe," then we could without any change of meaning replace "Persons have a right to live their own lives" with "The bourgeoisie believe that people have a right to live their own lives." Yet, these are clearly not the same claims, and so the question of what it is to say that a claim is an ideological claim remains. Indeed, unless one takes the expression "P is an example of X ideology" to mean "X-ists believe P," or unless one intends to use "ideology" pejoratively and thereby contrast what is believed from what is in fact the case, saying that such claims as "Persons have a right to live their own lives" is an example of ideology is fundamentally confused. It treats the modes or acts of awareness used to make this claim as the direct objects of awareness and thereby conflates the use of ideas, propositions, conceptual schemes, systems of belief or language with their mention. The non-pejorative use of "ideology" is a conceptual monstrosity.

When philosophers propose to study ideas, propositions, conceptual schemes, systems of belief or language, or whatever, we should, therefore, be on our guard. Are they concerned with their objects—what they are about—or are they concerned with the modes or acts of awareness themselves? When they propose to examine the concept of "objectivity," are they concerned with the concept itself or its object? Regardless of the philosophic period being studied, we should be aware of the ambiguity inherent in the non-pejorative use of "ideology" and always distinguish between what Aiken calls the mode of awareness and the object of awareness. We should apply this distinction to all discussion of ideas, propositions, conceptual schemes, systems of belief or language. When this is done, the arguments against objectivity will not appear as overwhelming as they once did.

2. When philosophers are concerned with modes or acts of awareness themselves and not what they are about, when they propose to examine a conceptual scheme itself, they are mentioning, not using the concept "conceptual scheme." (Or if some prefer, they are mentioning, not using, the words "conceptual scheme.") Yet, if this is the case, then the claim, so popular among advocates of ideology, that one cannot know anything independent of some conceptual scheme, can be disarmed. To say that we must use a conceptual scheme to know what, for example, a human being is does not imply that what we know is the concept "human being" and neither does it imply that what we know is something less than what a human being really is. To claim that it does is a *non sequitur*. Of course, if philosophers confuse mentioning a concept (or word) with using a concept (or word)—namely, confuse the mode of awareness with the object of awareness—then they could make such a claim. However, if the distinction between mode or act of awareness and the object of awareness is maintained, then there is no reason to assume that we are cut off from knowing what something really is by the fact that we must know via some conceptual or linguistic scheme.

3. When philosophers are concerned with what the modes or acts of awareness are about, when they do not propose to examine the conceptual scheme itself, they are *using*, not *mentioning* the concept "conceptual scheme." (Or if some prefer, they are *using*, not *mentioning* the words "conceptual scheme.") Yet, if this is the case, then it is clear that one is no longer merely concerned with a conceptual scheme. Rather, one is trying to know what, to return to our example, a human being is and is not, contrary to what some "analytic" or "linguistic" philosophers have claimed, trying to analyze the concept "human being" or the use of the words "human being." Of course, if the philosophers confuse using a concept (or word) with mentioning a concept (or word)—if they forget to distinguish between the object of awareness and the mode or act of awareness—then they could make this mistake. If the distinction between the object of awareness and the mode of awareness is maintained, however, then there is no reason to assume that in trying to know what something really is one must analyze concepts, words, systems of belief, or whatever.

4. Destutt de Tracy's science of ideas took much of its inspiration from Condillac's development of the "new way of ideas" which was first formulated by John Locke in his *Essay Concerning Human Understanding*. Tracy accepted the proposition that ideas were direct, self-contained objects of human awareness. This assumption, which starts with Descartes[35]

and which characterizes so much thinking since, is crucial to the rejection of the claim that objectivity cannot be grounded in the awareness of an extra-mental reality. If ideas—be they sensory or conceptual—are what we directly know, how do we know if there is anything else? How could we ever move from the "inside" to the "outside?" And if ideas are self-contained objects, e.g., objective essences before our minds, then why cannot we analyze concepts in order to know what something is and thus treat conceptual knowledge as something *a priori* and separate from any empirical investigation of the nature of things? And finally, and maybe most importantly, how could sense perception ever provide the basis for conceptual understanding? Would it not have to be that concepts are applied to sensory knowledge but never based there? The Cartesian assumption that ideas are direct, self-contained objects of human awareness need not, however, be accepted. There is an alternative. As Aquinas states:

> The intelligible species is to the intellect what the sensible species is to the sense. The sensible species [i.e., the percept] is not what is perceived but rather that by which we perceive. Similarly, the intelligible species [i.e., the concept] is not what is understood, but that by which we understand.[36]

When percepts and concepts are treated not as direct, self-contained objects of human awareness but as the acts by which awareness occurs, then many of the foregoing problems can be avoided, and cognitive realism becomes once again possible. It is not so easy to be forced down that slippery slope into the abyss which makes objectivity a function of one's conceptual scheme. In fact, once it is recognized that all forms of awareness are fundamentally of or about something, that awareness is inherently relational, then it is not possible to claim (*à la* Descartes) that all the objects of awareness could in the last analysis be nothing more than a creation of our awareness. Rather, the existence of beings *in rerum natura*, beings that exist and are what they are independent of awareness, is evident. They are given *in* awareness but not ultimately *by* awareness.

Though the many twists and turns of modern philosophy cannot be discussed here, it is fair to state that the assumption that ideas (whether perceptual or conceptual) are what we know makes possible and maybe even necessitates the Kantian "transcendental turn." The Kantian picture of cognition treats sense perceptions as if they were "raw materials," and concepts as if they were "molds," and knowing as if it were a process of creating an artifact. In effect, Kantian cognition amounts to saying that the mode of human cognition determines the content of human cognition. This account requires that percepts are treated as formless contents and concepts are treated as contentless forms. In either case, percepts and concepts are treated as direct, self-contained objects of human awareness. Yet, and just as before, there is an alternative. Kant assumes that the empiricist maxim, "*Nihil in intellectu quid non prius erat in sensu*," must be interpreted to mean: all objects of knowledge are presented *in* sense perception and are also and necessarily recognized *by* sense perception. Kant correctly regards empiricism in this sense as inadequate as a foundation for human knowledge and claims there must also be *a priori* concepts—contentless forms—in order for there to be human knowledge. Yet, the empiricist maxim need not be interpreted so strongly. Rather, it could mean: all objects of knowledge are presented *in* sense perception but are not thereby recognized *by* sense perception. To use Étienne Gilson's metaphor, "The senses carry a message which they cannot interpret." Human reason, man's conceptual capacity, is needed to discover and interpret what the senses present. Conceptualization is more than production of weak copies of percepts; it is the identification and integration of what sense perception reveals but does not itself recognize.[37] This weaker interpretation of empiricism is found in Aristotelianism. In this version of empiricism there is no bifurcation of human knowledge into the rational/conceptual and the sensory/empirical. Rather, human knowledge is regarded as involving both the rational and sensory, the conceptual and empirical, and though they can be distinguished, they never exist apart. In Aristotelian empiricism there is no need to posit *a priori* concepts that must be imposed on sense perceptions to render human knowledge possible. Sense perception, not *a priori* forms, is the basis for our conceptual knowledge. There are, of course, many difficult issues involved here,[38] but it can at least be seen how this weaker, Aristotelian empiricism is an important alternative to the type of empiricism Kant considered and found wanting.

It might be objected that even if Aristotelian empiricism is true, there is still a difference between our conceptions of reality and reality itself. Our concepts are classifications, products of our minds, and thus cannot be "read off" from the world. The concept "man," for example, is not part of the world's furniture, and so despite all that we say, there is still a fundamental difference between our concepts and reality. We cannot claim to know what things really are in themselves. Yet, this objection assumes that the mode of human cognition must be the same as the mode of that which is known in order for knowledge to occur. This is the fallacy of Platonism, and as Aquinas notes:

> Although it is necessary for the truth of cognition that the cognition answer to the thing known, still it is not necessary that the mode of the thing known be the same as the mode of its cognition.[39]

There is, of course, a difference between X as it exists in cognition, and X as it exists independently of cognition, but this is a difference in mode of existence—that is, X as related to a knower and X as not related to a knower. This difference does not establish some unbridgeable gap between our concept of X and X itself. Rather, it only underscores that knowledge is a relation. Our knowledge is *of* the real, but it would be wrong to say that it *is* the real. Yet, what this difference in mode of existence does imply is that one should never identify the concept of X or the features of the concept of X with those of X. We must distinguish between the mode and content of our knowledge and not assume that the mode of our knowing must enter into the content of our knowing.

5. The realism and empiricism of the kind that are being claimed here as necessary for any natural rights argument to succeed do not have to consider knowledge to be merely a passive reflection of reality. Human interests and needs can play a role in conceptual awareness. When confronted by the multifarious features of the world, we do tend to pick out those features that are relevant to our interests and needs; for example, the snow dweller's account of snow as compared to the non-snow dweller's reflects the former's greater concern for the features of snow. This is not something that neo-Aristotelian realism and empiricism need to deny; for the fact that our interests and needs can play a role in determining which features of reality we will examine first (or more closely) does not imply that our mind, our concepts, or our language play an active role in molding reality. It does not imply that the object of human awareness is changed in our knowing it. Only if we assume a Kantian view of cognition and reality, and thereby conflate the mode of cognition with the content of cognition, is it necessary to hold that such an admission is impossible for realism. In this regard, it is revealing to note what Henry Mansel, a nineteenth-century student of Kant, wrote regarding what was implied in Kant's transcendental turn:

> With him [Kant] all is phenomenal [mere appearance] which is relative, and all is relative which is an object to a conscious subject. The conceptions of our understanding as such depend on the constitution of our thinking faculties, as perceptions of the senses do on the constitution of our intuitive faculties. Both might be different were our mental constitutions changed; both probably are different to beings differently constituted. The *real* thus becomes identical with the absolute, with the object as it is in itself, out of all relation to a subject; and

as all consciousness is the relation between subject and object, it follows that to attain knowledge of the real we must go out of consciousness.[40]

The Kantian approach to epistemology demands that cognition not be a relation, and the Kantian approach to metaphysics demands that the real be absolute—be something which stands out of *all* relation to a subject. These demands in turn make knowledge of reality by definition impossible. Yet, realism does not have to accept the identification of the real with the absolute. All that is required is that the real exist and be what it is independently of a subject; it is not necessary that the real be incapable of standing in any relation to a subject. Thus, the real can stand in a cognitive relation to a subject. Kant, of course, believed that when the real stands in a cognitive relation to a subject the nature of the real thereby becomes, at least partially, the creation of a subject. Yet, the implicit assumption behind Kant's account of cognition is that "any knowledge acquired by a process of consciousness is necessarily subjective and cannot correspond to the facts of reality since it 'processed knowledge.' "[41] To hold this assumption, however, means that legitimate knowledge of reality has to be acquired without any means of cognition.[42] Knowledge of reality has to be something miraculous. In effect, to hold this assumption is like saying that a man cannot see because he has eyes and could only see if he had no eyes. Certainly, this is not an assumption that the realism recommended here holds or needs to hold.

Acknowledging that human interests and needs can play a role in determining which features of reality we will investigate only shows that human knowing "starts somewhere" and that we cannot claim to know everything in all its detail all once.[43] Thus, there is a sense in which our knowledge is relative—namely, in the sense that we cannot claim to know *sub specie aeternitatis*—but this in no way requires that the real be determined by theory or that our theory be barred from describing the real. As Roger Trigg has noted:

> Our knowledge *is* still correct, since partial, or relative, knowledge is knowledge, and the mere use of the term "relative" need not make us fear that we are lapsing into the kind of position which makes truth and reality themselves relative matters. "Relative" is in fact being opposed to "absolute" rather than "objective."[44]

Human knowledge is achieved in pieces, step by step, and thus need not be regarded as a static, timeless snapshot or picture. Human knowledge can change and develop.[45] Realism of the kind that is being advanced here requires that man is *not* the measure of all things, but it does allow that man is the measur*er* of all things. Our knowledge can thus be objective without having to be absolute.[46]

Since there is no privileged position, no "God's vantage point," from which to determine truth, the procedures for discovering the truth are to be determined by the subject matter of particular cognitive enterprises; and the truth or falsity of a proposition is to be determined by the evidence and methods currently available.[47] To hold that the real must be known in an absolute manner is to suppose that knowledge could be achieved without a subject that possesses a mode of cognition or particular needs which determine where the investigation of reality begins. This supposition, however, relegates epistemology to fantasy and forgets that an omniscient being would have no need for epistemology. There is no reason to assume that knowledge of reality must be attained absolutely. The meaning of truth is, as Aristotle noted, "to say of what is that it is and of what is not that it is not," but this understanding of truth does not require any *a priori* method or standard by which to attain truth or determine whether a claim is true or false. If we understand this, as well as that there are no good reasons for assuming that we are cut off from reality if we accept neither Cartesian nor Kantian approaches to cognition, then we can save ourselves from the futile task of trying to discover some "method" or "standard" by which we can determine whether we "really" know reality.

6. Finally, it simply seems that realism is crucial for everything that man needs to do; and if it is abandoned, we face an existence in which Mussolini's "inference" is no worse than any other's. Once more, as Roger Trigg has noted:

> It is a paradox that man can demand the centre stage, insisting that everything should depend on him, and yet in the end find that in doing so he has lost his rationality and his freedom. Realism takes the possibility of error and ignorance seriously, but it also gives men the chance of notable success in extending the range of their understanding. It gives them something to reason about, while acknowledging that they are free to make mistakes.[48]

Conclusion

If the foregoing observations have merit, then it seems that there might be a way to differentiate philosophy from ideology. Objectivity need not be a function of one's system of beliefs. The basis for objectivity can be found in the existence of a self-subsistent reality which affords human beings the opportunity to know it, as well, of course, as to make mistakes about it. If a basis can be found in reality for values, if some facts are inherently value-laden,[49] then a philosophical argument on behalf of the natural rights claims is possible. We need not assume that talk of the nature of man is merely the expression of some bourgeois ideology, or, for that matter, any other ideology. If the foregoing observations are without merit, then it is not only very difficult to see how one could differentiate philosophy from ideology, it is hard to see how anything could qualify as knowledge—including the Marxist account of the forces that move history.

NOTES

1. Bernard Bailyn, *Ideological Origins of the American Revolution* (Cambridge, Massachusetts: The Belknap Press of Harvard University Press, 1967), p. 27.

2. Henry D. Aiken, *The Age of Ideology* (New York and Toronto: The New American Library, 1956), p. 17.

3. Ibid., pp. 19–26.

4. Ibid., p. 23.

5. Can Kant intelligibly talk of the existence of a noumenal, but an inherently unknowable, world? Exactly how does the unity of consciousness require that appearances must be capable of connection according to universal necessary laws as opposed to merely capable of connection?

6. Milton K. Munitz's *Contemporary Analytic Philosophy* (New York: Macmillan, 1981) gives an excellent account of the different attempts in analytic philosophy to find a standard for determining objectivity.

7. Willard Van Orman Quine, "Two Dogmas of Empiricism," in *From A Logical Point of View* (New York and Evanston: Harper & Row, 1963), p. 44.

8. Willard Van Orman Quine, "Ontological Relativity," in *Ontological Relativity and Other Essays* (New York and London: Columbia University Press, 1969), p. 50.

9. Willard Van Orman Quine, *Word and Object* (Cambridge, Massachusetts: The M.I.T. Press, 1960), p. 22.

10. Willard Van Orman Quine, "Identity, Ostension, and Hypostasis," in *From A Logical Point of View*, pp. 78–79.

11. Quine, *Word and Object*, p. 23.

12. Quine reexamines the claim that natural science is empirically underdetermined in his article, "On Empirically Equivalent Systems of the World," *Erkenntnis* 9 (1975): 313–28. Quine's last ditch version of the thesis of underdetermination asserts that "our system of the world is bound to have empirically equivalent alternatives which, if we were to discover them, we would see no way of reconciling by reconstrual of predicates " (p. 327).

13. Willard Van Orman Quine and J. S. Ullian, *The Web of Belief*, 2nd ed. (New York: Random House, 1978), chaps. 6 and 7.

14. Quine, *Ontological Relativity*, p. 82. It seems that Quine's approach to epistemology is in the same vein as Destutt de Tracy's radical empirical analysis of ideas!

15. See Roger F. Gibson, Jr., *The Philosophy of W. V. Quine* (Tampa/St. Petersburg/Sarasota, Florida: University Presses of Florida, 1982), p. 173.

16. Munitz, p. 364. Also, see my article, "Quine and Aristotelian Essentialism," *The New Scholasticism* 58 (Summer 1984): 316–35.

17. Quine, *Word and Object*, p. 22.

18. Roger Trigg, *Reality At Risk* (Totowa, New Jersey: Barnes & Noble Books, 1980), p. 71.

19. Paul Feyerabend, *Against Method* (New York: Schocken Books: 1977), p. 195.

20. Paul Feyerabend "How to Defend Society Against Science" in *Introductory Readings in the Philosophy of Science*, ed. Klemke, Hollinger, and Klein (Buffalo, New York: Prometheus Books, 1980), p. 61.

21. Paul Feyerabend "Consultations for the Specialist" in *Criticism and the Growth of Knowledge*, ed. I. Lakatos and A. Musgrave (Cambridge: Cambridge University Press, 1970), pp. 228–29.

22. Ibid.

23. Henry B. Veatch, *Two Logics* (Evanston, Illinois: Northwestern University Press, 1969), argues, in effect, that the type of "logic" or conceptual system that science uses (must use?) is not capable of discovering what something really is, while the type of "logic" or conceptual system used, or at least capable of use, by philosophy (and the humanities in general) can discover what things really are.

24. See my article, "Rorty, Wittgenstein, and the Nature of Intentionality," *Proceedings of the American Catholic Philosophical Association* 57 (1983): 152–62, for an assessment of this claim.

25. Richard Rorty, *Philosophy and the Mirror of Nature* (Princeton: Princeton University Press, 1979), p. 182.

26. One might cynically add the qualifier, "beyond job security."

27. Rorty, *Philosophy and the Mirror of Nature*, p. 379.

28. R. Young, "Man's Place in Nature," in *Changing Perspectives in the History of Science*, ed. M. Teich and R. Young (London: Heinemann Educational, 1973), p. 429. Quoted in Trigg's *Reality At Risk*, p. 133.

29. Ibid.

30. This is, of course, not to say that Marxism is the only theory that could be attractive for the sociology of knowledge.

31. The Marxist might argue that there is no distinction between thought and reality. Rather, they are but two aspects of the same historical process by which truth is created, not discovered, and the involvement of men in concrete historical processes is all there can be. One cannot separate oneself from the process and abstractly judge it. Yet, what are we to make of *these* claims?

32. Basil Mitchell, *Morality, Religious and Secular* (Oxford and New York: Oxford University Press, 1980), p. 152.

33. Aiken, p. 14.

34. The problem is, however, not primarily a linguistic one. Rather, it is a conflation of any mode or act of awareness with the object of awareness, and this can take various forms. In traditional Aristotelian logic such conflation is avoided by distinguishing the types of supposition that a term can have. Supposition is defined as the way a term is used in a proposition to stand for something existing. For example: "Man is three-lettered" illustrates material supposition. "Man is a universal concept" illustrates logical supposition, and

"Man is an animal" illustrates real supposition. The rule to be followed is simply that once a term is used in a proposition with a certain supposition that supposition is not to be changed. Given that P signifies "People have a right to live their own lives," P can be used in "P is an example of ideology" with either material, logical, or real supposition. Depending on how P is used, and depending on what "ideology" signifies, one obtains very different propositions with very different truth values. The error found, then, in the non-pejorative use of "ideology" is that it allows P (or similar concepts) to be used *without regard to its supposition* as the subject of a proposition in which "ideology" is truly predicated of it. Yet, in such a case no one can be sure what is intended by the proposition, and so the confusion is complete!

35. Descartes states: "I see clearly that there is nothing which is easier for me to know than my mind." *Meditations*, II, trans. Haldane and Ross, *The Philosophical Works of Descartes* (Cambridge: Cambridge University Press, 1911–1912), 1:157. He further states in *Meditations*, III, that "the light of reason causes me to know that the ideas in me are like pictures or images. . . . " (Ibid., p. 163.) For further documentation of the claim that Descartes believes that ideas are direct and self-contained objects of human awareness, see Joseph Owens, "Is Philosophy In Aristotle An Ideology?" in *Ideology, Philosophy and Politics*, ed. Anthony Parel (Waterloo, Ontario, Canada: Wilfred Laurier University Press, 1983), p. 174, n. 4. Owens notes that in the Latin text "more evidently" is coupled with "easier."

36. Thomas Aquinas, *Summa Theologica*, I, q. 85, a. 2.

37. See Ayn Rand, *Introduction to Objectivist Epistemology* (New York: Bantam Books, 1979); also, see Michael Polanyi's *The Tacit Dimension* (Magnolia, Massachusetts: Peter Smith Publishing, 1983).

38. See Thomas S. Russman's article, "Selective Perception," *Reason Papers* 7 (1981): 51–60, as well as my article, "Quine and Aristotelian Essentialism."

39. Thomas Aquinas, *Summa contra Gentiles*, II, 75.

40. "On the Philosophy of Kant" in Henry Mansel's *Letters, Lectures, and Reviews*, ed. H. W. Chandler (London: John Murray, 1873), p. 171.

41. Rand, p. 108.

42. It should be noted that knowledge which is acquired without a means seems to be just what is meant by "absolute knowledge."

43. Realism and empiricism of the kinds that are being advanced here acknowledge that human beings make mistakes. Does this involve the acceptance of fallibilism? This depends, of course, on how fallibilism is interpreted. One should not infer from the fact that human beings make mistakes that it is always (or necessarily) possible that human beings make mistakes; rather, one should only infer that it is *possible* that human beings make mistakes.

There is a difference between saying "X is possible" and "X is always (or necessarily) possible." We should, then, be careful not to interpret fallibilism too strongly: being human does not require the possibility of error; rather, it merely allows for the possibility of error. Thus, it would be wrong to assume, as some fallibilists do, that the possibility of error penetrates everything humans do.

Possibility claims, as much as any other sort of claim, require that evidence be given, and the fact that humans make errors shows that it is possible that humans err, but this does not show, to repeat, that it is always (or necessarily) possible that humans err. When considering any particular human judgment, then, one should not assume, *simply because it is a human judgment*, that there is a possibility of error. To make such an assumption is a *non sequitur*. Rather, one must wait for some reason to assume why one may be in error in this case. As J. L. Austin once noted: "being aware that you may be mistaken doesn't merely mean that you are a fallible human being; it means that you have *a concrete reason* to suppose that you may be mistaken in this case." (Emphasis added.) "Other Minds," *Philosophical Papers*, 2nd ed. (London: Oxford University Press, 1970), p. 98.

As regards the objection, "How do you know that this is not the particular time which makes the general statement 'It is possible that humans make mistakes' true?" it can be responded that the onus of proof is on that person who claims that you may be making a mistake. This objection provides no reason for saying that this may be the time that makes the general statement true. Showing that you may not be making a mistake requires that you, at least, know in what such a possibility consists, and in the absence of evidence as to why there is a possibility of error at this time, there is nothing to refute. Proving that you may not be making a mistake in this context is senseless. There is nothing you can or need to do. As said before, possibility claims require that reasons be given. Merely asking, "How do you know that you are not . . . ?" in and of itself does not establish anything (even possibilities) and does not require a response.

Yet it might still be objected that this only shows that the possibility that you are making a mistake at this time has not been established, but this does not show that you know that there is no possibility of making a mistake at this time. This objection is true, but why must anyone who claims to know some proposition, P, also claim to know "There is no possibility of making a mistake regarding P"? Unless one assumes that the possibility of error permeates every human judgment, there is no good reason to assume this burden. See my article, "Open-Question Argument and the Issue of Conceivability," *Proceedings of the American Catholic Philosophical Association* 56 (1982): 162–72.

Putting the entire matter a little differently, it is possible *for* human beings to err, namely, human beings *can* make mistakes, but this implies that it is possible that one is *not* mistaken just as much as it implies that it is possible that one is mistaken regarding any particular case. Yet, if the human capacity to err implies both that one may *not* be in error as well as one may be in error, then clearly it does not imply anything regarding the possibility of someone's being wrong in a particular case. It does not constitute any evidence. See my article, "Austin and Wittgenstein On 'Doubt' and 'Knowledge,' " *Reason Papers* 1 (Fall 1974): 51–60. Also, see Susan Haack's "Fallibilism and Necessity," *Synthese* 41 (1979) for a discussion of various interpretations of fallibilism. She notes that "fallibilism is a thesis about *our liability to error*, and not a thesis about *the model status* (possible falsity) *of what we believe*." (p. 309).

44. Trigg, p. 196.

45. Knowledge claims, as J. L. Austin once noted, are not predictive in such a way that the future can always prove them wrong. "Other Minds," *Philosophical Papers*, pp. 88–89.

46. Portions of the last two paragraphs are taken, with certain additions and modifications, from my critical review of Roger Trigg's *Reality At Risk* in *Reason Papers* 9 (Winter 1983): 85–90.

47. See Michael Devitt's recent work, *Realism & Truth* (Princeton, New Jersey: Princeton University Press, 1984).

48. Trigg, p. 197.

49. See my article, "Essentialism, Values and Rights," in *The Libertarian Reader*, ed. Tibor R. Machan (Totowa, New Jersey: Rowman and Littlefield, 1982), pp. 39–52.

III

The Republican Ideology

ANDREW J. RECK

and authoritarian democracy.''[1] *The International Encyclopedia of the Social Sciences*, published in 1968, is even less considerate of republicanism. For its entry under republicanism, it offers a three word imperative: "*See Democracy, Monarchy.*"[2]

On the present occasion I will attempt to examine the republican ideology in the conviction that it is vigorous in American civilization, although our neglect of its meanings handicaps us when we seek to appreciate the dynamic but always imperiled empire of law and liberty under which we live. I will attempt to elucidate what I think are the major conceptual and valuational components of the republican ideology.

The concept and function of ideology are subject to numerous and conflicting interpretations,[3] and its roles in social systems are various.[4] Unfortunately a pejorative meaning envelops the word "ideology"; it stems from Marx, who construed the term to signify the concealment of economic interests, and is perpetuated by Shils, who has stressed the rigidity and authoritativeness it connotes. However, a positive, legitimate sense of the term is possible, originating with its inventor, Destutt de Tracy, and appreciated by Thomas Jefferson, whose Declaration of Independence epitomizes American ideology.

At the beginning of this paper it is therefore proper that I clarify my use of the term. By "ideology" I mean here a system of ideas, values, and beliefs, both normative and allegedly factual, which purport to explain complex social phenomena and which also aim to justify and direct public policy and action. An ideology may be implicit rather than explicit, although it should be a task of the philosophers to explicate it. It need not be rigid and unchanging; its dynamic is often consonant with the nature of the political society to which it belongs. For a free people facing an indeterminate future, an ideology would be a flexible and open system. While an ideology is general in character, it should not be confused with a metaphysics or a philosophical cosmology; it may share ideas and values with these branches of philosophy but, unlike them, it is necessarily linked to a particular society in a specifiable historic epoch. An ideology, moreover, differs from a political philosophy. Individuals—say, Plato and Morton Kaplan—have political philosophies, whereas political societies—say, the United States and the USSR—have ideologies.

My conception of ideology is akin to Clifford Geertz's characterization of ideology as a "schematic image of social order."[5] However, it cuts across Karl Mannheim's contrast between ideology and utopia: an ideology expresses an ideal that existed in the past but masks present interests while a utopia projects an ideal that has never existed.[6] In appealing to classic models in Greece and Rome, the republican ideology does refer to the past. At the same time it is, as I will contend, immanent in the present American social, economic, and political system, where it persists in large measure as a set of norms which American society approximates but never perfectly attains. Utopianism pervades the system insofar as the system strives for an order that is perennially progressive. Talcott Parson's classification of ideologies into four types—conservative, counter, reform, and revolutionary[7]—reveals the structure and dynamics of the republican ideology by virtue of its inapplicability. For none of these types quite captures the republican ideology. The type designated counter-ideology does not even merit consideration. In regard to the other three types, republican ideology was revolutionary in America and Europe in the seventeenth and eighteenth centuries and is now revolutionary in Eastern Europe and the Third World, although today in America it is simultaneously conservative and replete with programs for reform.

The republican ideology as the schematic image of social order, both factual and normative, consists of five component ideas. They are: (1) law, (2) liberty, (3) property, (4) the people, and (5) the mixed polity. They are reflected in five descriptions of the republic as (1) a government of laws, (2) a free government, (3) a commonwealth, (4) a popular government, and (5) a mixed government. It is my contention that the republican ideology, spelled out by these five characterizations, guides and ought to guide public policy and political action in the United States of America both domestically and in its foreign relations. Let us consider each of the five component ideas or descriptions in turn.

A Government of Laws

It is commonplace that a republic is a government of laws, not of men. It was Aristotle who first formulated the accepted dictum that "the rule of law . . . is preferable to that of any individual," and he implied that the rule of law derives from the rule of Nature, God and Reason.[8] Aristotle's suggestion was expanded and rendered explicit in the Stoic doctrine of natural law. Cicero has endowed this doctrine with his exceptional eloquence in a passage from *The Republic* that is the *locus classicus* of the concept.

77

> [T]rue law is right reason in agreement with nature; it is of universal application, unchanging and everlasting; it summons to duty by its commands, and averts from wrongdoing by its prohibitions. And it does not lay its commands or prohibitions upon good men in vain, though neither have any effect on the wicked. It is a sin to try to alter this law, nor is it allowable to attempt to repeal any part of it, and it is impossible to abolish it entirely. We cannot be freed from its obligations by senate or people, and we need not look outside ourselves for an expounder and interpreter of it. And there will not be different laws at Rome and at Athens, or different laws now and in the future, but one eternal and unchangeable law will be valid for all nations and all times, and there will be one master and ruler, that is, God, over us all, for he is the author of this law, its promulgator, and its enforcing judge. Whoever is disobedient is fleeing from himself and denying his human nature, and by reason of this very fact he will suffer the worst penalties, even if he escapes what is commonly considered punishment.[9]

In this passage Cicero condensed a multiplicity of themes that unraveled in later philosophical discussions and even became slogans for reform and revolution. He affirmed the transcendence—that is, the universality and immutability—of natural law, distinguishing it from positive laws and existing political institutions, which he subordinated to its norms. He implied the equality of all men before the law. He grounded the law in the nature of man himself, so that in violating it man punishes himself. And he attributed the law to God as its promulgator and enforcer, thereby identifying natural law with a branch of divine law, cited in our Declaration of Independence as "the Laws of Nature and of Nature's God."

The definition of a republic as a government of laws may seem at first to contradict the doctrine of the sovereignty of the people, which is also deemed essential to a republic. To this topic I will return later. Here I will focus on some implications of the law as transcendent—that is, as immutable and universal.

First, this conception excludes rule by men as capricious and arbitrary, subjecting all, no matter how elevated in rank, to its imperatives. So Tom Paine during the period of the American Revolution could exclaim:

> [W]here, say some, is the King of America? I'll tell you, friends, he reigns above, and does not make havoc of mankind like the Royal Brute of Great Britain. . . .
> [I]n America the law is king. For as in absolute governments the King is law, so in free countries the law ought to be king; and there ought to be no other.[10]

And again, nearly two centuries later during the period of Watergate, Richard Nixon could be compelled by a judgment of the Supreme Court to release tapes that led to his resignation. No matter how high a person's station or great his power, he is under the law in a republic. Even a king or a president is but an officer with limited powers and assigned duties, and his failure to comply with the legal definition of his office is justification for his removal.

Secondly, the law as a commanding obedience endows those who tend to laws a special measure of prestige. Respect for law psychologically leads to respect for lawyers. It is a respect manifest in the esteem the Founding Fathers had for members of "the learned professions," as the participants in the ruling elite who would effectuate, in their regard for the rule of law, the compromise of special interests on behalf of the common good. It is a respect evident in the preponderance of lawyers not only in all the branches of government but even in the governance of other institutions. It is a respect conspicuous in the way youth flock to laws schools and also the way employers prefer law graduates to others in the marketplace.

Thirdly, Cicero's conception of natural law as the discovery of "right reason" presupposed a cosmology and an epistemology that became embroiled in incessant philosophical controversies. The philosophers never resolved whether the law is founded on the will or the intellect, whether or not it holds independently of God's existence, whether it is known *a priori* by reason or by the moral sense or *a posteriori* by experience. However, going back to Aristotle, an indefatigable student of constitutions, and to Polybius, a world historian, a consensus developed that natural law could be discerned historically in those political organizations whose constitutions were mixed. So natural law found its historical embodiment in a special kind of constitutional law—the constitutional law of mixed polity superbly exemplified in the unwritten British constitution and the written American Constitution. I will return to the topic of the mixed polity later. Now I will briefly focus on the notion of constitutional law as continuing growth of the norms guiding and judging a society, a notion embodied in the role of the Supreme Court and its function of judicial review. It is remarkable that the ideal of a higher law has persisted in American civilization despite its secular character, which has undermined the theological and metaphysical foundations of natural law. John Dewey, America's secular philosopher *par excellence*, has suggested an explanation for the survival of the higher law ideal when, in praising Jefferson's political philosophy, he recommended that wherever Jefferson used the word "natural" we substitute the word "moral."[11]

A Free Government

The most ancient sense of liberty, discernible in the writings of Plato, pertained to political communities. A city-state was described as free when it was not subjugated by an alien city-state or subordinated to an imperial system. Resurrected during the era of the American Revolution as a motive for the rebellion that culminated in American independence, this ancient sense of liberty is expressed today in the widely acknowledged right of peoples to self-determination, and it has been a causative factor in the emergence of the new states in the Third World. Although the meaning of liberty was first glimpsed by the philosophers at the level of states rather than individuals, it has radiated from its locus in the state to the individual members themselves. And historically the medium of freedom's spread has been the laws. Montesquieu's statement is illuminating: "Liberty is a right of doing whatever the laws permit."[12]

The fate of many Third World states has been an irony of history tragically illustrating the necessary connection between law and liberty. Independence has not liberated their peoples. The filtering down of freedom from the state to the people has been obstructed by a process that the French journalist Jacques Julliard has accurately diagnosed: "The peoples of the Third World may be free as long as they are fighting for their independence, but as soon as this is won they tend to fall into the hands of pitiless dictators who use ideology essentially as an instrument of power." Hence he has called for a new *Internationale* as the remedy—an " '*Internationale* of human rights'—the only response to the '*Internationale* of sovereign states.' "[13]

Thus the liberty essential to a republic has historically evolved from the freedom of the state in regard to domination by external powers to signify that the citizens are secured in their freedom by the laws. Fundamental to this sense of law's securing freedom is the idea of a constitution. A free state—that is, a republic—embodies a structure of institutions; this incorporated structure is its constitution. Constitutional law, implicit or explicit, establishes the functional stations of the members of a state; it assigns duties and rights and prescribes the procedures for making other laws. So it can be said that a republic is autonomous. No other political power imposes its laws upon it. Rather, the laws by which it lives are of its own nature and making. That is the essence of its liberty.

The constitution of a state, establishing the stations of its members and assigning rights and duties to each class of members, renders by legal deduction to each a sphere that is its own, and this sphere is secured by law and the force of law. Historically intrusions by the state and by others into the individual's sphere, implicitly or explicitly grounded in the constitution, have roused the cries of concern for natural (or human) rights and triggered revolutions.

The republican strategy of securing liberty in law has two major aspects. First, there is the guarantee furnished by the explicit formulation of bills of rights within constitutions. Theoretically this safeguards rights from infringement by positive laws enacted by legislative organs of government and by decrees, regulations, and actions of executive organs. Practically, however, the constitutional safeguard of rights, to be effective, requires not only eternal vigilance but incessant litigation. The second aspect of the republican strategy is to provide that the citizen participate in the process of making the laws. Richard Price expressed the point succinctly when, in anticipation of Kant's formula for the autonomy of the human agent in morality, he declared: "In every free state every man is his own Legislator."[14]

In regard to liberty, however, law is ultimately limited by the fact that it cannot beneficially comprehend the entire range of human action. Joseph Priestley grasped the difficulties in determining how far laws, regulations, decrees, and executive orders can be extended in consonance with human freedom. He prudently observed:

> We are so little capable of arguing a priori in matters of government, that it should seem, experiments only can determine how far this power of the legislature ought to extend; and it should likewise seem, that, till a sufficient number of experiments have been made, it becomes the wisdom of civil magistracy to take as little upon its hands as possible.[15]

A Commonwealth

Cicero linked the concept of the republic to the concepts of property and of the people. For the Roman senator the term "republic" meant literally the "public thing" or "public property," and this in turn signified "the property of the people." In his *Republic* Cicero defined the republic (*res publica*) as "the property of a people," and he continued, "a people is not any collection of human beings brought together in any sort of way, but an assemblage of people in large numbers associated in an agreement with respect to justice and a partnership for the common good."[16]

I will defer discussion of the concept of the people until later, and attend now to the notion of "public thing." Cicero formed this notion within the perspective of an aggrandizing, militant society. There existed public lands and monuments, highways, temples, and aqueducts. As Roman legions foraged the territories they conquered, treasures, trophies, and booty flowed back to the mother city to enrich her treasury. As the Roman system of law prevailed over the other states that were absorbed within its empire either by conquest or alliance, tribute and taxes were paid to Rome. In the ancient world victorious war paid off— it increased the property of the victorious people. It became imperative that this property, belonging to all, not be despoiled by a few to gratify their special interests. The shaking of the republic by civil wars and its tragic degeneration into a dictatorial empire stemmed from a collapse of concern for the public good as a result of the competition of the factions for greater shares of the public property.

Cicero's considerateness for the public property, however, did not embrace the private right to property. Indeed, it is not easy to find among the thinkers of classic antiquity much consideration of individual rights. The intellectual elite in a civilization that rested on slavery was generally insensitive to human rights. This absence of a moral foundation for entitlement to private property in the ancient world crops up in unexpected writings. Even Aristotle condoned piracy as a method of acquiring property.

Perhaps the long Christian process of intensifying the worth of the individual that transpired in the Middle Ages was necessary to inculcate a respect for the individual and what is his own by right. By the late Middle Ages the love of the individual for *temporalia*, material possessions in lands, houses, animals, precious jewels, art objects, clothes, and other artifacts, was conspicuously displayed in an acquisitiveness unmatched in earlier times. The trait is all the more startling when it is recognized that in the context of the medieval belief system an individual gathered material possessions at the risk of losing his immortal soul. Of course the escape from hell to heaven by these rich acquisitors was conveniently arranged by the church, which received the cherished material wealth and exchanged it for coinage from the Treasury of Grace. So even if you could not literally take it with you, your progress through purgatory toward heaven could be financed by the values it returned in special masses, prayers, and other rites. Although this ecclesiastically sponsored strategy may have slowed the development of capitalism, by delaying the formation of durable stock-companies or corporations, it bequeathed concepts that were indispensable to capitalism, not the least of which are the notions of "private property" and of the legitimate use of property as an investment that yields profits in the future.

On the passage from Cicero, it is pertinent to remark that the translator renders *res publica* in English as "a commonwealth." The term "commonwealth" in English has a special historic significance; it invokes memories of the Puritan revolution and the antimonarchical movement that nevertheless installed Cromwell to protect "the commonwealth." James Harrington superbly articulated the republican fervor of the time, and his judgments are durable contributions to the understanding of the links between government, people, and property. He defined *de jure* government as an empire of laws, not of men, "and erected it upon the foundation of *common* interest."[17] The motivation of government by the common interest, the public interest, rather than by the private interests, makes possible a government of laws rather than men. Although Harrington meant by "property" primarily land, his doctrine that "empire follows the balance of property, whether lodged in one, a few or many hands"[18] is relevant today. Whoever owns property reduces to a servile condition those who depend upon it for a livelihood. Because for Harrington property was tantamount to land and the quantity of land in the realm was limited, he favored an agrarian law that, in regulating and restricting ownership, had a leveling effect.

Transfer Harrington's insight concerning property and politics to an industrial society consisting of corporations, and the result is the opposite of an agrarian that levels. The right to private property, subject to regulation by law, is an indisputable ingredient in any free, republican society. While property embraces a realm of things that extends from, on the one hand, what is rightfully public—e.g., public monuments, lands, police and military equipment—to, on the other hand, things that are unquestionably private—e.g., the clothes I am wearing—there stretches between them a range of things that may be defined as either public or private, depending upon the orientation of a given society toward socialism or individualism.

Particularly noteworthy are the so-called private corporations that make up industrial society—e.g., General Motors, Bellarmine College, The Washington Institute. In one sense, these institutions are private property. Ownership of shares in General Motors entitles the owner to dividends and voting that cannot be wrested from him without due process of law. In another sense, they are public, operating under a charter issued by the state and subject to its regulations as well as its protections. I wish to suggest that this quasi-private, quasi-public property is part of the commonwealth, part of the thing that is public and belongs to the people. As the concept of a republic evolved from a band of people who pursued a common good that consisted, for the most part, in predations upon their neighbors' goods to expanding politico-economic systems which, harnessing technology instead of slaves, can benefit all at no cost to any, it has been discovered that the best care of the people's property, the commonwealth, the wealth of a nation, is provided by the people themselves as shareholders spread out across the land, and the worst care occurs when this property is nationalized and owned and managed by the state. These discoveries, I submit, are a matter, not of *a priori* reason or of willful preference, but of empirical fact. The test for this empirical fact is simple; it is found in the comparative wealth enjoyed by citizens of capitalist vs. socialist societies. Additional to the material benefits, even superior to them, is the fact that liberty flourishes best in the society where wealth, instead of being concentrated in the public purse, which after all is in the direct care of a few, is distributed among the citizenry, and no system of distribution, compatible with the preservation of capital requisite to industrialized economies, has been erected that is superior to the capitalistic system, which rests on the private ownership of shares in corporations. Where wealth is concentrated, or where it is stagnant, the people decay. Where wealth accumulates and the people partake in its ownership as shareholders, the republic flourishes.

A Popular Government

Essential to the republican idea is the political primacy of the people. It is recognized by all advocates of republicanism; it is explicit, for example, in the Ciceronian definition of a republic. Republican government is traditionally popular government; the people are sovereign. However, this is not tantamount to equating a republic with a democracy, which theoretically raises people above law.

Strictly speaking, a democracy is a society in which all power belongs to the people (*demos* meaning people, and *kratos*, power). A pure democracy requires direct participation of all the citizens in political decisions, by means of an assembly in which, after debate, issues would be decided by voice vote and by means of the rotation of offices.

Democracy in this pure sense has existed for brief periods in the Greek city-states and has been projected as normative in the visionary utopianism of Rousseau. Yet it not only lacks feasibility in contemporary mass societies, it is also undesirable from the standpoint of human rights. It easily degenerates into a totalitarianism that represses and persecutes minorities not attuned to the majority will.

Nevertheless, republics rest, in part, upon the democratic tenet of popular sovereignty. This tenet, in turn, rests upon a particular moral conception of what a people is. The people, to reiterate a quotation from Cicero, is "not any collection of human beings brought together in any sort of way." Cicero insisted that a people is an assemblage of human beings united by a shared sense of justice and a partnership in a common good. A people is, therefore, a collectivity in fundamental moral unity. Here perhaps is to be found the kernel of Montesquieu's interpretation of virtue as the spring for a republic.

Montesquieu distinguished the nature of a government from its principle. The nature of a government is its structure, or constitution, of which there are three sorts: republican, monarchical, and despotic. Whereas in a monarchy supreme power resides in a single person who is nonetheless subject to the laws, and in a despotism it again resides in a single person who rules according to his own will and caprice, republican government locates supreme power either in a few families (that is, aristocracy), or in the collectivity of the people (that is, democracy). The principle of a government is that by which it acts—that is to say, "the human passions which set it in motion."[19]

In regard to popular republican government, Montesquieu contended that virtue is the principle. Montesquieu's interpretation of virtue reflects the influence of Machiavellianism; it stresses political virtue rather than private virtue, and as political virtue it is power—the power to move the state. What is this virtue? It is, Montesquieu declared, "the love of our country."[20] Political virtue, then, is tantamount to patriotism. It transcends the satisfaction of our particular passions and addresses itself to the general good. And it "is conducive to a purity of morals," which is reciprocally supportive of political virtue.[21]

In esteeming patriotism a virtue, republicanism is incompatible with much contemporary liberalism, which criticizes allegiance to particular groups or national interests at the expense of moral interests. Patriotism dwells in particular communities; it is a specific form of loyalty, a generic virtue that ties together particular individuals and institutions for partial, personal regard—e.g., the fidelity of husband and wife. In the case of patriotism, loyalty assumes the form that binds together individuals and institutions in order to constitute a state and/or a nation. In his penetrating lecture, "Is Patriotism a Virtue?," Alasdair MacIntyre has argued that the morality that fosters patriotism as a virtue is inconsistent with the liberal morality that prescribes impersonal norms of disinterested universality, but that each morality has its right. On the one hand, the liberal moralist is able to charge that "patriotism is a permanent moral danger because of the way it places our ties to our nation beyond rational criticism," while, on the other hand, the moralist who defends patriotism is able to respond that "liberal morality is a permanent source of moral danger because of the way it renders our social and moral ties open to dissolution by rational criticism."[22] MacIntyre, moreover, concludes that the program of the seventeenth- and eighteenth-century republicans, who sought to synthesize the moral scheme in which patriotism flourishes with the liberal scheme of universal morality, "can never be carried through without coherence."[23] However, the confusions and incoherences are MacIntyre's, springing in large measure from the academic traditions in moral philosophy that are obsessed by the viciously false dualism of duty and interest, of deontology and utilitarianism. Republicanism, grounded in the antecedent tradition of natural law, need not succumb to this dualism. MacIntyre himself recognizes that a true patriot may critically oppose or resist the *de facto* government or governors of his nation by appealing to the national project which allegedly has been distorted or abandoned by its official caretakers.[24] Hence it is the project —the norms articulated in the ideology—which is paramount, and in the case of the republican ideology this project, transcending the partial principles of any particular community, points toward a future of liberty, equality, and property for all, a sociopolitical order in which duty and interest are rightly intertwined.

The republican ideology grounded on the virtue of patriotism emphasizes characteristically the sovereignty of the people. Popular sovereignty in a republic is first manifest in the establishment of the government itself. For government always involves a distinction between ruler and ruled, governors and governed, sovereign and subject, and this distinction exhibits a hierarchical order in which one part commands and the other obeys or else. How government that is derived from the people can then legitimately stand over and subordinate the people from which it sprang is the major problem that confronted the liberal Western political thinkers of the seventeenth and eighteenth centuries. It is the problem of justifying how, in Rousseauean rhetoric, men, who are born

Republicanism has its roots in antiquity. It flourished in actuality as well as in the minds of the philosophers when the Greek city-states marked the highest level of political organization compatible with liberty. Then it succumbed to force of arms when Alexander violently welded the city-states together in a world empire. It had a magnificent rebirth in Rome until Caesar vanquished her. It bloomed again, although perilously, in the Italian cities of the Renaissance. It spread to the monarchical and aristocratic polities of northern Europe, restructuring the constitution of Great Britain during the seventeenth century and overturning the *ancien régime* in France during the eighteenth century. And it inspired the founding of the United States of America.

In the twentieth century, however, republicanism has retreated from the center of our political reflections. It has been shoved aside by concern with other less definable notions, such as liberalism, conservatism, and democracy, and by post-Marxist flirtations with, or aversions from, the totalitarianisms of the right and of the left—fascism and communism. The entry on republicanism in the *Encyclopedia of the Social Sciences*, published in 1934, closes with the judgment that republican sentiment, targeting monarchy as its adversary, has "lost both its opponents and its significance." The author concluded that, since Italian fascism, initially republican, had finally accommodated the monarchy and since German National Socialism had remained constantly vigorous in the rejection of monarchy, the real issue of politics is "no longer the idea of democracy, but how it is to be realized. In place of the antithesis between monarchy and republic has appeared that between parliamentary free, are everywhere in chains. Now these thinkers solved the problem by means of the well-known contract theory of political society. The essence of this theory, however variant the versions of different authors were, is that men joined together and entered into a compact that established a government over them, deriving its powers from them, and in turn securing them in their lives, liberties, and properties. The theory legitimates political authority by referring back to a putative contract into which men originally entered freely and to which their successors now tacitly consent. It is a theory that became historical fact in the establishment of the Constitution of the United States. In implementing the theory, the American people invented a new mechanism, omitted by the philosophers but indispensable if they were to wield their sovereign power—namely, the constitutional convention.[25]

The second aspect of popular sovereignty within a republic consists in the norm that the people participate in the political process. In this sense a republic may be regarded to be a *representative* democracy but is incompatible with a totalitarian democracy.

In the first place, the concept of political participation by the people implies that they have a voice in who governs them and how. This requirement is institutionalized by extension of the suffrage and by provision for regular elections.

In the second place, it entails the public offices, perhaps all public offices, be open to persons without regard to birth, party affiliation, or other invidious qualifications irrelevant to the competent performance of the duties of the office. Here, of course, we encounter one of the fundamental meanings of republicanism that sets it apart, in the popular mind, from aristocracy and monarchy. It is a meaning, moreover, that is closely linked to the cherished republican value that men are equal before the law.

In the third place, a republic provides that the people participate indirectly in political decisions and consequently resorts to the principle of representation. Sometimes representation is implemented by specifying a separate assembly composed of members elected by the people of particular localities for brief terms, as for example, the Constitution of the United States has provided with the establishment of the House of Representatives. This device, however, provokes further questions concerning the nature of representation. Practically, the questions are often posed as follows: Should a representative simply act according to the wishes of his constituency? Or should he follow his own conscience as to what is best?

Ab initio representation seems to be a dyadic relation. Obviously it involves two terms—represented and representative. Since the quantity of the people excludes the possibility of their presence in a political assembly, some few are elected or chosen to stand for them. The people are the represented; the few are their representatives. Soon it becomes obvious that a third term is required; representation is a triadic relation, the representative standing for the people before some third term. What is this third term? Originally perhaps the third term was a king, or a council of nobles. The representative, who was accountable to the people he represents, was also accountable to the king or council. Today we tend to recognize the accountability of the representative to his constituency and consequently overlook the need of a third term. Political realism, however, suggests that while the people, as they are now, are originally the represented to whom the representative is responsible, he is also responsible to the people as they ought to be in the future. For a representative in politics is weighed historically by his efficacy in advancing the progress of the people toward what they ought to be. An essential difference between ancient political theory and modern theory is that whereas for the former the people exist for the state, for the latter the state exists for the people. Republicanism in modern times has always sought to promote commerce, industry, agriculture, the arts, the sciences, and education as ways of enriching and improving the people. Further scrutiny of representation uncovers still a fourth term, showing the relation to be tetradic. The representation of the people as they are by a representative who stands before the people as they ought to become, while dynamic, is also unstable. To endure, such representation must be grounded in some principle that formulates the goals of the people specifying what they ought to be. This ground is the fourth term; it is the constitution of the political society. In the American ideology this function is explicitly served in the Preamble to the Constitution.

The virtue that the people must possess for the effective operation of popular republican government must be even more intensely concentrated in their representatives for the system to work. Algernon Sidney, a martyr for republicanism, pinned the stability of the state to the wisdom and virtue of the people, and added: "The stability . . . that we seek, in relations to the exercise of civil and military powers, can never be found, unless care be taken, that such as shall exercise those powers, be endowed with the qualities [wisdom and virtue] that make them stable."[26]

A Mixed Government

In the *Politics* (Book III, Ch. 5) Aristotle defined constitution as government and further defined government as the supreme power in the state. Such power, he added, must be held either by a single ruler or a few or the mass of the citizens.

Plato had preceded Aristotle in distinguishing types of polity. In the *Republic* Plato had recognized only one perfect type—the ideal republic as the rule of the best (the wisest)—and had considered the other types as degenerations from the pure type—timocracy, oligarchy, democracy, and tyranny. The degenerate types devolved in succession from the pure type through each other. And Plato enunciated a major theme of later republican theory when he offered a sociopsychological explanation of the degeneration of polities in the moral terms of corruption and vice.

Aristotle divided polities into three pure types based on the number of rulers—monarchy, aristocracy, and constitutional government, each susceptible to degeneration into tyranny, oligarchy, and democracy, respectively. When Aristotle characterized government as constitutional, he intended to indicate that it is a government of laws rather than of men. By "constitutional government" he meant, in effect, what the term "republic" has traditionally signified.

An inconsistency in Aristotle's theory surfaces. Constitutional government, a republic, is one of the pure polities. But as the best kind of government it is also identified in actuality with a mixed polity. The inconsistency in Aristotle's formulation is insignificant, however, by comparison with his discovery of the mixed polity as the best actual government for the effective establishment of a constitutional government of laws.

In the ancient world, as in the modern, polities were threatened not only by external foes but also by the internal dissensions between the few wealthy and the many poor. The mixed polity promises durable stability because it seeks to balance the internal factions within the framework of law. While the ideal of the mixed polity, on the one hand, accommodates realistically the interests of the competing factions or blocs and effectuates a compromise, it proceeds on a foundation of constitutional law and hopes to discover and promote within the clash of particular interests the public interest or the common good, like the fire generated by the sparks that fly from the rubbing and striking of stones.

Polybius, whose world history centered on Rome, combined the insights of Plato concerning the role of virtue and vice in the historical evolution and degeneration of polities and of Aristotle concerning the mixed constitution. A fragment on the Roman Constitution in Book VI of Polybius's *Histories* lauded the Roman constitution as the best actual polity, a lasting republic that would endure.[27] Polybius's interpretation of the structure of the Roman constitution as a mixed polity and his assessment of the causes of its durability deeply influenced later republican thought. Thus Cicero portrayed the Roman republic as the embodiment of the ideal, mixed constitution, and also like Polybius, correlated organs of the Roman government with the principles of monarchy, aristocracy, and democracy—namely, the consuls representing the monarchical principle; the senate, the aristocratical principle; and the tribunes, the democratic principle.[28] Machiavelli paraphrased Polybius,[29] and through the influence of Machiavelli on modern republicanism the ideal of the mixed constitution has persisted. In the eighteenth century the British constitution, which attributed sovereignty to Parliament, consisting of king, lords, and commons, was perceived as the most perfect constitution, an historical evolution in which natural law found its concrete realization in an actual existing state. This ideal of a mixed polity guided the Founding Fathers of the American Constitution.[30]

Polybius's justifications for the moral superiority and durability of the mixed polity, historically vindicated in the example of the Roman republic, have been reiterated in modern political theory. On this score John Adams, an author of the Declaration of Independence and first vice-president and second president of the United States, is informative. In his remarkable anthology of the philosophers and historians who influenced American constitution making, *A Defence of the Constitutions of Government of the United States of America* (1787), Adams paraphrased Polybius; he emphasized that "the generation and corruption of governments" stems from "the progress and course of human passions in society."[31] He further recorded the evolution (or devolution) from monarchy to kingly rule to tyranny to aristocracy to oligarchy to democracy back to monarchy, explaining the processes of change by reference to human features such as weakness and passions such as envy. "This," Adams declared, "is the rotation of governments, and this the order of nature, by which they are changed, transformed, and return to the same point of the circle."[32] To this extent at least Adams merely copied Polybius:

> . . . [E]very form of government that is simple, by soon degenerating into that vice that is allied to it, must be unstable. The vice of kingly government is monar-

chy; that of aristocracy, oligarchy; that of democracy, rage and violence; into which, in process of time, all of them must degenerate . . . . [33]

Adams differed from Polybius in refusing to concede that a pure type, no matter how brief the period, is without abuse of power. He suggested instead that "perhaps it might be more exactly true and natural to say, that the king, the aristocracy, and the people, as soon as ever they felt themselves secure in the possession of their power, would begin to abuse it."[34]

The remedy for the political instability palpable in the incessant circular change of polities was, in Adams' words, to be in

. . . government not of one sort, but . . . [incorporating] all the advantages and properties of the best government; to the end that no branch of it, by swelling beyond its due bounds, might degenerate into the vice that is congenial to it; and that, while each of them were mutually acted upon by *opposite powers*, no one part might incline any way, or *out-weigh* the rest; but that the commonwealth, being equally *poised* and *balanced*, like a *ship* or a *waggon* [sic], acted upon by *contrary powers*, might long remain in the same situation; while the king was restrained from excess by the fear of the people who had a proper share in the commonwealth; and, on the other side, the people did not dare to disregard the king, from their fear of the senate, who being all elected for their virtue, would always incline to the justest side; by which means, that branch which happened to be oppressed because always superior, and, by the occasional weight of the senate, outbalanced the other.[35]

Adams's conception of the ideal polity as a mixed constitution in which an aristocracy of virtue held the balance of power to check the classes in conflict and keep the state in dynamic balance has been dismissed as "already an historical freak."[36] The orders of mankind—kingly, aristocratic, and democratic—it assumes no longer existed, if ever. Gordon S. Wood has contended that the "classical politics," based on virtue, had to yield to a politics of factions or group interests.[37] When, however, it is considered that the natural aristocracy Adams and even Jefferson cherished was never deemed to be hereditary and that the virtue they praised signified merit and ability, readily evidenced in wealth, the classical politics of virtue may survive and even dominate interest group politics.

Perhaps Aristotle, the father of the ideal of the mixed polity, should be our guide, for the Greek philosopher grasped the politico-economic actualities without sacrificing ideals. His entire philosophy articulated the dual principles that every ideal has a natural basis and that every natural process has an ideal goal. The mixed, constitutional government he envisaged as the best actual government man could attain was not the Polybian, Ciceronian type; rather it was a blend of the deviant types of oligarchy and democracy. Aristotle's mixture, while remote from the vision of John Adams, notably anticipates the politico-economic structure of capitalistic democracy. In still another striking regard, Aristotle anticipated contemporary political society when, after dividing the orders or classes of men into high, middle, and low, he urged a numerous middle class as the safeguard of constitutional government, since the middle class balances in the distribution of property the extremely rich and the extremely poor classes which otherwise disrupt society. The evolution of republicanism from a mixed polity dependent upon an aristocracy to one grounded in a numerous middle class is a return to Aristotle's political wisdom. Indeed, the success of a state in promoting the growth of a middle class has become the measure of its excellence. Far from freezing the classes or degenerating into some pure type that menaces liberty, the republican mixed polity evinces stable, historical progress toward a middle class society characterized by a love of individual liberty and a sense of personal enterprise.

This is not to say that the goal of the republican ideology, like that of Marxism, is a classless society, or even a one-class, middle class society. On the contrary, republicanism, unlike the utopianism of Marxism, recognizes that, because of the ineradicable scarcity of goods, there will always be higher and lower classes, although a person with initiative may rise from the lowest to highest class just as another may fall from the highest to the lowest. Nor can equal distribution of goods secure social justice. When government discourages production, it will inevitably promote human misery. When, however, production of goods is enhanced, as in the United States today, then with minimal government-managed redistribution the lower class will possess wealth unapproached by the higher and middle classes of earlier times or even in contemporary socialist societies.[38]

Concluding Remarks

My exposition of the republican ideology focused on the essential ingredients of a republic as a government. The idea involves a particular philosophy of man, but I have omitted an examination of this philosophical anthropology because I wish to emphasize the political

meanings of this ideology without too much indulgence in abstract speculations. The theses concerning the idea of a republic I have established
are:

(1) That a republic is a government of laws. The republican concept
of law is complex; it involves ideas of natural law and of constitutional
law, while it subordinates all persons equally to the governance of laws.

(2) That a republic is a free government. The concept of liberty pertains not only to the freedom of the state from domination by external
powers but also of the members. The liberties of the people, moreover,
are secured within the framework of laws.

(3) That a republic is a commonwealth. Understanding this notion
required investigation into concepts of property as public and as private,
and the distinction between private and public interests.

(4) That a republic is a popular government. Here examination of
popular sovereignty led to the recognition of the people as a moral unity,
and the need for virtue as a spring for popular government.

(5) That a republic is a mixed polity. Paramount to this notion of mixed
polity is the sense of competing orders of men with different interests
kept in balance within a framework of law.

My exploration of the republican ideology, drawing upon the insights
of the philosophers, is offered within the context of reflections upon
history and contemporary social realities. Dynamic in character, the
republican ideology has evolved without losing its core-meanings.
Discovered by the Greeks, expanded by the Romans, cherished by the
moderns from Machiavelli to the Founding Fathers, the republican
ideology is embodied in American political society. The elucidation of
the republican ideology, particularly since it is the American ideology,
is of paramount practical importance in these critical times. The United
States and the Soviet Union are engaged in a perilous competition for
the minds and allegiances of peoples throughout the world. While
military and economic forces will play the decisive role in the outcome,
the role of ideas and values should not be underestimated. Whereas the
professed ideology of the Soviet Union is so discrepant with the actual
conditions that prevail in Russia and her tributary states as to become
empty rhetoric, the America republican ideology contains the principles
that guide, sometimes by means of criticism and reform, our society
domestically and internationally. A clear grasp of the principles of the

American republican ideology is useful to policy makers and persons of social, political, and economic action; it illuminates the American way and provides a comprehensive and coherent vision of where we have been, where we are, and where we hope to go. It informs the mind of a free people facing an indeterminate future but resolute in the determination to endure and to prevail.[39]

NOTES

1. Peter Richard Rohden, "Republicanism," in *Encyclopedia of the Social Sciences*. (New York: Macmillan, 1934), 13:321.

2. *International Encyclopedia of the Social Sciences*, ed. David L. Sills (New York: The Macmillan Company & The Free Press, 1968), 13:479.

3. Edward Shils, "Ideology: The Concept and Function of Ideology," in Ibid., 7:66–76.

4. Harry M. Johnson, "Ideology: Ideology and the Social System," in Ibid., 7:76–85.

5. Clifford Geertz, "Ideology as a Cultural System," in *Ideology and Discontent*, ed. David E. Apter (New York: Free Press, 1964), pp. 47–48.

6. Karl Mannheim, *Ideology and Utopia: An Introduction to the Sociology of Knowledge*, trans. Louis Wirth and Edward Shils (New York: Harcourt, 1954).

7. Talcott Parsons, "An Approach to the Sociology of Knowledge," in *The Transactions of the Fourth World Congress of Sociology*, ed. Milan and Stresa (Louvain: International Sociological Association, 1959), 4:25–29.

8. Aristotle, *Politics*, Bk. III, Ch. 16, 1287a, trans. Benjamin Jowett in *The Basic Works of Aristotle*, ed. Richard McKeon (New York: Random House, 1941), p. 1202.

9. Cicero, *De Re Publica*, III, XXII, in *De Re Publica, De Legibus*, trans. Clinton Walker Keyes (New York: Loeb Classical Library, 1928), p. 211.

10. Thomas Paine, *Common Sense* (London, 1776), pp. 28–29.

11. John Dewey, *Freedom and Culture* (New York: Capricorn Books, 1963), pp. 153–56.

12. Montesquieu, *The Spirit of the Laws* (New York: Hafner Publishing Co., 1949), Bk. XI, p. 150.

13. Jacques Julliard, "For a New 'Internationale'," *The New York Review of Books*, XV (July 20, 1978), p. 3.

14. Richard Price, *Two Tracts on Civil Liberty* (London, 1778; reprinted in New York by Da Capo Press in 1972), p. 6.

15. Joseph Priestley, *An Essay on the First Principles of Government* (London, 1771), p. 58.

16. Cicero, *De Re Republica*, I, XXV in Keyes, p. 65.

17. James Harrington, *The Commonwealth of Oceana* (1656), in *The Political Works of James Harrington*, ed. with an introduction by J. G. A. Pocock (Cambridge: Cambridge University Press, 1977), p. 161.

18. This formula was actually composed by Harrington's eighteenth-century editor, John Toland. It is quoted often in later political literature, as, for example, by John Adams, *A Defence of the Constitutions of Government of the United States of America* (New York: H. Gaine, 1787), p. 157.

19. Montesquieu, Bk. III, Ch. 1, p. 19.

20. Ibid., Bk. V, Ch. 20, p. 40.

21. Ibid.

22. Alasdair MacIntyre, *Is Patriotism a Virtue?*, (The Lindley Lecture, University of Kansas, 1984) p. 18.

23. Ibid., p. 19.

24. Ibid., p. 15.

25. See Andrew J. Reck, "The American Revolution, A Philosophical Interpretation," *The Southwestern Journal of Philosophy*, 8 (1977): 95–104, and R. R. Palmer, *The Age of the Democratic Revolution* (Princeton: Princeton University Press, 1959), 1:214–15.

26. Algernon Sidney, *Discourses on Government* (New York: Deare and Andrews, 1803), Vol. II, Ch. II, Sec. XI, p. 86.

27. Polybius, *Histories*, Bk. VI, 3–9, 11–15.

28. Cicero, *De Re Republica*, in Keyes, passim.

29. *The Discourses of Niccolo Machiavelli*, trans. Leslie J. Walker (New Haven: Yale University Press, 1950), Bk. 1, Ch.2., pp. 211ff.

30. See Paul Eidelberg, *The Philosophy of the American Constitution* (New York: The Free Press, 1968).

31. Adams, p. 175.

32. Ibid., p. 179.

33. Ibid., p. 168.

34. Ibid., p. 180.

35. Ibid., p. 168–9.

36. J.G.A. Pocock, *The Machiavellian Moment* (Princeton: Princeton University Press, 1975), p. 572.

37. Gordon S. Wood, *The Creation of the American Republic, 1776–1787* (Chapel Hill: University of North Carolina Press, 1969), pp. 606–15.

38. It is noteworthy that in the *Politics* (Bk. IV, Ch. 11) Aristotle also enunciated the tripartite division of government into deliberative, executive, and judicial departments, foreshadowing the contemporary divisions into legislative, executive, and judicial departments. Sometimes this division is construed to be the import of the mixed polity, but to elucidate the senses in which this construal is and is not correct would be to tell another story.

39. Research for this paper was originally undertaken when I was a Liberty Fund Senior Scholar, Institute for Humane Studies, Menlo Park, California, Summer, 1982, and Visiting Scholar, The Poynter Center, Indiana University— Bloomington, January-July, 1983, during sabbatical leave from Tulane University. I wish to thank these institutions for enabling me to pursue my studies in freedom. An earlier version of this paper was presented to the American Association for the Philosophic Study of Society, meeting in conjunction with the Eastern Division, American Philosophical Association, in Boston, on December 29, 1983. I am grateful to the participants for their comments.

PART II

IDEOLOGY AND THE
AMERICAN ECONOMY

IV

Self-Interest and
American Ideology

Douglas J. Den Uyl

The American ought therefore to love this country much better than that wherein either he or his forefathers were born. Here the rewards of his industry follow with equal steps the progress of his labour; his labour is founded on the basis of nature, self-interest; can it want a stronger allurement? Wives and children, who before in vain demanded of him a morsel of bread, now, fat and frolicsome, gladly help their father to clear those fields whence exuberant crops are to arise to feed and to clothe them all; without any part being claimed, either by a despotic prince, a rich abbot, or a mighty lord.

———

J. Hector St. John de Crèvecoeur, 1782

Perhaps no other president since Franklin Roosevelt has had as significant an impact on the American political and social conscience as Ronald Reagan. Whether one is sympathetic to his programs or not, the fact remains that Reagan's presidency marks a significant shift in the character of public policy debate. The overwhelming defeat of Walter Mondale suggests this point, and numerous public opinion polls indicate that Reagan's vision is generally not out of touch with that of the rest of the country. In rhetoric, if not in fact, the Reagan vision contains both an economic and a moral component. "Free enterprise" defines, albeit somewhat ambiguously, the economic component, while "traditional moral values" characterizes (again, ambiguously) the moral component. What is the relationship between these two components? Although we cannot explore this question by speculating on how Reagan or his followers might connect the two, we can discuss the components in a broader philosophical context and analyze the bearing their relationship may have on the concept of American ideology.

It is perhaps America's economic system that best characterizes the essence of our civilization, for it is here that our social values are expressed in the concrete. Our nation, however, was founded as a moral and not as an economic order. The Founding Fathers knew nothing of the debate between capitalism and socialism, and yet it has been claimed that their principles favor the former sort of economic system over the latter.[1] But if the "traditional values" of our Founding Fathers constitute a moral vision, then we must be able to reconcile that vision with what is taken to be the central feature of our economic order—self-interest.

101

Since self-interest is commonly considered to be antithetical to moral values, some exploration of the relationship between self-interest and morality is needed in a setting devoted to the theme of "American Ideology."

To get a handle on the idea of self-interest, the opening part of the paper discusses Adam Smith. Although Smith was not an American, his "system of natural liberty" is thought to be the theoretical defense of our economic system and the values associated with that system.[2] After a discussion of Smith's views, I shall mention what I take to be a problem in his conception of human nature and self-interest and the effect this problem might have on ideology. Finally, I shall try to relate the preceding sections of the paper to the American experience.

Before beginning, a word needs to be said about "ideology." This concept has a wide range of meanings and uses from the positive to the neutral to the negative. Ordinary usage, however, has turned "ideology" into a negative term rooted in the Marxist traditions of class interest.[3] In this case "ideology" constitutes a set of beliefs which serve to rationalize one's own or one's class (or group) interests. A good simple definition of the term might therefore be: "An ideology is a set of beliefs or values that can be explained through the (non-cognitive) interest or position of some social group."[4] One's beliefs or values are in essence epiphenomenal to one's underlying interests and are not the motivating force behind one's actions. For reasons that should become evident as the paper continues, I will retain this negative interpretation of "ideology." I do this for the special purposes of this paper and make no claim that this is the "correct" or only understanding of the term.

Adam Smith and the Problem of Self-Interest

Traditionally there has been a problem in presenting a coherent interpretation of the role self-interest is meant to play in Smith's philosophical system. We can see this problem by comparing two passages from two of Smith's works. The first one is perhaps the most famous passage from his *Wealth of Nations*:

> It is not from the benevolence of the butcher, the brewer, or the baker, that we expect our dinner, but from their regard to their own interest. We address ourselves, not to their humanity but to their self-love, and never talk to them of our own necessities but of their advantages. Nobody but a beggar chuses to depend chiefly upon the benevolence of his fellow-citizens.[5]

This next set of passages is perhaps less well known today, but it comes from Smith's *The Theory of Moral Sentiments*—a work on which he made his reputation during his lifetime.

> That wealth and greatness are often regarded with the respect and admiration which are due only to wisdom and virtue; and that the contempt, of which vice and folly are the only proper objects, is often most unjustly bestowed upon poverty and weakness, has been the complaint of moralists in all ages. . . . Two different roads are presented to us, . . . the one, by the study of wisdom and the practice of virtue; the other, by the acquisition of wealth and greatness. . . . The great mob of mankind are the admirers and worshippers, and, what may seem more extraordinary, most frequently the disinterested admirers and worshippers, of wealth and greatness. . . . It is scarce agreeable to good morals . . . that mere wealth and greatness, abstracted from merit and virtue, deserve our respect. We must acknowledge, however, that they almost certainly obtain it; and that they may, therefore, be considered as, in some respects, the natural objects of it.[6]

Consider also:

> If he would act so as that the impartial spectator may enter into the principles of his conduct, . . . he must upon this, as upon all other occasions, humble the arrogance of his self-love, and bring it down to something which other men can go along with.[7]

If self-interest, expressed through a desire to obtain wealth and "greatness," is the engine of economic prosperity and economic prosperity is to be valued, then how does one reconcile that with the critique of wealth and self-interest to be found in *The Theory of Moral Sentiments*? It would seem that Smith is forced to give up prosperity for the sake of morality or morality for the sake of prosperity. Traditionally, this has been labeled *Das Adam Smith Problem*. And even if it should turn out that there is not much of a "problem" here as far as Smith is concerned, ordinary moral discourse and debate often dichotomizes morality and self-interest. The way in which Smith attempts to reconcile the two might, therefore, be helpful in our own thinking about the relationship between them.

The Dilemma of Self-Interest in Smith

To deal with the concept of self-interest in Smith it should be instructive to examine the views of one of Smith's critics—George Gilder. Gilder is most useful for our purposes because, (1) as a leading "supply side" theorist he is sympathetic to the Smithian conclusions about the value of a free economy, (2) his book, *Wealth and Poverty*, has been widely read and thus can offer insights into "popular" economics and culture, and (3) his criticisms focus on defects in Smith's moral justification of the "system of natural liberty." We shall not, however, analyze Gilder's own thesis that "capitalism"is the economic expression of altruism. In the first place, that thesis tends to confuse altruism with entrepreneurial creativity. Secondly, as an ethical theory altruism is thoroughly "demand-sided." The value of one's own life or actions is dependent upon their favorable reception by others. A "supply side" ethics,[8] on the other hand, would see a person's life as having value quite independently of any contribution it makes towards the welfare of others. Nevertheless, Gilder's reflections on Smith do raise the appropriate questions about Smith and the role of economic self-interest in general.

Gilder claims that the Smithian conception of society is founded on a dilemma.[9] On the one hand, Smith and the intellectuals who follow him do not approve of businessmen. They are seen as vulgar, self-serving, amoral, and uninteresting when compared to intellectuals.[10] On the other hand, many social benefits come from these businessmen's operating in an environment of free economic exchange. Businessmen are allowed the freedom to pursue their own greed and avarice because the market is a "great machine" directed as if by an "invisible hand," such that the greed of the businessman is transformed into something that serves the public good. Thus businessmen, who mean only to satisfy their own selfish desires, are led to produce results which were really no part of their intention. Gilder calls this arrangement a "Faustian pact" between society and businessmen. Furthermore, this pact is bound to create a kind of "moral schizophrenia," since the actors in the system are seen as amoral or immoral while the system itself is thought to be for the public good.

The Smithian model is sure to be unattractive to the "young," "idealistic," and/or morally sensitive individual. After all, how can we possibly create a good society by placing it in the hands of those regarded by the theory itself as being predatory philistines? Nevertheless, the theory has attracted a number of intellectuals for two main reasons: (1) it allows them to like capitalism without liking capitalists, and (2) economists liked the theory because it tended to reduce productive activities to scientific formulas, since Smith and others reduced man to a mere mechanism of self-interest amenable to mathematical calculation.

In general, Smith made two basic errors according to Gilder—one economic and the other moral. On the economic side Smith thought that wealth was created by the efficient *distribution* of resources, rather than by creative entrepreneurial production (the correct view). On the moral side, Smith failed to see that the morally sound endeavor of creative effort was not reducible to a (morally improper) Hobbesian conception of man. In other words, by seeing man as an essentially self-interested mechanistic and atomistic utility maximizer, Smith was mistaken in believing that positive effects alone could nullify the amorality or immorality of such a foundation of the economic order.

In Defense of Smith

It is my position that Gilder's critique of Smith is generally mistaken or misleading, although Gilder does intuit a problem I shall discuss later on. Our attention, however, must be directed to Gilder's moral claims about Smith's theory of self-interest rather than to Gilder's economic critique.[11] The defects in Gilder's characterization of Smith[12] can be summed up under two main categories: (1) his failure to appreciate the importance Smith's theory of justice plays in both *The Wealth of Nations* and *The Theory of Moral Sentiments*, and (2) his failure to see that the economic phenomenon of "self-interest" in *The Wealth of Nations* is complex and subject to two different (and opposing) characterizations.

Recent scholarship has demonstrated the importance of Smith's theory of justice to understanding (and reconciling) his two major works.[13] Justice for Smith was a moral concept of limited application.[14] It referred to principles that were minimally necessary for social life to take place. Thus justice was essentially negative, because it was concerned with restraint from harming others rather than with positive acts of beneficence. Justice also defined the limitations on the use of force or violence. Consider the following:

> Mere justice is . . . but a negative virtue, and only hinders us from hurting our neighbour. The man who barely abstains from violating either the person, or the estate, or the reputation of his neighbours, has surely very little positive merit. He fulfills, however, all the rules of what is peculiarly called justice, and does every thing which his equals can with propriety force him to do, or which they can punish him for not doing. We may often fulfill all the rules of justice by sitting still and doing nothing.[15]

The foregoing indicates that although justice is a moral concept, it is not the same thing as moral virtue(s) in general. Indeed, other moral virtues cannot be coerced as conformity to the rules of justice can be.

Douglas J. Den Uyl

And as Teichgraeber points out, this conception of justice caused Smith to de-emphasize the moral importance of politics[16] and, I might add, to emphasize the social and moral value of liberty.

The significance of all this for our purposes is that *The Wealth of Nations* presupposes a concept of self-interest that is constrained by justice. Smith is not saying that self-interest is the foundation of the "system of natural liberty," but rather that self-interest constrained by the rules of justice is the foundation of the system. If this is correct, self-interest takes on rather different connotations from those given to Smith's theory by Gilder and others. Smith is *not* endorsing unqualified greed for the sake of its beneficial effects.[17] "Faustian pacts" are not the sort of thing that can be constructed under strict adherence to the rules of justice of the kind Smith advocates.[18]

In fact, however, it is by no means clear that Smith thought greed had beneficial social effects. This, of course, brings us to our second objection to Gilder's characterization of self-interest in Smith. If self-interest must be understood as an anti-social passion that is manifest in the advancement of the self at the expense of others, then Smith neither favors this nor understands it to be the motive force behind the system of natural liberty. Consider the following passage which appears just before the more famous one we examined earlier:

> In almost every other race of animals each individual, when it is grown up to maturity, is entirely independent, and in its natural state has occasion for the assistance of no other living creature. But man has almost constant occasion for the help of his brethren, and it is in vain for him to expect it from their benevolence only. He will be more likely to prevail if he can interest their self-love in his favour, and shew them that it is for their own advantage to do for him what he requires of them. . . . and it is in this manner that we obtain from one another the far greater part of those good offices which we stand in need of.[19]

This passage not only indicates that it is not atomistic individualism that grounds the Smithian system, but also that self-interest is the vehicle *for* socialization, rather than a hindrance to it.

Furthermore, writers such as Gilder fail to appreciate the fact that self-interest in an economic context is actually a term with dual implications. For the most part self-interest in *The Wealth of Nations* translates into the desire a person has to "better his own condition"[20]—a desire that is a long way from greed and avarice. When Smith thinks of self-interest in terms of such negative values as greed, he is usually referring to those conditions subversive of his system of natural liberty. Economic

106

greed for Smith can be viewed as the willingness to use the coercive powers of the state to secure one's own economic advantage at the expense of others.

> To widen the market may frequently be agreeable enough to the interest of the publick; but to narrow the competition must always be against it, and can serve only to enable the dealers, by raising their profits above what they would naturally be, to levy, for their own benefit, an absurd tax upon the rest of their fellow-citizens.[21]

> Corporation laws enable the inhabitants of towns to raise their prices, without fearing to be under-sold by the free competition of their own countrymen. . . . The enhancement of price . . . is every where finally paid by the landlords, farmers, and labourers of the country, who have seldom opposed the establishment of such monopolies. They have commonly neither inclination nor fitness to enter into combinations; and the clamour and sophistry of merchants and manufacturers easily persuade them that the private interest of a part . . . is the general interest of the whole.[22]

These passages help demonstrate that economic self-interest as greed has little, if anything, to do with the system of natural liberty Smith advocates. Indeed, the greed which results in the desire for "combinations" is the essence of mercantilism—the system Smith opposes. Smith chastises businessmen not because their pursuit of self-interest is a necessary evil one must accept in order to receive the social benefits, but because that self-interest, unchecked by justice, may result in an economic advantage at another's expense.

It is my conviction that Americans traditionally have seen self-interest much the way I have described Smith as seeing it. Self-interest is partly a fact of human nature and partly a value which, when grounded in justice, is by no means a greedy or anti-social passion. Adherence to the rules of justice (e.g., as it was understood by the Founding Fathers) serves to check the excesses to which self-interest may be prone. But to admit that self-interest may have unwanted tendencies is a long way from the Faustian pact presented to us by Gilder and others.[23] Given this more accurate representation of the role of self-interest, we are now in a better position to examine the implications and questions self-interest may raise about the topics of ideology and American values.

Self-Interest and "Moral Dualism"

Although we may have saved Smith from the easy attacks on self-interest so common among his critics, other issues remain. Perhaps these issues are in part expressed by the feeling of uncertainty one has when reading The Theory of Moral Sentiments. Is this a book of moral theory proper (where criteria or principles are explained and justified on how to evaluate actions), or is this work in what could be called "moral sociology" (a descriptive account of how moral norms arise)? This is not an easy question to answer. In the last part of the work Smith discusses the defects of various traditional moral theories. The reader, however, is left only with criticisms and little by way of positive alternatives. If one searches the earlier part of the book for those alternatives, the most plausible candidate seems to be the "impartial spectator." The impartial spectator arises in Smith's moral theory within a context rooted in sentiment—specifically, the human propensity for sympathetic feelings towards others. Unfortunately, "spectating" impartially poses a kind of dilemma: Either the standards of right and wrong are derived from the sentiments one impartially "spectates" about (in which case the impartial spectator cannot function as a *standard* for evaluating those sentiments but only as a means to their discovery) or the impartial spectator uses standards not founded exclusively on those sentiments (in which case we are left wondering what the standards are and where they come from). Of course, this dilemma can be solved if we read the work as a treatise on moral sociology and not moral theory. However, Smith gives us the impression that he is doing more than moral sociology.

The problem here stems generally from the Humean tradition of moral philosophy (of which Smith is a part) that dichotomizes human nature into reason and desire (or passion, or sentiment). Hume regarded reason to be the seat of impartiality and objectivity but incapable of discerning the difference between what ought to be valued and what ought not to be valued or of directing one's desires.[24] The issue is somewhat more ambiguous in Smith, especially given his critique of Humean utilitarianism.[25] But however refined or subtle Smith may get, he never quite moves out from under the Humean umbrella. Feeling or desire remains at the foundation of human nature and moral theory. Reason is an entirely different, and disconnected, feature of our nature in the service of sentiment or desire. For lack of a better expression, let us call this "moral dualism," and let us make the concept Humean by agreeing that "reason is and ought only to be the slave of the passions."[26]

Given the presence of moral dualism, I wish to provide a brief justification for two theses: (1) self-interest (when understood in the Humean context) does, after all, produce paradoxical moral conclusions, and (2) ideology, in the negative sense described earlier, is a likely spin-off of this moral dualism. The impact of both these theses will be discussed later.

"Self-interest" refers to the desiring side of our nature and not to reason and such cognate concepts as "impartiality." This generates a certain paradox, the foundations of which are described by Henry Veatch in contrast to an Aristotelian anthropology and ethic:

> The moral life is no longer thought of as consisting principally in the individual's pursuing his rightful end or goal or telos just as a human being and trying not to be deflected therefrom by the myriads of chance impulses and drives and inclinations and likings and preferences that never cease to manifest themselves in the life of any one of us. No, morality will instead be largely an affair . . . of the individual's having to try to bring himself to be other-regarding rather than exclusively self-regarding. His duties . . . are not towards himself at all, but only towards others, in that morally he must needs be careful to try not to impede or wrongfully interfere with others in their pursuit of their ends and interests, just as they in turn are in duty bound not to interfere with him in his pursuit of his ends and interests.[27]

Veatch's claim, that modern ethics has turned away from the concept of *self*-perfection that was central to antiquity, is founded upon the recognition that the passions, interests, sentiments, drives, etc., are taken as givens in human nature. We do not concern ourselves with altering these givens, but rather with controlling their "neighborhood effects" upon others. Ethics, then, is exclusively other-oriented.

The paradox all this generates is as follows: Although the system of natural liberty is said to depend upon (the now-constrained version of) self-interest, the *best* that can be said for self-interest in a moral context is that it is amoral! Our moral choices concern how we let our desires or interests affect others, but our passions and their satisfaction are without moral import because they are the givens upon which moral reasoning is based. We therefore reach a position where a system that encourages the free pursuit of self-regarding actions must be justified exclusively in other-regarding terms. Self-interest must be legitimized by selflessness. If this is not a contradiction, it is certainly a paradox.[28]

It is interesting to look at those sections of *The Theory of Moral Sentiments* where Smith employs the impartial spectator to combat weakness of the will.[29] Here impartiality (or reason) is understood as being devoid of the influence of passion or interest upon judgment, anticipatory of

Kant's prescription to act "from duty." But if Hume is right, it seems to be the case that reason will lose the battle. And because of this conflict Kant found it necessary to posit a noumenal self as the seat of impartiality and to remove all traces of self-interest from morality. Moreover, if reason and passion are at odds or require differing moral evaluations, we seem to generate what Gilder called "moral schizophrenia"—an inability to encompass our *whole* being within the moral framework.[30] The attempts to solve this problem are usually similar: find a way to remove self-interest from morality, so that only one side of the dualism is given to morality. The Kantians do this by purging the phenomenal self from the "kingdom of ends." The utilitarians do it by separating actions from motivations. Gilder does it by arguing for the (in my opinion absurd) idea that self-interest really is not self-interest after all, but giving. Yet there is, finally, a different alternative as well—moral skepticism. Here one does not get rid of self-interest, but rather morality.

I am not convinced that these various alternatives (for example, deontology versus consequentialism) remove the schizophrenia or the paradox. People not only do pursue that which they regard to be in their own interest, but also tend to place positive moral value on many of those pursuits. I would regard the Aristotelian solution to be the appropriate one, namely, self-interest refers neither to the passions nor to reason, but to some combination of these aspects of our nature (for example, rational desiring) guided by some standard of self-perfection.[31] Unfortunately, the Aristotelian paradigm is not highly regarded in academic circles and is beyond defense in this paper. We have, in any case; supported our first thesis that there is something paradoxical about the relationship between morality and self-interest in a system which equates self-interest with the satisfaction of desire.

With respect to the second thesis, that ideology—negatively understood as essentially rationalization—will be commonplace, we can see this best within a Humean context. If reason serves the passions, then all reasoning becomes a form of rationalization for our desires. The surface justifications offered by people are really epiphenomenal to their deeper motivations, and it is to these hidden motivations that one must look in order to gain an understanding of social life and action.[32] What this theory leaves for theoretical dispute is whether these rationalizations are done with respect to our individual interests, our economic interests, our class interests, or whatever. In the end, however, we are all ideologists because we can be nothing else.

We might, on the other hand, deem it possible and desirable to be completely *dis*interested, to reject the Humean paradigm altogether. It is not clear, though, whether this removes the problem of ideology or strengthens it. The Humeans seem to be right in their insistence on the reality and force of desire—a point noted long ago when Plato argued that the appetitive part of the soul was the strongest and the rational part the weakest. Complete impartiality, understood as reason devoid of any connection with interest, is thus a myth. And if this is true, then the tendency will be for people to invest a great deal of passion and interest in abstract causes under the illusion that the abstract is the same as the impartial or the selfless. The result might be a society that is actually *more* ideological than the Humean one, because there would be a greater tendency to ignore or refuse to recognize the self-interested elements underlying those causes. Either way, our second thesis gains some theoretical support and does not seem contradicted by contemporary experience. When the individual's own desires are considered beyond the pale of morality, ideology is the likely side effect.

The American Rejection of Ideology

We have argued that Americans generally favor Smith's system of natural liberty, including the pursuit of self-interest, when that system is properly understood and presented. We have also argued that there nevertheless remains a kind of moral paradox about self-interest based upon what we have labeled "moral dualism." This dualism encourages ideological thought. I wish to argue here, on the other hand, that Americans are generally not very ideological, choosing instead to meet pragmatically the problem raised in the last section.[33] The pragmatic attitude is suspicious of both claims to impartiality and of interested behavior. Instead of judging behavior or proposals on their own merits, one considers an action or proposal as incomplete and unjustified until it has confronted its opposite and a compromise has been reached. The compromise is then put in force and final judgment is reserved until we have a chance to see how it works. The pragmatic attitude is thus a results-oriented approach grounded in a skepticism that any person (or group, or position) can be in possession of the "truth." Absolutist and moralistic stands are avoided; and this is coupled with an equally strong suspicion that whenever a moral stand is taken, that stand masks a deep self-interest that serves as the real motive and explanation.[34]

It is difficult to prove that Americans generally lack an ideology, especially since part of my case in the last section is made plausible by the rise of ideological attitudes in this century. Nevertheless, it has long been a truism of American politics that the middle of the road wins elections. That center shifts to the right or left from time to time, but seldom does it wander far from center. Even Reagan and Roosevelt do not represent counter-examples, but rather shifts in the tilt of the center brought on by social problems inherited from previous administrations (the Depression or the failure of the Great Society). There are indeed ideological wings to the various parties which have an impact on the shifts. But that influence is a long way from saying that Mr. and Mrs. Front Porch are moved by anything beyond a pragmatic feeling about the shift in the direction of the center.

In academic circles the recent rise in various forms of social contract theory seems at least partially to support my point. Social contract theory, as it is done by Rawls, Buchanan, Ackerman, and others, begins by explicitly rejecting "absolutist," "moralistic," or "ideological" approaches to social theory. It focuses instead upon compromise and agreement, and regards the "correct" moral values to be those that *result* from the bargaining process of the social contractors. Moreover, these approaches to political and social theory seem to be natural responses to the ideological fervor of the late sixties and early seventies.

If a pragmatic attitude is the response to having to choose between sanctifying self-interest and adopting the myth of disinterested impartiality, then the remaining question concerns explaining how traditional values—such as liberty, property, free expression, and so forth—can be made consistent with our thesis that Americans are pragmatic. After all, these are the traditional values thought to be held sacred by all and beyond reduction to self-interest or compromise. It must be asked, however, whether the pragmatic attitude, in the process of avoiding ideology, engenders its own problems. For example, do these traditional values contain much substantive and guiding content anymore? They certainly have such content when contrasted to Soviet-style communism. What is not clear, on the other hand, is whether they now function as much more than slogans to which everyone gives assent but which otherwise fail to guide actions or policies. Property rights, for example, have been so eroded by the courts and government regulation (with apparent public approval) that it is no longer clear what one is committed to when one says he or she favors our economic system of "private property."[35]

If certain traditional values have indeed become vacuous, it can only be because they have come to be understood pragmatically. One implication of this pragmatic attitude is the resolution of conflicts through compromise and mutual concession. If this is done with basic values, those values are bound to lose their power as guides to behavior. They are likely to become instead slogans which offend no one and include the interests of everyone. The result will be less a guiding moral vision than simply a moral sentiment. We are thus brought back to the problem surrounding *The Theory of Moral Sentiments*: Are moral values prescriptive standards for guiding behavior and limiting action or are they simply expressions of agreed-upon feelings? Perhaps Smith's message is that the two are the same thing.

Conclusion

We began by exploring a concept that seems central to the American economic system—self-interest. We attempted to clarify that concept from the standpoint of the theorist most often associated with it, Adam Smith. We saw that the usual characterization of the concept was faulty, and we implied that Americans traditionally understood it much as Smith himself did. Although self-interest could not be subjected to the standard and easy attacks leveled at it from both the right and the left, we noted that there may, nonetheless, be some paradoxical features to the concept. This led to an attempt to explain how the phenomenon of ideology might be related to those problems and the impact that may have on the pragmatic attitude Americans have towards politics. In this connection we saw that such an attitude was a response to a dualism that made integration of self-interest and morality difficult or impossible and which rejected the attempt to move too much towards one side or the other. But we also saw that the pragmatic attitude opened up its own set of problems.

As a final question we might ask whether the pragmatic reaction is an improvement upon tendencies towards ideology or moral skepticism. Indeed, it might be worth considering whether the pragmatic attitude itself could become a kind of ideology—one where definite interests and values are masked by an appearance of practicality sometimes legitimized by technical sophistication.[36] Indeed, there is a real possibility that the pragmatic attitude collapses back into the ideological attitude it was a reaction against. If the content of basic values is gutted by compromise and defined by mere agreement, then one seems left with only one's own interest. And in the absence of alternatives to modern moral dualism, the attempt to recapture moral values will likely take on the character of equating morality with selflessness or the impartial with the abstract. In other words, we would be back in the position the pragmatic attitude was meant to correct. It seems plausible to conclude by saying that America today is caught in a tension between ideology and the pragmatic reaction to it. And if what we have just said is true, the tension seems almost inescapable, since each side of that tension feeds and nurtures the other.

We have not offered a solution to the problems raised in this paper, other than to agree with Smith that one of the links between self-interest and morality will come through a theory of justice. Offering a solution, even if one could be found, would carry us beyond this essay's limits. Nevertheless, the American concept of individualism, without the atomistic overtones, seems to offer us some direction. For example, if supply-side economics (whatever its merits as a macro-economic program) has forced us to pay attention to the central role of individual initiative and entrepreneurship in economic prosperity, then perhaps an analogous point can be made in the realm of values. A supply-side approach to moral values would recognize the centrality of the self as both the source of moral values and as the ultimate seat of responsibility for those values. Neither "the state," nor "others," nor "the cause," nor "tradition" can replace or supersede the individual. The value of individuals is not a function of their contribution to these collective forces, but rather the vitality and legitimacy of these forces is a function of the values instilled in them by individuals. A difficulty with ideology is that it reverses this priority. Individuals are made a means to an end (the cause), instead of the cause being a means for enhancing the growth of individuals. Therefore, moral and political doctrines which either seek to eliminate or substantially reduce the importance of the individual's own interests or goals would be foreign to a supply-side conception of values.

In practice, the foregoing requires the recognition of the *moral* propriety of individual freedom. To paraphrase our discussion of Smith, individual freedom is not justified because of the social benefits that arise from having, for example, free markets. It is rather because individual freedom accords with the demands of justice that the benefits of the market can be realized.[37] The following passage from Smith well expresses our general theme. The "man of system" is the counterpart to our term "ideologist."

The man of system . . . is often so enamoured with the supposed beauty of his ideal plan of government, that he cannot suffer the smallest deviation from any part of it. He goes on to establish it completely and in all its parts, without any regard either to the great interests, or to the strong prejudices which may oppose it. He seems to imagine that he can arrange the different members of a great society with as much ease as the hand arranges the different pieces upon a chess-board. He does not consider that the pieces upon the chess-board have no other principle of motion besides that which the hand impresses upon them; but that, in the great chess-board of human society, every single piece has a principle of motion of its own, altogether different from that which the legislature might chuse to impress upon it.[38]

NOTES

1. The term "capitalism" is a term of derision given to the system by Marxists. I shall try to use alternative expressions, such as Smith's "system of natural liberty," after this introduction.

2. *The Wealth of Nations* was first published in 1776 and thus had little, if any, influence upon the American founding. However, Smith was known to a number of the Founding Fathers and his book *The Theory of Moral Sentiments* was widely acclaimed throughout Europe and thus probably known to some of the Founding Fathers.

3. See, for example, Koula Mellos, "The Concept of Ideology in Marx," *Social Praxis*, 7, no. 1-2, pp. 5-19; and also for a different view of the negative character of ideology see: John A. Guegen, "Modernity in the American Ideology," *Independent Journal of Philosophy*, 4, no. 1, p. 79. But a number of papers in this volume argue for a more positive interpretation of the concept of ideology. Moreover, these papers also correctly identify the origin of the concept as De Tracy and not Marx.

4. Jon Elster, "Belief, Bias and Ideology," in *Rationality and Relativism*, ed. M. Hollis and S. Lukes (Cambridge: MIT Press, 1982) p. 125. I apply the definition to individuals as well as groups in this paper.

5. Adam Smith, *An Inquiry into the Nature and Causes of the Wealth of Nations*, ed. R.H. Campbell and A.S. Skinner (Indianapolis: Liberty Classics, 1981), p. 27. Henceforth WN.

6. Adam Smith, *The Theory of Moral Sentiments*, ed D.D. Raphael and A.L. Macfie (Indianapolis: Liberty Classics, 1982), p. 62. Henceforth TMS.

7. TMS II, ii, 2, p. 83; quoted in Michael Novak, *The Spirit of Democratic Capitalism* (New York: Simon and Schuster, 1982), p. 147. The quotation that opens this paper from Hector St. John Crèvecoeur was taken from Novak's citation, p. 149.

8. The term "supply side," when applied to ethics, is somewhat artificial and misleading because it suggests an economic approach to moral values; but the label can serve a useful purpose within the limited confines of this paper, since we are talking about the connection between economics and ethics, and because it brings into focus some issues that deserve attention.

9. George Gilder, *Wealth and Poverty* (New York: Bantam Books, 1982), Ch. 3. Portions of this chapter, especially those dealing with Smith, can be found in "Capitalism is for Givers," *The American Spectator*, 15 (February 1982): 7-13.

10. An economist friend of mine once challenged me to find a single passage in *The Wealth of Nations* where Smith has something nice to say about businessmen. If there are such passages, I have not found them. Consider, for example, this passage: "People of the same trade seldom meet together, even for merriment and diversion, but the conversation ends in a conspiracy against the publick, or in some contrivance to raise prices." (WN, I, x, p. 145)

11. Gilder is quite mistaken to see Smith as focusing only upon the efficient distribution of resources and not upon savings, capital investment, and productivity. This mistake stems from Gilder's apparent belief that Smith's economics can be reduced to advocacy of deregulation and the benefits of the division of labor. One passage should be sufficient to indicate this misunderstanding:

> As the accumulation of stock must, in the nature of things, be previous to the division of labour, so labour can be more and more subdivided in proportion only as stock is previously more and more accumulated. . . . The person who employs his stock in maintaining labour, necessarily wishes to employ it in such a manner as to produce as great a quantity of work as possible. He endeavors, therefore, both to make among his workmen the most proper distribution of employment, and to furnish them with the best machines which he can either invent or afford to purchase. . . . The quantity of industry, therefore, not only increases in every country with the increase of the stock which employs it, but, in consequence of that increase, the same quantity of industry produces greater quantity of work. (WN, II, Introduction, p. 277.)

12. I might add here that Gilder's characterization of Smith is more common than unique. Thus what I say below applies to all similar characterizations of Smith.

13. L. Billet, "The Just Economy: The Moral Basis of the Wealth of Nations," *Review of Social Economy* 24 (December 1976): 295-315 and R. Teichgraeber, III, "Rethinking *Das Adam Smith Problem*," *Journal of British Studies*, 20 (Spring 1981): 106-23.

14. Smith's view of justice as described in *The Theory of Moral Sentiments* can be found in Pt. II, Sec. II, Chs. 1-3.

15. TMS, p. 82.

16. Teichgraeber, p. 123.

17. Incidentally, Smith offers a critique of merely utilitarian justifications of social practices. See TMS, IV, Ch. 2.

18. This is true whether or not one approves of Smith's theory of justice. The point is that it is not self-interest, but morally constrained self-interest that Smith endorses.

19. WN, p. 26.

20. WN, II, 3; III, 3; IV, 5; IV, 9.

21. WN, I, p. 267.

22. WN, I, p. 144.

23. In a related capacity see my "Self-love and Benevolence," *Reason Papers*, 9 (Winter 1983): 57-60.

24. David Hume, *Treatise on Human Nature*, Bk. III, Sec. 1.

25. TMS, VII, ii, Ch. 3.

26. I add this latter clause about the relation of reason to passion because Hume is clearer than his students and to help clarify the argument that follows.

27. Henry B. Veatch, "Telos and Teleology in Aristotelian Ethics," in *Studies in Aristotle,* ed. Dominic J. O'Meara (Washington, D.C.: The Catholic University of America Press, 1975), p. 287.

28. The paradox is not removed by recalling that Smith requires that self-interest be constrained by rules of justice. The relationship between those rules and the self-interested pursuits they permit raises the same paradox as we have just described in a more specific or limited way.

29. TMS, VI, iii, pp. 237-49.

30. Here we have the insight I mentioned earlier, though Gilder's interpretation of it is different from the present argument.

31. Obviously, to speak of "self-interest" with reference to Aristotle is somewhat anachronistic, since this is a modern problem. But I did say "Aristotelian" and not "Aristotle," which I take to mean using a framework like Aristotle's to address modern issues.

32. This is not necessarily a critique of certain methods in the social sciences that try to explain behavior by examining underlying incentives (e.g., Public Choice economics). It is rather a critique of the philosophical absolutizing of such theories.

33. I make no claims either for or against the idea that what I call the "pragmatic attitude" below is related to the school of philosophical thought labeled "pragmatism." I believe some elements of this attitude are so related while others are not. A discourse and debate on this question, however, would take us too far afield.

34. For example, in recent years I have disucssed with my business ethics classes the Proctor and Gamble decision voluntarily to remove Rely Tampons from the market, even though certain competitors (e.g., Tampax) did not. None of my students have felt that P&G did so for moral reasons, but rather because of the impact on future litigation or "PR."

35. For a history of this erosion, see B. Seigen, *Economic Liberties and the Constitution* (Chicago: University of Chicago Press, 1980).

36. I wish to thank Professor James Valone of my department for pointing out this possibility and for making a number of helpful suggestions on a first draft of this paper. In addition to Professor Valone, I should thank all the participants at a conference on American Ideology (sponsored by The Washington Institute) for their helpful criticisms. Of these participants, I am especially indebted to Morton Kaplan, Andrew Reck, and John Roth.

37. It is even possible to translate this perspective into practical public policy recommendations. Consider a simple example. Suppose we agree that corporations cannot continue to dump their wastes indiscriminately into the "public domain" (e.g., air and water). In trying to solve such a problem two basic approaches, summarized by the labels "design-based" and "performance-based" standards, might be considered. In the former, the state dictates the means and

specifications for reducing "pollution" levels. In the latter, a desirable level of pollution is set, leaving it up to the participants to choose their means of compliance. The performance-based approach obviously permits greater individual choice and freedom and thus better accords with a perspective that gives primacy of place to individual choice.

This simple example helps to illustrate the general point that economic and moral values, if not the same, are at least intimately connected in some way. And other recent work suggests that more comprehensive analyses of public policy issues can be undertaken with this vision of the priority of individuals in mind. See, for example, *Instead of Regulation*, ed. Robert W. Poole, Jr. (Lexington, Mass.: Lexington Books, 1982); and *Rights and Regulation*, ed. M. Bruce Johnson and Tibor R. Machan (Cambridge, Mass.: Ballinger Publishing Co., 1983).

38. TMS, VI, ii, pp. 233-34.

V

Property Rights and the Decent Society

—

TIBOR R. MACHAN

. . . In a society where everything is nationalized and is the property of the state, anybody can be expropriated and subject to export. The East German Minister of Culture once announced in Leipzig that "Unsere Literatur gehört uns (Our literature belongs to us!). . . . " What he meant was that it didn't belong to you, or to some "common national culture of two separate states" (which the DDR's constitution still mentions), certainly not to the shared language or the outside world. In Germany the phrase for chattel slaves or indentured servants was Leibeigenen, for the bodies belonged to their owners; now we have the new concept of Geisteigene, for minds and spirits are also part of the new social property relations. When a bureaucracy considers itself to be the owner of literature, then it has the absolute personal right not only to cultivate its own garden but also to remove ruthlessly such weeds as it deems harmful.

—

François Bondy, "European Diary: Exit This Way"
(Encounter, April, 1981)

A merica is searching for itself in our time, and this essay is aimed at helping in that task. Whether in domestic or in foreign policy matters, and some of the rhetoric to the contrary notwithstanding, this country no longer has a distinctive identity.

Of course, America has always been a diverse, many-faceted, pluralistic society. There has never been a culture with greater variety of religions, fashions, races, philosophical viewpoints, customs, lifestyles, and whatever else can make a difference among human beings. Yet, despite its great diversity, the United States once had a fledgling identity. It was a society with a discernible direction which set it apart, some would say quite drastically, from all other human communities at any time in human history.

The United States of America was known, for good or for ill, as an individualist society. Elsewhere it had been the state, the culture, the people, the race, the tribe, the clan, the spirit, or some other being that counted for the most, whereas in America the individual was supposed to be the main focus of political value.

Accordingly, America came to be identified with a general social philosophical viewpoint, namely, individualism, though as a nation it fell considerably short of fulfilling the requirements of the viewpoint. Clearly, slavery was America's greatest betrayal of its individualism, but other contradictions between its guiding vision and its practice could be identified. Still, compared to all other human communities in history, America stood out—and does so still today, rhetorically—as the society of individual rights and liberties.

Today, however, not even the direction of America's institutions points toward individualism. This has resulted in an identity crisis for this country. And without an identity, a country is difficult if not impossible to guide toward some kind of future. That is especially true when it happens also to be the one country to which much of the rest of the world looks for philosophical guidance.

In this essay I wish to explain why one element of individualism, the right to private property, is indeed a vital part of a good human community and therefore worthy of full understanding and preservation. I will discuss and defend the unique American political idea of the right to private property.

Is Individualism an Ideology?

First, an annoying distraction needs to be handled. It is one which deserves little respect yet has acquired enough of it within the intellectual community so as to require some attention. I refer to the fact that individualism has been dubbed an ideology, in that insidious sense of the term which refers to a system of ideas serving to rationalize (that is, make artificially palatable) preexisting wants, interests, or socioeconomic roles. Even the technical sense of "ideology" invites some curious prejudices, of course, since it means, roughly, the investigation of the source or material origin of ideas in the human mind. Within a historicist framework this immediately implies that ideologies must be narrow and bound to specific historical periods. The sense in which I wish to endorse the use of the term owes little to this legacy. When I speak of an American ideology, I have in mind a policy-guiding system of ideas and norms, not the Marxian or even the supposedly neutral sense that has gained currency.

Karl Marx treated all his serious intellectual adversaries as ideologues who were not worth arguing with, whose ideas he simply explained away as historical phenomena. Ideologies for him were reflections of essential features of prehuman societies involving the oppression of one class by another, with the hidden purpose of legitimizing this oppression. Thus those who argued for these principles of political economy were really to Marx not honest thinkers worthy of having their mistakes corrected. They were agents of a class, apologists, mouthpieces of the oppressors—even when others would consider them major theorists. Thus for Marx,

Adam Smith, the founder of modern economics, was not a scientist or theorist but merely a man engaged in elaborate, sometimes brilliant, rationalizations.

Under Marx's influence, but with the support of many non-Marxist outlooks, American individualism has been characterized an ideology by many social commentators. Some only mean by this that individualism, when expressed in simplistic terms, does not deserve to be called a serious social philosophy. But others really think the doctrine merely serves to rationalize the status quo—especially when there is little evidence that a society actually embodies individualist principles and policies, as is the case in ours at the present time.

For Marxists a system of laws based largely on the "rights of man"— for example, the right to private property—had a limited function in human history, namely, to facilitate production and technological development. Once this function had been achieved, these principles would be abolished by a new phase, and eventually by the last phase of human history, communism:

> Communism is for us not a state of affairs which is to be established, an ideal to which reality will have to adjust itself. We call communism the real movement which abolishes the present state of things. The conditions of this movement result from the premises now in existence.[1]

The movement in question can be viewed on analogy with the way a human individual develops from infancy to childhood, then to adolescence, and finally to maturity. Marx was extremely clear about this: "[From] my standpoint . . . the evolution of the economic formation of society is viewed as a process of natural history. . . . "[2]

Marx lay claim to having a "God's eye" perspective on humanity, a growing "organic body."[3] He spoke of early Western civilization as a stage of childhood when he wrote that "the Greeks were normal children."[4] His method of analysis supposedly entitled him to pinpoint the stages of humanity's development from its beginning through to its full emancipation. And thus for him capitalism was humanity's adolescence. As in adolescence, so in capitalism we experience joys and sorrows, costs and benefits, all quite unavoidably but only temporarily, with better times to come.

There are immense problems with the Marxian perspective; yet Jean-Paul Sartre was right to regard Marxism the dominant way of thought in our age. The reasons for this are complicated, but they have to do mainly with Marx's valiant but unsuccessful attempt to merge two indispensable and yet apparently incompatible human concerns, namely, science and values. In the end Marxism fails to be a theoretically successful system. Still, it is the most powerful, intellectually appealing, and widely discussed system of thought in our time.

This is not the place to take on Marxism. But it will be necessary to suggest some of its major flaws before we can appreciate why individualism is far more than an ideology in the Marxist sense of that term.

First, Marxism conceives of human beings collectively, as if humanity, not you or I, were the individual person, with purposes, intentions, ideas, health and illness. Marx discounts the importance of individuality and measures all values by reference to an idea of collective human essence. As he says, "The human essence is the true collectivity of man."[5] The foundation of this essence is material production, hence the labor conception of value and the messianic role of the working class.

Contrary to Marxian views, human nature must include our individuality. *Human beings are unique in being self-motivated and thus self-differentiating or self-defining.* The entire Marxist edifice rests on a monumental misunderstanding of human nature which ultimately undermines not only Marxian historical analysis—which is its most influential part—but also the practical prospects of socialism and communism.

Second, Marxian characterizations of capitalism and its social-philosophical foundation, individualism, are unfounded. If humanity does not undergo the developmental process of a biological organism, as Marx suggests, then his understanding of human history on the model of that process is unsupported. In turn, the various arguments about how human society should be organized, the right way for people to live in company with one another, cannot be dismissed as mere ideology. Rather, these are serious contenders for the answer to the perennial question of how we should live with one another, the central political question from time immemorial. The belief that in tribal societies human beings were at their stage of infancy, whereas in capitalist times they are in their adolescence, is an appealing, progressivist notion; but it turns out to be an unwarranted extrapolation. Human nature is far more stable than this view would have it. The question is what human nature is and how we must accommodate it, not at what stage of humanity's growth period or maturation we happen to be, as Marx and many of his conscious and unknowing followers suppose. This does not deny change in human life, but it does deny that the basic nature of human beings— albeit not likely eternally fixed—lacks stability through time.

Having discussed these two serious flaws in Marxism, we can now consider that an American ideology may have existed and might again exist, and what its features should be. We may talk of an ideology not because we are considering the framework in a pejorative way but because we are considering it from the point of view of its practical utility as a relatively simple—that is, not philosophically complex—public policy-guiding system of ideas.

The Nature of Property

We arrive now at our key topic, private property rights. With Marxism as the guiding dogma for many intellectuals, the principle of private property rights must always remain in doubt. Under Marxism's influence it has indeed suffered relegation, not just by Marxists but also by many others, to the field of intellectual archaeology. I wish to defend private property rights as a very good, indeed indispensable, idea and social principle.

Property—any just or rightful and exchangeable belonging—cannot include human beings. In the strict sense of that term one cannot thus own oneself: a person is not two beings, one the self who owns, the other the self who is owned. Of course it may at times be convenient to talk of owning oneself or, rather, owning one's life. This is the sense in which John Locke spoke of the property one has in one's person, meaning that the individual, not others, may be the final authority for guiding or governing what he or she will do. "Property," the relationship of rightful possession, means that some items, skills, or other valuables may belong to someone.

Property can be land—or *estate*, to use Locke's term—as well as furniture, paper, machinery, or other physical items. But property can also include poetry, computer programs, musical arrangements, paintings, works of fiction, reports, designs, roles, and so forth. *Property can be anything exchangeable that may be of value to persons, but it is not itself a person.*

Let us turn now to privacy. The term comes from the Latin, meaning "separate, not public or belonging to the state." Because throughout much of human history human beings had been considered by prominent thinkers as part of the whole—for example, part of the Greek *polis*—personal privacy did not receive paramount attention and treatment, although some exaggerate this point and draw unwarranted conclusions from it.[6] When finally the individual came into focus, a rather extreme characterization of individuality came to dominate. Marx was right to protest this Hobbesian conception of the human being as "the limited individual who is limited to himself."[7]

There is no need for such extremism, namely, the doctrine that everyone is wholly individual—unique and separate from everyone else. Rather, we can more realistically conceive of human beings as multifaceted, with characteristics which are indeed fundamentally private, and with others that are familial, fraternal, social, and political. What matters here is that the concept of privacy indicates that aspect of a person which *is* separate from others, capable of being, for better or for worse, autonomous, and on which the person's self-direction in life may have to depend. As such, one's private self may ultimately govern one's whole life.

"Private property," then, means any valuable item or service which may be separated off from the public or state for individuals to manage or control. The concept of a right to private property presupposes a moral standpoint suggesting justification for the individual's authority within a social context to decide on the disposition of a certain range of valued items.

An early expression of this standpoint can be found in William of Ockham, writing in the twelfth century. Heinrich A. Rommen has characterized Ockham's idea of the right to private property as "a dictate of right reason."[8] Ockham believed that "natural right is nothing other than a power to conform to right reason."[9]

Rights in Focus

The doctrine of natural rights rests on the possibility of identifying the nature of something, including human nature, and the moral aspects of human life whereby each individual is responsible to live morally, in accordance with dictates of human reason.[10] Because we are all personally responsible to achieve our human excellence—our moral success or happiness as human individuals—when considering the proper conditions of our social existence, the main issue must be to make this task possible in light of the presence of other people. Natural rights are those conditions which everyone must help secure so as to enable everyone to live morally or ethically.[11] Natural rights, when upheld, do not guarantee human moral conduct but are necessary conditions of it.

Of course this is not an uncontroversial thesis. The very idea of "the nature of X" has been in dispute for centuries, with many holding, I think wrongly, that no clear sense can be made of it.[12] Skepticism about the very possibility of an objective moral framework which would guide all human beings has also been widespread.

Both these views are flawed because both rest on demands of a theory of natures and moral truth that cannot be met. However, this is not the only way to understand what is required for a sound theory.[13] Indeed, the centrality of the natural rights to life, liberty, and property is required for the possibility of a full moral life for everyone in human communities; and this is discoverable by an understanding of human nature and the basic requirements of morality.[14]

I leave these very large issues aside for now, however, and turn to the troublesome enough idea of the right to private property, which I argue is indispensable for the moral life of human beings. To the extent that the right to property—which is not the central natural human right—is eroded, the prospect for a moral life will also erode.

Our Moral Task and Our Sphere of Authority

A central tenet of any morality is that we are responsible to choose our course of conduct correctly.[15] We ought to choose what we will do in a way that accords with the moral standards applicable to human life. Concretely, this means we ought to guide ourselves properly with respect to the reality that we encounter.

As a minimum, such an idea is implied by all genuine moral systems and by our common sense understanding of what it is to blame and praise persons for how they conduct themselves, regardless of place or historical period. All the details of morality must ultimately presuppose this element of personal responsibility, whether in modern or in ancient times. The assumption of voluntary self-responsible conduct can be found in ethics from Aristotle to the most recent moral philosophy, from hedonism to rational altruism.

This also means that we are committed to the exercise of rationality which will enable us to identify our moral responsibilities. I have in mind "rationality" not in a Cartesian or economic sense of that term but in the sense that we mean it when we refer to thinking clearly, being perceptive and aware of how we should act. We are committed to being thoughtful, to applying ourselves to concrete tasks in a basically principled fashion. Work, communication, integration of goals, choice of friends and country, concern for long-range tasks, and so on, are all part of the varied moral tasks of every individual capable of rationality.

One characteristic of rational living is the conscientious consideration of available alternatives. A person should choose the right course of conduct, and this means that he or she must know what alternatives are open to choice. For example, the questions might be: Should I attend church or go to the golf course? Should I purchase a car or a new encyclopedia? Should I invest my earnings in stocks or Care packages? Should I spend my time with my children or doing extra work at the office? Should I move from my present quarters to new ones? In each case the availability of the alternative is presupposed: Going to church or to the golf course both have to be available for the question to arise, and often, of course, numerous options are available. Should I take swimming lessons, send my child to dancing school, purchase a new tire for the family car, contribute to the homeless children's welfare fund, write a philosophy paper, or send a gift to my parents? Given that at any time I have a fixed budget or other limited resources, I would have specific options.

In any case, if, as any conception of human moral life supposes, persons are responsible for the decisions or choices they make from among alternatives, these alternatives have to be clearly available to them. To put it another way, jurisdiction over the alternatives is required to make a determinate choice about them. In the absence of such jurisdiction, the moral situation is systematically ambiguous, and just what a person ought to or ought not to do is impossible to clearly specify. While approximation may be possible, the possibility of clear assignment of blame or praise will be rare.

We can put it another way: Without a clear idea of what is ours, what belongs to someone else, and so forth, we must remain morally confused and ultimately lose confidence in our ability to live a moral life. That in turn can produce a demoralized society.

All this should begin to indicate the moral significance of private property rights. Suppose that my available options are unclear. I do not hold membership in the church and the golf club. Whether I may—that is, am authorized to—select either as an alternative is indeterminate; membership is largely at the discretion of the congregation and the city athletic association, respectively. Then whether I will go to one or the other is not something I *can* decide. "Ought" implies "can." If it is not up to me whether I will be going to one or the other place, I cannot be responsible for where I shall go—and so on down the line with every option involving two or more alternatives.

One way of interpreting the famous doctrine of "the tragedy of the commons" is to realize that when common ownership *and* authority attach to some valuable option, individuals who are responsible to make morally right choices cannot make them. They are unable to determine what they *should* do because the various alternatives are not theirs to select. With this goes the more widely recognized problem that when no individual authority is recognized with respect to some alternative (the choice of going to the club does not impose responsibilities of doing this carefully, prudently, and so forth), the ramifications, consequences, implications, and so on will be unattended.

Suppose I may personally select some portion of land with no obligation to admit others to share it, at least for a given time period. Now it is also clearly my responsibility whether I take good care of or neglect this land while using it. But if "we all" or some other indeterminate group has this authority, it becomes inherently ambiguous whose responsibility it is to take care. As Aristotle observes:

> For that which is common to the greatest number has the least care bestowed upon it. Every one thinks chiefly of his own, hardly at all of the common interest; and only when he is himself concerned as an individual. For besides other considerations, everybody is more inclined to neglect the duty which he expects another to fulfill; as in families many attendants are often less useful than a few.[16]

Yet even Aristotle misses the full story. What is ultimately tragic in "the tragedy of the commons" is that even if one were determined not to neglect any of one's responsibilities *it cannot be clear what one's responsibilities are*.

One might suppose there is a way out of this problem by finding an overriding common interest, so that when no personal sphere of authority is evident one would know to aim at this common concrete goal. But no such alternative is possible. The common or public interest, though capable of being specified, takes care of only a part of the concerns human beings have in life. The common interest or good is limited to values people in fact share, based on their nature as human beings. But all alternatives must be linked to actual or actually possible outcomes, only a few of which can effect the common good.

When considering the public interest apart from the protection of the rights of everyone—for example, the upkeep of what are called public parks or beaches—it might be thought that it is clear enough what our duties are: Public property must be used with proper care. Public facilities should be kept clean. When we administer so-called public education, it often sounds as if there is a very clear purpose at hand. Appearances to the contrary notwithstanding, attempting to deal with societies along these lines poses insurmountable difficulties.

In anyone's life, sound decisions are required pertaining to what will be attended to, what will be cared for considerably, and what will be neglected. No one has infinite time and resources. For example, during any timespan a parent may have to choose between attending fully to a baby, to work, or to other responsibilities. Because of the fully dependent status of the baby, its care will rate most attention, with other matters having to be relegated to lesser significance.

When, however, we do not have full authority over our sphere of activity and a choice presents itself, we often cannot determine what we should do about the common sphere. Say, we are suddenly called away from a public beach because our child needs us and we do not clean up after ourselves. We might, of course, spend time cleaning up before we rush away, but that could turn out to be irresponsible in light of the parental obligations we would thus neglect. If we have such a situation in our own bathroom, there we have jurisdiction and impose our decision only on those within its sphere—for instance, our family. The beach is left for others, unrelated to us, to care for. But they too have pressing matters calling on them, and eventually collective spheres become neglected, not because people fail to do their duty but because in public places duties are indeterminable.

These have also been called "uninternalizable negative externalities," meaning that apparently legitimate activities taking place in or adjacent to the commons have negative impact on others who have not agreed to suffer them. All this may appear to be quite manageable. We may elect politicians and appoint bureaucrats to take care of collective affairs. Yet they administer these matters with the resources of others— some of whom sincerely, and possibly rightly, judge the allegedly collective purpose morally or otherwise objectionable and thus will resist it. Accordingly, discord is inherent in the management of virtually all but the most specific and determinate sorts of collective affairs.[17]

Even the most conscientious individuals will find it impossible to avoid the tragedy of the commons. Few individuals will be morally perfect or consistently responsible, and exacerbation of the problem is unavoidable without establishing a sphere of individual dominion and the corresponding legal machinery to keep track of it for purposes of making self-responsible conduct possible, as well as for resolving disputes among human beings.

The right to private property is indispensable for a decent human community, one in which the moral life of individuals can flourish. Individuals cannot conduct themselves morally without a determinate sphere of authority.

None of this is touched by such red-herring considerations as that the right to private property is not absolute—meaning, one may suppose, that we are not omniscient about its full extent and implications and would need constantly to be vigilant about its clear, practical determination, its implementation, and its protection. What is clearly evident is that by any reasonable conception of the moral nature of human life, the right to private property is a necessary—though by no means sufficient—condition of morality within human communities.

It might be asked, then, just what the full extent of the right to private property must be for a society to satisfy the requirement of creating the fullest possible realm of personal authority for all persons. And without going into the details of the matter, the answer is that private property rights must prevail to the extent that the realm of public administration of justice is also secure. Thus, aside from the property needed to uphold the law—including provision for defense against domestic and foreign aggression, the necessary bureaucracy, and so on—the rest of the society's valued items would all be subject to private acquisition and holding.

Mirages of Collectivism

Despite doctrines contending otherwise, advanced by both the left and the right,[18] there is a very serious problem with collectivism and statism. Even if individuals who compose the state were not flawed, the state would be. The reason becomes evident from one socialist argument given in support of extensive state powers:

> The idea of social planning seemed to socialists to be inherent in their definition of rationality, indeed, in their definition of man. To be human was to be rational, and rationality consisted in planning one's conduct and environment in a way that helped realize one's consciously formulated purpose. The bourgeois view of man also defined him as a rational being, and rationality as a capacity

for planning, but for socialists there was a contradiction. They thought it odd
that men should plan their lives individually but not collectively, that they should
live as men individually but as "animals" collectively, and wondered if it was
ever possible for an individual to act rationally in a society that was not itself
rational.[19]

The essence of this argument is that if individuals can rationally plan
their lives, so can societies, and it is as vital to do this in the case of
societies as it is in the case of individuals. Socialism is the way that
societies can be rationally organized.

This general line of argumentation has subsequently led defenders of
capitalism to argue against the value of rationality. F. A. Hayek, for example, developed an elaborate attack on constructive rationalism, the
idea of "reason . . . conceived as . . . a capacity of the mind to arrive
at the truth by a deductive process from a few obvious and undoubtable
premisses."[20] This modern idea of reason, made prominent under the
very strong influence of René Descartes, has dominated both individualist
and collectivist thinking. The difference between individualists and collectivists seems here to amount to nothing more than the difference
between planning and laissez-faire. Socialists believe society, too, ought
to try to implement efficient means for its goals, namely, rational central
calculation.

Several problems confront both these arguments, however. For one,
there is far more to reason than mere efficiency. The narrow idea of reason
derives from a totally illegitimate, unscientific assumption, namely, that
human motivation is identical to the principles of mechanical motion.
By that Enlightenment idea the difference between persons and other
things was thought to be a matter of mere complexity, not of kind.
Therefore, principles of motion applied to persons, only in a somewhat
more complicated fashion, and could be extended to societies as well.

But how is this idea to be proven? By extrapolation and hope. Marx
realized that its proof had to involve an entire metaphysical edifice. We
have already seen some of its flaws. We were very successful in identifying the principles of mechanical motion, and that success led to optimism as far as our control over nature was concerned. By extrapolating
those physical principles to human nature and to human societies, we
were given the hope that we could control all human life just as we
have managed to control much of the rest of nature.

Since the time of this reckless optimism much scientific change has
occurred. Some of it points to the inadequacy of the early mechanical

framework even for the sphere of nature where it had been thought to be most successful in the first place, namely, physics.

Human nature gives clear evidence of being fundamentally different from the rest of nature. Furthermore, there is great variation within the various spheres of nature before we ever come to consider human nature. A monkey is vastly different from a bee, a shark from an ant, an oak tree from a tulip, a pebble from a mountain, a planet from a star, and so on. One reason the familiar and pervasive extrapolation is unjustified is that nature contains very different kinds and types of entities. A pluralism, permitting great diversity in the types and kinds of beings, as well as in their principles of motion, is most likely true.[21]

If a pluralistic metaphysics is sound, and if the evidence for a distinctive human nature is sufficient, then principles of motion or motivation applicable to human beings could be fundamentally different from the principles of motion to be applied to rocks and machines. In that case the modern conception of rationality is flawed, and both modern individualism and modern collectivism must be rethought in that light. The antecedents of these conditional statements seem true. Let us then see how to rethink rationality and the two political outlooks which invoke it.

Reason Reconsidered

In *Essays on the Laws of Nature*, John Locke, who himself made powerful use of the concept of reason within political thought, states:

> By reason . . . I do not think is meant . . . here that faculty of the understanding which forms trains of thought and deduces proofs, but certain definite principles of action from which spring all virtues and whatever is necessary for the proper moulding of morals.[22]

Hayek, who mentions Locke's observation, notes that "to the medieval thinkers reason had meant mainly a capacity to recognize truth, especially moral truth, when they met it, rather than a capacity of deductive reason from explicit premises."[23] And he notes that it is against this older "natural law" theory of reason that the modern instrumentalist or positivist conception—proposed by Francis Bacon, Thomas Hobbes, and René Descartes—had been advanced. The older conception, in contrast to the modern, did "recognize that much of the institution of civilization was not the product of deliberate human design."[24]

I will not go into a discussion of Hayek's general philosophical outlook.[25] What is crucial is that Hayek advances a very valuable lesson about political economy based on the above recognition of one of the main fallacies of modern thought, namely, its scientism.

Once we understand that human reason is not mainly the calculating kind but is instead our conceptual capacity for recognizing truth—for integrating and differentiating the evidence of the senses, for guiding action in the light of such truth, and thus for moral conduct—the complaint of collectivists against individualists turns out to be unjustified.

We should recall that complaint, namely, that socialists "thought it odd that men should plan their lives individually but not collectively." So long as rationality is viewed instrumentally, there might be something to this complaint. Surely, given certain set goals, efficient means may be found for pursuing them whether the goals are those of individuals or those of the entire society. Collectivists think, as do now even many who really cannot be easily labelled, that these set goals *for society* exist, and they are designated by such notions as the public purpose, the public interest, the public good, the full emancipation of humanity, and so on. So long as some such goal for society *as a whole* exists—so long as there is some "end state" for humankind, to use Robert Nozick's apt phrase[26]—there need be no good reason to refrain from planning for its achievement from above, by central direction.

But as soon as it is seen that reason must engage in the discovery of individual or social goals, the story changes drastically. Discovering what principles we must adhere to and what our individual goals are or should be, is something that can only be done through the use of the individual human faculty of reason, something collectives do not possess. This does not deny general principles of human conduct, of course. Identifying such general principles and choosing to live by them is, however, necessarily a private task, albeit possibly the work of many individuals. Others can only aid in carrying out the task. This is Hayek's and the Austrian economists' main point, although they put it in economic or "praxeological" terms. Hayek notes:

> . . . how little the individual participants need know in order to be able to take the right action. In abbreviated form, by a kind of symbol, only to those concerned. It is more than a metaphor to describe the price system of telecommunications which enables individual producers to watch merely the movements of a few pointers, as an engineer might watch the hands of a few dials, in order to adjust their activities to changes of which they may never know more than is reflected in the price movement.[27]

Let us now add to this. From what Hayek says individuals clearly can take the right action, since he thinks all activities can be adjusted with such available information. This is the idea that I discussed earlier, namely, that each person has moral responsibilities, to be individually fulfilled. To attempt to fulfill them, one must have a determinate sphere of authority for action. If so, then the idea of collective planning is not only impossible but, indeed, quite reprehensible. It implies the undermining of the moral nature of human beings.

The reasons for this conclusion may now be summarized from what has gone before in this essay:

1. Rationality *must* be exercised by individuals. Collective bodies do not possess this capacity; there is no such thing as a collective cerebral cortex. The initiation of the process of thought is necessarily an individual human task. Collectivism is a mistake because no collective capacities exist apart from those which individuals create through pooling their individual faculties and other resources.

2. The truths which rationality can unearth for individuals are mostly about individuals and their individual traits, needs, opportunities, goals, and fortunes. And it is in terms of such information that the moral guidelines by which individuals should conduct themselves must be identified. Here is where the Hayekian point about central state planning is brought home very clearly. The individual's plans are very different in kind from any sort of collective plan, in part because individuals may face different sets of challenges in life, and so, of course, may have different goals. (This, by the way, does not preclude the *possibility* of the harmony of interests. It does preclude the possibility of their uniformity, which is what collective planners must assume so as to be able to ignore the facts pertaining to individuals as individuals.)

3. By collectivist strictures, as Marx puts it, "the human essence is the true collectivity of man." So rational social-economic planning does not consider individual traits, goals, and talents as crucial. Only our common traits matter to collectivists. But this is a drastic and devastating metaphysical and moral oversight. Individuality is essential to being human precisely because every person is a rational animal, a concrete biological individual with the capacity for original, creative rationality. Both one's concrete biological individuality and one's capacity for rationality are necessary to being human. So when one considers the nature of a human polity—as Marx and Plato did—one must treat as vital what any person must be, namely, a human *individual*.[28]

Being rational does not in the least undermine, indeed it powerfully supports, one's individuality, contrary to what socialists believe. But the matter cuts both ways. Neither is the Hobbesian—or what today is known as the *homo economicus*—conception of individuality right. Persons are not able to escape their humanity; they are *human* individuals. Treating them as isolated monads or atoms—an idea promptly seized upon and denounced by socialists—has to be rejected. And with this we must reject the possibility of any degree of political-economic collective "planning," the notion from Hayek that gives anarchists so much intellectual fuel. With respect to their equality as moral agents, individuals must be understood to possess certain features requiring human social orders to be constituted in certain ways—namely, they must rest on natural, individual, human rights to life, liberty, and property, and be protected in an integrated, principled manner.

Based on a clear understanding of our human nature, certain natural rights may be identified and a political order *can* be planned or designed. The Constitution of the United States is thus a possibly suitable general plan or design. What is different in such a plan from those spoken of in connection with socialist planning is this: Socialists model their planning on the business firm or social club; they treat all property and persons as if they had a common purpose and were available for use in the realization of this purpose. Socialist planning is, then, regimentation, not economic planning!

But a constitution only spells out certain prohibitions and procedural rules, not goals. It does not specify the goals for society but makes goal seeking possible to all members of society. If we can consider a constitution as a design, its purpose is to serve the innumerably varied purposes of individuals with equal respect for everyone's task of pursuing the best possible purpose that he or she has come to identify. And the rule in terms of which a constitution aims for this purpose is to make it possible for everyone to follow through practically on his or her moral task.

It is just at this point that we return to our main topic, that is the role of the right to private property in a good human community.

Individuality, Morality, and Liberty

Let me now simply reiterate some of the points made at the outset of this essay. The task of a good society is to enhance the moral life of its members. This is best achieved if individuals are understood to require and are in fact secure in their proper sphere of authority to govern themselves. The best way to achieve this end is to identify and protect the individual right to private property.

The law of property of such a society could, of course, be very complicated. Real estate to copyright law, fences to patents, the justice departments of various levels of government to the police departments and the military—all these must keep a constant vigilance about the task of identifying and protecting the individual right to private property. The central purpose of such a system of law—not its sole end—is to make it possible for individuals to carry out their moral tasks in life.

The moral task of every individual is to succeed in his or her individual life. This places no priority on equal attainment in terms of prosperity, education, artistic endeavors, and so on, so fairness in such a society, contrary to widespread impression, is not the main feature of justice. Instead it is individual liberty—the negative freedom whereby individuals may not be interfered with by other individuals. And this condition is most directly enhanced by the clear identification and protection of the right to private property, the individual's sphere of personal authority.

Many objections to this distinctively American outlook or ideology might be considered, among them that we have been defending here a reactionary and obsolete framework. But a progressivist bias is just another case of extrapolating from science and technology to all human concerns. We should resist such jumps, even when prominent opinion inclines toward them. Some aspects of human life progress quite smoothly; some, such as art and literature, do not; and there may be positive regression, for example in the conduct of governments, which clearly belies the doctrine of historical progress in political matters. Progress makes sense when taken to represent some areas of existence but by no means can do justice to all of it.

I am urging that we once again appreciate that the American Revolution still identifies the most radical and sensible ideals available to human beings during our species' short history: Individual persons are important, indeed irreplaceable; a good society must provide a moral opportunity to each and every citizen who does not violate the principles by which persons of diversity are fully able to live a morally decent life.

Conclusion

The American ideology of individualism is not an apology for the exploitation of some by others. It is the soundest conception of social life yet rationally formulated by human beings. It will not do to try to brush it aside by calling it reactionary. It has to be confronted in argument, not analyzed away in the fashion one may expect when visiting a psychologist.

Universal, unrestrained collectivism, which is individualism's main intellectual adversary, is a mistake. It distorts the kind of rationality involved in human planning. Bona fide rationality can only be exercised by individuals. The values identified by human reason relate to human individuals. Only individuals can have determinate goals or purposes, such as getting to play at Carnegie Hall, or running in the Olympic Games, or curing AIDS, cancer, or malaria. Societies cannot have these sorts of plans. Constructing social plans as if they were goals of individuals must lead to disaster. Thus the collective or public domain is a very limited, specific realm of concern, properly restricted by a sound constitution to the administration of justice.

In turn, the way that individuals can best secure for themselves the conditions of living a moral life is clearly and publicly to have their private property rights identified. This will provide them with the actual framework for moral decision making. It will avoid, as much as institutionally possible, the tragedy of the commons and the calculation problem. It will preserve among human beings one *necessary* condition of civility, decency, and morality, provided that they attend to the maintenance of those legal principles which do help to identify private property rights. The right to private property is, then, a necessary, indispensable—though by no means a sufficient—condition for a good human community.

Ultimately the task of a moral life for human beings includes their political mission. As the late Leo Strauss pointed out:

> The good life simply is the life in which the requirements of man's natural inclinations are fulfilled in their proper order to the highest possible degree, the life of a man who is awake to the highest possible degree, the life of a man in whose soul nothing lies waste. . . . Political freedom, and especially that political freedom that justifies itself by the pursuit of human excellence, is not a gift of heaven; it becomes actual only through the efforts of many generations, and its preservation always requires the highest degree of vigilance.[29]

The right to private property is not the most fundamental right. The right to life and the right to liberty are conceptually prior, thus more fundamental. But for practical policy purposes the right to private property—concerned as it is with concrete features of our lives, the particular, actual, specifiable dimensions of living—is central: Through its protection we can secure those more fundamental rights, as well as the conditions for a decent human life within human communities.[30]

NOTES

1. Karl Marx, *Selected Writings*, ed. D. McLellan (London: Oxford University Press, 1977), p. 171.
2. Ibid., p. 417. See, however, George G. Brenkert, *Marx's Ethics of Freedom* (London: Routledge & Kegan Paul, 1983). Here Marx is made out to be a moralist. He was, rather, a value theorist, not someone who could consistently ascribe moral responsibility to individual human beings.
3. Karl Marx, *The Grundrisse*, ed. D. McLellan (New York: Harper Torchbooks, 1971), p. 33.
4. Ibid., pp. 45–46.
5. Marx, *Selected Writings*, p. 126.
6. Alasdair McIntyre, *After Virtue* (Notre Dame: University of Notre Dame Press, 1981).
7. Marx, *Selected Writings*, p. 53.
8. Heinrich A. Rommen, "The Genealogy of Natural Rights," *Thought* 29 (1954): 419.
9. Ibid. Thomas Hobbes, too, spelled out his conception of natural rights along these lines, but for him "right reason" had a purely materialistic, physicalist meaning, so that by Hobbes's theory, that is naturally right which accords with the innate drives which motivate some living being.
10. As John Locke observed, it is by the use of reason that we apprehend the natural law. See, also, Tibor R. Machan, "A Reconsideration of Natural Rights Theory," *American Philosophical Quarterly* 19 (1982): 61–72; "Human Rights: Some Points of Clarification," *Journal of Critical Analysis* 5 (1973): 30–39; and "A Rationale for Human Rights," *The Personalist* 52 (1971): 216–35.
11. Ayn Rand, "Value and Rights," in *Readings in Introductory Philosophical Analysis*, ed. John Hospers (Englewood Cliffs, N.J.: Prentice-Hall, 1968), p. 382.
12. Tibor R. Machan, "Epistemology and Moral Knowledge," *The Review of Metaphysics* 36 (1982): 23–49.
13. This point is stressed by Renford Bambrough, *Scepticism and Moral Knowledge* (Atlantic Highlands, N.J.: Humanities Press, 1979).
14. These are widely debated issues. I am here invoking the account associated with the Aristotelian tradition, although any doctrine which postulates the possibility of moral knowledge would have to adhere to the point at issue. I go some lengths toward defending these matters in my *Human Rights and Human Liberties* (Chicago: Nelson-Hall Co., 1975).
15. The scientific bases of free will are discussed in Roger W. Sperry, "Changing Concepts of Consciousness and Free Will," *Perspectives in Biology and Medicine* 20 (Autumn 1976): 9–19.
16. Aristotle, *Politics*, Bk. II, Ch. 3. 1261b34–1261b38.

17. For a discussion of how to determine the nature of public affairs, see Tibor R. Machan, "Rational Choice and Public Affairs," *Theory and Decision* 12 (September 1980): 229–58.

18. Michael Harrington, "Corporate Collectivism: A System of Social Injustice," in *Ethics, Free Enterprise, and Public Policy*, ed. R. T. De George and J. A. Pichler (New York: Oxford University Press, 1978), p. 44; Russell Kirk, *The Conservative Mind* (Chicago: Henry Regnery Co., 1953). Consider, also, Charles Baudelaire, who wrote, in *Intimate Journals*, "Commerce is satanic, because it is the basest and vilest form of egoism." Quoted in Robert Beum, "Middle-Class Power and its Critics," *University Bookman* 18(1978):76. We may suppose that what Harrington calls "collectivist" about corporations is that much of the business they do involves the voluntary mutual effort and investment of large numbers of people. But no individualist has even objected to such voluntary "collectivism."

The sort of collectivism which individualists regard as morally objectionable is probably best called natural collectivism, whereby, following Marx and others, human beings are seen to be *species-beings*, tied through and through to everyone else and independent in no meaningful way whatsoever. Collectivism is distinctive in regarding individuals as parts of a larger, *more important* whole! A recent exposition of conservative hostility to individualism may be found in George Will, *Statecraft as Soulcraft* (New York: Simon and Schuster, 1982).

19. Bhikhu Parekh, "Introduction," in *The Concept of Socialism*, ed. B. Parekh (New York: Holmes and Meier Publishers, Inc., 1975), p. 6.

20. F. A. Hayek, *Studies in Philosophy, Politics and Economics* (New York: Simon and Schuster, 1967), p. 85.

21. Machan, "Epistemology and Moral Knowledge."

22. John Locke, *Essays on the Law of Nature*, ed. W. von Leyden (Oxford: The Clarendon Press, 1954), p. 111.

23. Hayek, *Studies*, p. 84.

24. Ibid., p. 85.

25. I discuss some of the pitfalls of Hayek's own philosophical underpinnings in my "Reason, Morality and the Free Society," in *Liberty and the Rule of Law*, ed. R. L. Cunningham (College Station, Texas: Texas A&M University Press, 1979), pp. 268-93.

26. Robert Nozick, *Anarchy, State, and Utopia* (New York: Basic Books, 1974).

27. F. A. Hayek, *Individualism and Economic Order* (Chicago: University of Chicago Press, 1948), pp. 86–87.

28. For a clear exposition of the ethical individualism see David L. Norton, *Personal Destinies* (Princeton: Princeton University Press, 1976).

29. Leo Strauss, *Natural Right and History*, 2nd ed. (Chicago: University of Chicago Press, 1971), p. 131.

30. I wish to thank the Reason and Progress Foundations for their support, which has made it possible for me to work on this and related projects. I also thank the participants of The Washington Institute Conference on Ideology and the American Experience, especially Professor Gordon C. Bjork, for valuable comments on earlier drafts of this paper.

VI

Ideology and the American Economy

GORDON C. BJORK

Any economic system depends on an ideology. An ideology is a belief system which explains the nature of the world and man's place in it. It explains the nature of man and the derivative relationships of humans to one another. From these basic beliefs come the organization for economic activities to provide the means of survival, growth, and security. From these basic beliefs come the structures of property rights, exchange relationships, and social control of individual activity.

The contemporary American economy is based on extensive private property and individual freedom to use one's property in a self-interested way. The contemporary Soviet economy, by way of contrast, is based on state ownership of natural resources and reproducible capital and on central direction of labor and control of the distribution of income. All modern industrial societies are somewhere along the continuum between individual and state control of economic activity. How does a society's social and intellectual history explain its economic ideology and organization?

American economic ideology is based on a conception of man as a free agent who voluntarily cooperates within a social framework with other *homi economici* to achieve individual objectives, and who exchanges goods and services with other men for mutual advantage. Soviet Marxian ideology, *per contra*, emphasizes that individuals have no economic rights or independent income security apart from their particular society. The state exercises complete control as the administrative agent of an organic society to organize all production and distribution because the alternative would be economic instability and the immoral exploitation of some groups or classes by others.

Marx argued that the individualistic institutions of private property, free markets, and limited states were a temporary transition between the corporate, collective conceptions of feudalism and socialism.[1] Capitalism was a *necessary* transitional phase to break down the inefficiencies of feudalism but would inevitably destroy itself through the malfunctioning of markets with their creation of class warfare and increasing macroeconomic instability. Thus, Marxian ideology had not only a theory of how man related to society but also a theory of dynamic change of institutional relationships. Capitalism, on the other hand, has never had any generally accepted theory of institutional change even though capitalist economists have generally had an optimistic belief that individual adaptation of private property and exchange relationships—in markets, courts and legislatures—would accomplish such change.[2]

I will argue in this paper that ideology has played a powerful role in the American historical experience as it relates to the structuring of economic organization. I will argue, as Marx did more than a century ago, that the institutions of capitalism have provided "a powerful engine of growth" but, unlike Marx, argue that they have been amenable to protean change to control conflict and instability.

I will identify the origins of American ideology in the Judeo-Christian tradition and the Enlightenment philosophy of John Locke and Adam Smith and conclude that Marx has been largely irrelevant to the American experience because of our religious heritage and the unique character of economic development in an empty land, unthreatened by the Malthusian pressures which have beset much of the rest of the world.

A Telescopic View of Change. How the American economy has changed in two centuries! In 1785 four million inhabitants scattered themselves along the east coast of the present continental United States from Maine to Georgia. Less than ten percent lived in towns, a majority engaged in subsistence agriculture. They lived in crude, unplumbed, poorly heated houses—three or four to a bed, frequently hungry, dirty, and cold. They worked three-quarters of their waking hours for three-quarters of their lives. Two centuries later, most Americans are spaciously housed, sumptuously clothed, and overfed. Less than three percent are left on farms and they feed a substantial portion of the world in addition to the remaining ninety-seven percent of the population.

Two centuries ago, nearly all of life's labors were concentrated on the production of food, clothing, and housing. Today, most of our labor is going to health, education, recreation, provision for national defense, domestic tranquility, and the support of a dependent population. Work now occupies half our waking hours for half our life.

In 1785 the average American's bread came directly from his own labors. Today, that bread originates on thousand-acre farms where university-educated farmers use hybrid seeds, agricultural chemicals, and sophisticated machinery purchased from transnational corporations and financed by transnational banks which collect their deposits from around the world on computer networks dependent on communications satellites. Yields per acre, per man-hour, and per dollar of employed capital have increased by factors of ten to one hundred.

Our pioneer ancestors heated and lighted their homes with hand-cut firewood and homemade candles. The contemporary householder buys decorative candles from an alternative-lifestyle college graduate who supplements his candle earnings with food stamps and subsidized housing. Heat and light come from a privately-owned but publicly-regulated utility which obtains its petroleum from the other side of the world in Japanese supertankers financed in Singapore, crewed by Koreans, insured in London, and registered in Liberia to a corporation based in Athens.

In 1985 a typical American family may live in a condominium in the suburb of a city. The dwelling has materials from thirty-five different states and was assembled on-site in two weeks. It was financed by a mortgage loan originated by a private company, resold through a government-chartered corporation to the pension fund of a public employees' union. The condominium stands on land leased for ninety-nine years from the endowment fund of a private university. In 1785 the site was occupied by a frame house built by the owner and his neighbors without financing (although a larger account-payable was run up at the local general store). The eighteenth-century occupant thought that he and his successors might occupy the house in perpetuity. The modern pension fund has assumed an average mortgage term of seven years.

The present occupants of the condo may hold jobs in neighboring cities and drive more miles in a week than the eighteenth-century occupants traveled in their lifetime. They will invest over $50,000 in current dollars per child for their care and education in addition to public expenditures on education and health. Modern social scientists are bemused by such intergenerational transfers based on motives more complex than self-interested insurance for income maintenance in an actuarially improbable old age. Modern parents are looking not to their children but to the government for Social Security and Medicare transfer payments in their retired years. Perhaps that is why they have dramatically reduced their savings rate, since there is no longer such a drive to accumulate an individual annuity for old age and a bequest for their heirs.

Over the last two centuries, the United States economy has changed from a primitive and precarious struggle at the edge of a "howling wilderness," to a complex and affluent role in an interdependent world. American social institutions, individual values, and economic organization have been both cause and effect of that change. What is remarkable is that American ideology has changed so little when the economy has changed so much. This essay will explore, first, the reasons for the performance of the American economy and, second, the relationship between ideology and the economy.

Sources of American Economic Growth and Change

From an economic point of view, I would distinguish four factors which have transformed American economic life: (a) the education, mobility, and attitudes of the labor force; (b) the security, flexibility, and transferability of private property rights in land, capital, and knowledge; (c) a primary emphasis in government on policies and programs which increased wealth rather than redistributing it; and (d) a scientific attitude toward the natural and human world which led men to seek to analyze how things worked so that *they* could be made to work more productively.

All of these factors have been profoundly influenced by the belief systems of the European immigrants who settled this land. They have been reinforced, expanded, and changed by our own unique historical experience in the New World. Let us first consider the economic consequences of the four factors and then identify their origins and articulation in our intellectual history.

Individualism, Education, and Mobility of the Labor Force. The United States started with a unique labor force. Many of the British settlers of the thirteen colonies in the seventeenth and eighteenth centuries did not come primarily for free land or economic opportunity. They came for religious liberty. The same was true, to a lesser extent, for some time of the German and Scandinavian settlers of the nineteenth century and the Jews in the late nineteenth and early twentieth centuries. Africans came involuntarily as a result of the slave trade. Others came primarily for economic opportunity. The religious faith of the earlier nonconformist and dissenting Protestant immigrants emphasized individual responsibility to a sovereign God unmediated by priest, bishop, or earthly sovereign.

The religious emphasis on the responsibility of the individual carried over into political and economic organizations. The state, like the temporal church, was viewed as the agent of voluntarily associated individuals. Economic relationships were individually established and only production gave a person a claim to income. The Bible and individual revelation were the source of truth. That made education important for all men—regardless of wealth or social station.

Education was important, even for farmers. It made them more aware of market developments and, therefore, opportunities. In the late nineteenth and early twentieth centuries it made them aware of scientific developments in genetics, soil chemistry, and biochemistry which were sources of increased yields.[3] Education was important to factory workers and craftsmen learning to master progressively more complex machinery and functions.

Perhaps the separation of immigrants from the settled communities of their ancestors has meant that Americans have always been more willing to leave one home and job for another. Family and community ties have not been as strong as in Europe, and resettlement in new communities has not been as difficult. The pattern of western settlement and other interregional migration in the United States involved moving from areas of lesser to greater opportunity—and from lower to higher productivity.[4]

Another spur to mobility was the lack of community and family acceptance of economic responsibility for the underemployed. In European parishes and the traditional societies of undeveloped countries, the individual has a claim on the community for support.[5] This not only lessens his incentive to leave for greater opportunity, it lessens the incentives of all members of the community to increase their income if other members of the family or extended family of the community have a claim on their income. One of the great failures in American economic history was the post-Civil War position of the black freedman who could not reap the benefits of his labor in a share-cropping system, could not compete with white labor because of Jim Crow laws, and could not migrate to the expanding northern cities until after the waves of European migration ended with World War I.[6]

Over the past century the rapid expansion of free public education, together with ever-increasing geographic mobility has been very important to the development of the American economy. Labor surplus in farm areas, created by high rates of natural increase and steady rates of growth in labor productivity, was readily absorbed into the expanding industrial labor force. In recent years the social freedom of American women to participate in the industrial and service sector labor force on a relatively equal basis with men has contributed to continuing growth in per capita incomes through increases in the participation rate. Current high rates of unemployment and underemployment in the declining iron and steel and manufacturing areas of the old Northeast reflect more the reluctance to abandon investments in homes and union seniority than lack of mobility based on education or lack of social acceptability elsewhere in the country.

From an economic point of view, educational accomplishments and social mobility which facilitate the movement of workers from areas and occupations of lower to higher productivity contribute significantly to raising the average level of output per worker. These factors—present in the United States for most of the population for two centuries—have increased in Europe only over the last three decades and have made a large contribution to the "catch-up" of their economies with the United States.[7]

Emphasis on individual freedom and responsibility has been a crucial element in the mobility and productivity of the American labor force. Individualism has its roots in ideological views about the nature of man and man's place in nature and society. American religious and philosophic beliefs are profoundly different from those of, say, China, India, or Africa. They have also diverged from the mainstream views of the European countries of provenience from which our population derived.

Property Rights. The security, flexibility, and transferability of private property in land, capital, and patentable ideas have contributed significantly to our economic performance. They were initially of great importance in agriculture. Investment in the improvement of agricultural land has a long-term payoff; in economic terms, the capital/output ratio is high. Occupants of land who have insecure tenure or problems in realizing their long term investment from sale in an efficient market will limit the investment of their savings and labor in agriculture. They will also have difficulty using the land as collateral for loans from financial intermediaries.

Apart from a few colonial experiments with common land in New England and feudal fees in the Hudson and Delaware river valleys, Americans have used freehold land tenure almost exclusively for the management of land. Settlers easily obtained grants of lands in freehold tenure from state or national governments, and when "squatting" preceded the application for title, the courts upheld the rights of squatters.[8] A primary economic activity throughout American history has been the improvement of land and the liquidation of capital gains for reinvestment. Courts and legislatures in the nineteenth and twentieth centuries have not been very favorable to the holding of undeveloped land.[9] "Beneficial use" has been a primary determinant in the assignment of property rights.

The economic superiority of freehold land tenure is dramatically illustrated by the relative productivity of public and private timber and range lands in contiguous tracts in the contemporary western United States or in the productivity of small private tracts in the Soviet Union. Private rather than public land-holding is conducive to efficient management.

The security of private assets and businesses from state seizure or even regulation has been an important spur to investment in the United States. The Constitution of the United States forbade the taking of private property for public use without due process and just compensation.[10] The interstate commerce clause of the Constitution has been widely used to prevent state or local interference with the property rights established by commercial practice and contract.

The decision of the Supreme Court in the Dred Scott case to uphold the validity of property rights in slaves even outside the slave states, was an extreme affirmation of the inviolability of individual property rights which led, inevitably, to the Civil War. Southern states protested the anticipated unwillingness of the Northern states to continue the protection of this type of property rights, which were instrumental in the growth and prosperity of chattel slavery in the ante-bellum South. Secessionist leaders argued that a primary function of the state was the enforcement of private property rights and inferred that if the Union would not offer property protection to Southern slave-holders they had no obligation or interest in remaining in the Union.[11]

An indispensable element in the capitalization of the industrial revolution in the United States was the creation of the limited liability, state-chartered joint stock corporation. This type of business organization spread rapidly in the last three-quarters of the nineteenth century and stimulated the flow of savings from a multitude of savers into areas of greatest economic opportunity. The economic result was an increased incentive for savers and the allocation of savings into investments with the highest returns.

The development of the corporation, and its progressively greater control by professional management lacking important personal stock ownership, have also contributed to a high rate of corporate retention of earnings rather than the declaration of dividends. The result may have been a higher rate of national saving and the allocation of that saving to investment may have been less productive.

Finally, the recognition of property rights in the productivity increases due to improved technology has been an important incentive to research and development. The establishment of a patent office to secure the benefits of new inventions to their inventors is one reason why the United States has historically been in the vanguard of technological change.

Secure and transferable property rights in various forms of assets are a necessary condition for high rates of capital formation in a market economy.[12] A sufficient condition is a low rate of time preference by individuals. This is true for an individual's investment in personal knowledge and skills as well as in holdings of physical and financial assets. Willingness to postpone present consumption for future consumption was an important characteristic of American society in the past. However, the decline of the family and the rise of the welfare state has led to questions about rates of private capital formation in the last quarter of the twentieth century.[13]

There is also a social dimension to a declining rate of time preference. American acceptance of substantial inequality in wealth distribution in the past has been based, first, on a belief that the *laissez faire* individualism which permitted greater wealth inequality would also lead to higher aggregate growth in income. Secondly, with low rates of time preference, the present poor would be willing to wait for economic growth to produce a share in future wealth which, even in discounted terms, would be worth more than the present income gain from wealth redistribution. Karl Marx scoffed at the masses' in capitalist societies being promised "pie in the sky" by organized religion. He should have noted an equally powerful secular faith in economic progress to make the discounted value of future gains worth more than the present slight gains from a socialist redistribution. In the past, with low interest rates and high growth rates it was a rational choice. In the future, with lower growth rates and/or higher rates of time discount, it might not be.[14]

The determinants of American practice in the assignment of property rights have been ideological. This ideology embraces the notion that land should be the freehold property of those who *use* it, and the notion that there should be procedural safeguards against social confiscation of individual property. It recognizes the utility in social confirmation of contractual limitation, specification, and division of property rights in productive assets, including ideas. All these characteristics of property rights in the United States have their ideological foundations in beliefs about the individual and the rights of the individual even against the society which guarantees and protects those rights.

Government and the Economy. Government does play a critical role in economic development—beyond the enforcement of property rights and contractual obligations. The War for Independence was, in part, a rebellion against the mercantilist policies of the British Crown. The writers of the Constitution saw that government would, inevitably, involve factional interests in attempting to use the powers of government to obtain economic advantage and redistribution of income. Part of their solution for balancing the factionalism and redistributive characteristics of mercantilism was federalism and the separation of powers. Part of it was limitation of the powers of the federal and state governments.[15] There has been a tension since the nation's founding between the Jeffersonian economic philosophy of a limited and passive government which merely enforces private property and contracts and the Hamiltonian advocacy of government activism in the promotion of the general welfare through the support of particular private interests.[16]

The division of powers between the states and the federal government was one way to check the power of factions. Division of powers between executive, judicial, and legislative branches was another. The Constitution specifically prohibited the states from interfering with interstate commerce and gave the federal government control over navigable rivers, the monetary system, and the post office. The national government was prohibited from imposing direct (income) taxes or specific legislation (bills of attainder). It was not given the power to charter corporations or interfere with exports. The most significant limitations of the Constitution (as opposed to the Bill of Rights, which was an attempt to secure *civil* rights) were limitations on the power of government to interfere with private economic activity.

The essence of governmental economic policy in Europe at the time of the American Revolution was participation in and control of markets.

It is of great historic significance that Adam Smith's *The Wealth of Nations*, a polemic against mercantilism and for *laissez faire*, was published in the same year as the American Declaration of Independence. *The Wealth of Nations* and the founders of the new nation both rejected the union of economic and political power and the regulation of economic activity by political power rather than markets.

The eighteenth-century European farmer and craftsman were protected from competition by imposts (and high transport costs), but they were also controlled by law and custom in their response to market forces. Manufacturing and commerce in particular trades were controlled by chartered guilds and local monopolies. The purpose of social control of trade is the creation of economic "rents"—returns to producers in excess of what they could earn in competitive markets where the rents would be dissipated by competition for customers.[17] Apart from the effect of controlled markets on income distribution, their inevitable effect is short-term inefficiency and long-term lack of innovation.

While the United States has used tariffs throughout its history to protect manufacturers from foreign competition, these imposts have had limited effect in retarding efficiency and innovation because of internal competition. Over the last half-century that consequence has been less true because of the growing concentration in some industries and the rise of industry-wide unions which have blunted the force of competition. In recent years intense foreign competition has once again led to pressure for tariffs as a part of "industrial policy."

At the same time that governments have not limited competition, they have expanded it by internal policies of transport improvement. First it was government participation in the building of post roads and canals. Then there were land grants and subsidies to the railroads along with the granting of powers of eminent domain to reduce land costs in the rights of way. The most recent developments have been aid to airlines and federal sponsorship of the interstate highway system. American government, like the governments of more mercantilist states, has seen the social advantage of subsidizing transportation improvement to encourage the social gains that result from the pricing of transportation services on a declining marginal cost basis.

Governments have always played an uneasy and controversial role in the chartering and regulation of the banking system and in the control of other financial intermediaries such as insurance companies and securities markets. Banks play an invaluable role in the reduction of transactions costs of intermediation between savers and investors, lenders and borrowers. The First and Second Banks of the United States had federal charters before the Civil War. National banks have been federally chartered and regulated since the Civil War. The Federal Reserve System has had an uneasy and controversial existence for the last three-quarters of this century.

One cannot conceive of a modern capitalist society without banks. Equally, it is difficult to conceive of one in which banks are free of government control over their operations. It is possible to argue that government control of banking is necessary without conceding that it has been done well. The American bias against the centralization of political or economic power has retarded concentration in banking and finance. The dispersion of financial power has always been an important element in American economic and political ideology and practice. Our fragmented banking system is presently undergoing consolidation and increasing governmental control because of the destabilization caused by inflation and "bad" regulatory policies. However, its instability is not due to the dispersion of power.

Americans have always been ready to use the powers of government to supplement the market—to remedy "market failures" rather than to supplant the market. In the nineteenth century this attitude had its basis in an optimistic view of the self-regulating forces of the market which Adam Smith and his followers adapted from the Newtonian view of the self-equilibrating universe. In the twentieth century the adoption of Keynesian macroeconomic stabilization policies seemed an acceptable response to the complications introduced by the human invention of money in what otherwise would have been a stable and self-equilibrating system.

The reformist tradition in American economic thought has always regarded economic regulation as an emendation to an economic system which would be self-regulating if the conditions for perfect competition could be achieved. Thus, tariffs were espoused as temporary measures to protect "infant industries" until they could be self-sustaining against "unfair" foreign competition. Railroads and utilities were chartered and regulated as "natural" monopolies. The unchartered monopolies to be regulated by the Sherman Anti-Trust Act were viewed as illegal *per se* because prevailing legal and economic doctrine held that they *only* could have grown powerful in control of markets through conspiracy. Labor unions were fostered and protected by the Wagner Act to counteract the unnatural power of large corporations. Environmental regulations were the substitute for the lack of property rights in the purity of air and water and the amenities of rural beauty and urban culture. The intervention of the state was always rationalized on the basis of "market failure" to provide the conditions of perfect competition—free entry, transferable and enforceable property rights, free information, and zero transaction costs. That these conditions *never* exist in the real world but only in the abstract economists' model does not seem to have harmed the *belief* in markets. Americans *believe* in market control rather than government control. In theory, government control has always been limited to aberrations. This is one element of the "Reagan counterrevolution" in economic policy. Belief in "the market" has always been an important part of American ideology and a distinctive characteristic of American economic policy and economic organization.

Science and Nature. When European settlers came to the New World they found native peoples who held the animist beliefs of most traditional hunting-gathering societies. They believed that they were an integral part of the natural world, that the natural world was a mysterious and arbitrary place, and that it was inappropriate and dangerous for man to modify it or attempt to bring it under his control.[18]

The European settlers who drove the native peoples from their ancestral lands did so with science, technology, and the belief that the land was given to them for possession and exploitation. Land was a commodity to be changed, exchanged, domesticated, and, if advantageous, abandoned. Americans have never had the mystic reverence for land typical of cultures for which continuity and the veneration of ancestors and nature is important.

Americans have always had a domineering attitude toward the natural world. Benjamin Franklin and Thomas Jefferson prided themselves on their scientific knowledge and their ability to apply their knowledge to practical invention. Nineteenth-century Americans were disdained for their poor craftsmanship but admired for their practical technological skills as a nation of "tinkerers."[19]

When land grant universities were started by the Morrill Act (1862), they were charged with responsibility for the discovery of scientific knowledge and the practical arts. They were also charged with the dissemination of their discoveries, and agricultural extension agents were viewed as an integral part of the university community responsible for seeing that the discoveries of the laboratory were channeled into practice on the farm.

Some European countries in the nineteenth century admitted science into the universities, but the emphasis was on "pure" rather than applied science. Research in natural science was viewed with some skepticism, and scientific inquiry in the European universities was more usually directed toward the explication of classic texts than observation in the laboratory.

American openness to innovation and empiricism in the search for better methods also extended into the management of business enterprise. Railroads, in particular, brought forward problems in coordination and control which went beyond the traditional methods of personal command management.[20] By the beginning of the twentieth century, businessmen were talking about "scientific management," and American universities recognized the development of management methods as they established schools of business administration. Training for business took its place beside professional training in medicine, law, and divinity. The place of business schools is sharply different in American and European universities.

The transformation of the economy from subsistence agriculture and handicraft entailed an ideology which saw man as the master of nature. It also required an ideology of man which emphasized the rational organization of strangers in planned and contractually controlled activity as a substitute for the bonds of family or clan.[21]

The Origins of American Ideology

The ideological basis of American capitalism is the belief that individual ownership of productive assets is just and that market transactions need to be controlled *only* by self-interest. These are the beliefs which distinguish capitalism from socialism. And it is the intensity and widespread acceptance of these beliefs which explains differences between the United States and other Western countries.

Christian theology has always been schizophrenic about these two principles. The commandments to "love your neighbor as your self" and "do unto others as you would be done to" have been construed as inimical to private property and self-interested exchange. Apart from New Testament references to the sharing of ownership and distribution of all to the poor, private property has been viewed by some Christian theologians as an unacceptable assertion of self-interest *contra* community interest. Self-interested exchange has, likewise, been seen as morally defective. Judaism, interestingly, has never had the same problem of reconciling self-interest and love of neighbor and has urged a balance between the two.

The moral justification of private property in the Anglo-American intellectual tradition receives its classic articulation in John Locke's *Second Treatise on Civil Government* (1688). Locke argues that since individual liberty is a natural right, assets which are created by the exercise of that natural liberty are, equally, a natural right. I have argued elsewhere, on the basis of textual analysis, that Locke's arguments were couched in terms of "natural rights" to accord with the philosophic and theological arguments and concepts of his time but are more appropriately placed in the utilitarian tradition.[22] Locke justifies private property because it will increase economic output and will make all members of a society which guarantees it more affluent. Whatever the intellectual tradition, Locke's ideas seemed ideally suited to the American historical circumstance of an empty land.

The Lockean proviso—that private property in land is justified as long as alienation from common ownership "left as much and as good for others"—seemed particularly appropriate in American history as long as there was unclaimed land at the frontier. The availability of free land was one element in the "frontier theory" of American history popularized by the American historian, Frederick Jackson Turner.[23] It has been argued that the existence of the frontier prevented both the exploitation of landless laborers and drained off potential radical support as the malcontents went west. Subsequent research by economic historians has demonstrated that the West never provided a "safety-valve" in the sense that large numbers of urban laborers moved west to claim land at the frontier.[24] Many farmers' sons and daughters and a few immigrants did. The economic importance of the frontier was the labor-intensive capital investment in projects such as railroads which kept wages up and employment full. What was ideologically important about the frontier was the strengthening of belief in the fairness of private property since even the unequal ownership of assets did not deny or preclude the promise of ownership to the industrious and frugal. This legitimized the inequality of wealth which was a conspicuous feature of American capitalism in the nineteenth century and satisfied the Lockean proviso that private property for some not preclude it for others.

Adam Smith based the moral, as opposed to practical, argument for unfettered exchange of labor services and commodities on Locke's arguments about man's natural right to liberty. The liberty of the individual to pursue his own self-interest has been one of the most basic American precepts since Jefferson's transformation of Locke's phrase about "life, liberty, and property" into "life, liberty, and the pursuit of happiness" in the Declaration of Independence—published in the same year as Smith's *The Wealth of Nations*.

Ideological Evolution. The year 1776 marked the transition from the American colonial period in which paternalism still dominated political and economic thinking to the nineteenth-century affirmation of individual liberty. The "natural harmony of interests" is a recurrent theme of nineteenth-century American thinkers. This is not to suggest that Americans accepted all of Adam Smith's *laissez faire* and anti-mercantilist notions. The early American economist, Henry Carey, advocated protective tariffs to nourish "infant industries" with a secure home market. At the end of the nineteenth century Richard T. Ely and John R. Commons, influenced by the German historical school of political economy, called for close scrutiny of the way in which markets and firms *actually* worked in industrializing America and for suspension of belief in their efficacy until supported by comparative analysis.

At the end of the nineteenth century, Henry George caught the popular imagination as no other American economist had in his classic, *Progress and Poverty*. George, methodologically following the British economist David Ricardo, argued that the inevitable result of economic progress and urban growth in the United States would be the redistribution of income toward urban landowners. He advocated a "single tax" on urban site values as a method of confiscating the unearned income of urban landowners whose wealth was due to industrial progress they had no part in creating. What is significant about George's ideology is his acceptance of the *overall* results of markets in directing rewards to contributors and his identification of urban lands as an exception to the rule that markets worked to produce just and harmonious outcomes.

During the last quarter of the nineteenth century, America was rapidly transformed from a nation of small farmers, craftsmen, and merchants into an industrial nation with great concentration of power in the hands of the railroads, industrial monopolies like Carnegie's U.S. Steel and Rockefeller's Standard Oil, and J.P. Morgan's "money trust." American reaction to concentration of wealth and monopolization of markets was double-edged. First, there was the assertion of government control over such "natural monopolies" as railroads and public utilities. Secondly, there was the application of the old common law doctrine against conspiracy in restraint of trade. The Sherman Anti-Trust Act (1890) emphasized that monopolies could *only* occur by conspiracy to stifle competition and, therefore, the state need *only* prevent conspiracy and break up the results of conspiracy to assure the protection of individuals from conspiratorially created market power.

In the period following the Civil War, economic liberty was transformed from pragmatic practice into moral principle. The Fourteenth Amendment to the Constitution, passed to protect the civil rights of the freedmen from discriminatory legislation by the States, ironically was used to protect powerful economic interests from State regulation. Corporations were held to be "persons" entitled to equal protection. Regulation was alleged to confiscate property (by limiting its economic value) and to abridge individual liberty (by limiting unilateral control over prices and conditions of service.)[25]

Economic liberty was viewed as a necessary part of the competitive process which would lead to the "survival of the fittest." The notion of market competition as a social counterpart of the Darwinian struggle for survival in the biological world was a mind-boggling transformation of Adam Smith's argument for free competition on the grounds that it afforded the protection of individuals. "Social Darwinism," progressively rejected by the courts in the early twentieth century and, finally, by the U.S. Supreme Court in the New Deal cases of the 1930s, still lingers on vestigially in the rhetoric of part of the business community.

The belief that competitive markets would protect workers from the economic power of employers was the basis for the legal bias against labor unions from the early nineteenth century until the passage of the Wagner Act in 1935. Labor unions were viewed throughout the nineteenth century as an illegal conspiracy in restraint of trade. Their prohibition was viewed as a protection of the public, who would be hurt by higher prices, and individual workmen, who would have their liberty to compete for employment constrained. The limitation of union powers was not undertaken for the protection of employers, who were *assumed* to be forced to pay fair wages as the result of competition in labor markets.

After the Clayton Act (1913) specifically exempted labor unions from the anti-trust provisions of the Sherman Act, unions gained the right to organize, engage in collective bargaining, and strike. Employers, however, had no legal obligation to bargain collectively, and they attempted to counter the growing powers of labor unions with two new legal strategies. First, workers were pressured to sign "yellow-dog" contracts guaranteeing that they would not join a union. This was justified on the grounds of freedom of contract. Second, strikes were stayed by court injunctions on the grounds that they represented a threat to the security of the private property of the employers. There was little recognition by the courts that workers might contractually establish property rights in their jobs. Labor was always the "variable" factor and capital always the "fixed" factor in social practice as well as economic theory.

The period from the end of the Civil War to the beginning of the Great Depression witnessed the flood tide of unbridled capitalism and capitalist ideology in the United States. The paternalist ideology of the slave-holding Southern aristocracy had been shattered by the Civil War. Karl Marx published *Das Kapital* (1868) warning that free markets would lead to the exploitation of labor, the elimination of small farmers and businessmen, and increasing macroeconomic instability. He was not taken seriously (if read) by American intellectuals, and the mainstream of labor unions looked to collective bargaining for "more" rather than revolution. Charles Darwin's *Origin of Species* (1859) was followed by Herbert Spencer's and Charles Sumner's theories of "Social Darwinism." They defined the struggle for natural survival and economic survival as parallel processes to ensure the "survival of the fittest."[26]

The relation of religious thought to social and economic practice during this period was complex. Faith in the inherent accuracy of the Scriptures was brought into question by Darwin's evolutionary theory. Archaeological discoveries and historical criticism of the biblical texts began to kindle controversy about various theological doctrines. One reaction of the American Protestant churches was a division into modernist and fundamentalist camps. The latter took little interest in issues concerning economic and social organization. The former, however, turned to the "social gospel" and began to criticize some of the effects of the operation of economic forces on the social welfare of the population. The Catholic church, growing very rapidly from the waves of immigration, was turning its energies toward the assimilation of the new immigrants and the financing of a separate system of education. With some notable exceptions, religious faith and doctrine during the period were either favorable or unquestioning in their support of the predominant ideology of capitalism. Horatio Alger was mingled with the Old Testament heroes in Sunday School lessons and Andrew Carnegie's *Gospel of Wealth* mingled with the gospel proclaimed from the pulpit in this period of socially unrestrained economic individualism.

The most trenchant American economist critic of the natural harmony of economic interests during the heyday of capitalism was the awkward and iconoclastic Thorstein Veblen.[27] Veblen raised doubts about the fundamental assumptions of the social utility of markets. He questioned whether markets were driven by consumer sovereignty or "conspicuous consumption" and he questioned whether workers could only be disciplined into productive behavior by omnipresent wage pressure. His questions were interesting anticipations of John Galbraith[28] and Herbert Marcuse on the consumer sovereignty question and current Japanese management practice on the industrial productivity question. Veblen did attract marginal political interest, and his ideas were propounded by the Technocracy movement. However, the idea that an economy can be run by a benevolent dictatorship of engineers was not an idea likely to appeal to the populist American character.

The New Ideology. The Great Depression of the 1930s marks a watershed in American economic ideology. While markets had been unstable in the previous century, they collapsed in the 1930s, and the belief in self-governing markets was shattered by events rather than ideological critiques. The political response to the economic breakdown was government assumption of responsibility for economic organization. In Europe, with a substantially different ideological and historical experience, the results were fascist syndicalism in Germany and Italy and left-led governments of national unity in France and England. In the United States, it was the New Deal.

The main thrust of the New Deal was the regulation rather than replacement of the market and private property. Banks and other financial intermediaries were regulated and their deposits were insured. Industrial competitors were joined into government-sponsored cartels to suppress competition until the National Recovery Administration was declared unconstitutional by the Supreme Court. Labor was assisted in organization, anti-union tactics by employers were declared "unfair," and management was required to bargain "in good faith" with labor unions. Social Security was introduced to supplement the individual's responsibility to provide for old age. Measures were initiated to limit agricultural production in order to raise food prices.

The ideological justification for government interference with the market and individual liberty was not long in appearing. J. M. Keynes's *General Theory of Employment, Interest, and Money* was published in England in 1935, but his ideas were already being widely discussed by economists and political advisors earlier in the decade. Keynes argued that the combination of rigid wage labor markets and unstable money markets might frequently lead to instability, low output, and high unemployment. His prescription of government borrowing and spending was welcomed by politicians as a wonderful justification for actions which would increase their power and popularity.

At Harvard, where Keynes's ideas were being taught to the next generation of university teachers, political officials, and leaders of public opinion, Edward H. Chamberlin produced a dry treatise, *The Theory of Monopolistic Competition* (1937), which "proved" that unregulated markets could turn out results likely to decrease rather than increase the benefits to consumers, producers, and employees. Intellectuals and managers were being moved toward an ideology in which government intervention in the market was a widespread and desirable responsibility rather than a regrettable exception to the general case for *laissez faire*.

Government control of the economy was remarkably ineffective in restoring full employment in the American economy in the 1930s. What pulled the nation out of the slump was the Second World War. At the end of the war there was widespread fear that the transition to a peacetime economy would cause the nation to revert to the chronic unemployment and price instability of the interwar period.

One effect of the fear of economic instability was legislation which embodied the revolution in economic thinking which had taken place— the Full Employment Act of 1946. While the Constitution had affirmed the power of the federal government to control the currency and interstate commerce, this Act affirmed the responsibility of the federal government to provide economic growth, price stability, and full employment. The role of government had changed from guarantor of market structure to manager of economic performance.

The controls necessitated by a wartime economy were relaxed after the war but not abandoned. The Works Progress Administration (WPA) was not continued, but price supports and acreage limitations for agriculture were. The powers of labor unions were lessened by the Taft-Hartley Act, but government responsibility for collective bargaining was maintained. The Federal Reserve abandoned its agreement with the Treasury to maintain the price of government bonds (and interest rates) but retained a primary responsibility for the administration of monetary policy rather than mere provision of liquidity to the commercial banking system.

A slowly growing labor force, rapid growth of government defense expenditures, and the replacement of capital stocks neglected during the

Depression and World War II made the maintenance of full employment easier than the maintenance of price stability in the first fifteen years after the 1946 Act. The election of a Republican administration in 1952 did not reverse the extension of government control over the economy which had been started by the New Deal and confirmed by the Full Employment Act of 1946. It completed its legitimation among conservatives and within the business community.[29]

Contemporary Ideology

The last half-century has seen accelerating and cumulatively important changes in the character and structure of the American economy which have necessitated modification of our traditional ideology. I will relate them to the four factors which I have identified as critical to our growth.

Labor Force Education, Values, and Mobility. Traditionally, Americans have placed great responsibility on the individual for assuring education and productive employment. Increasingly, the state has assumed responsibility from the family for the education of children. Ironically, the focus of education has shifted from basic education for literacy and employability to socialization for greater cultural homogeneity. It would be unrealistic to assume that the public schools could educate the whole population to the high standards of literacy and general competence to which the elite aspired in the past. Nevertheless, the rising educational demands of employment and the specificity of skills in many branches of employment have led to an increasing mismatch between jobs and workers. The failure of education to keep up with job requirements now poses a significant limitation on productivity growth and achieving low unemployment levels.

Coupled with the education/employment "mismatch" has been a change to an ideology which now asserts that society, rather than the individual, bears responsibility for assuring employment. This is a modern market counterpart to the assumption of social responsibility for income maintenance in more traditional societies. One concurrent change in social ideology recognizes that workers have "property rights" in their jobs. Another asserts that employers have a legal responsibility to recruit and hire workers from groups presumed to be disadvantaged in labor markets by past discrimination. A third ideological change asserts a legitimate public interest in restricting access to employment in particular areas by enforcement of restrictive agreements. I refer, for example, to the limitation of employment to practitioners who have satisfied the requirements established by their own professional associations or of, say, plumbing to journeymen admitted to the union.

I am not making any value judgments about the changes in ideology which have accompanied these changes in labor markets as they affect education, responsibility for employment and income security, property rights and access rights to particular jobs. I will generalize, however, in saying that the particular income stream and income security possessed by an individual is now viewed as a social, rather than private, creation. It then becomes reasonable for the state to modify what the state has created. The readjustment of claims in a rich and rapidly changing economy is increasingly taken out of the impersonal market and assigned to political decision. Individual responsibility has been replaced with social responsibility in education and employment.

Property Rights. Property has been depersonalized. The nineteenth-century farmer felt a personal attachment to his land because he had "mixed his labor with it." The ownership of productive assets is now widely dispersed in the portfolios of pension funds, trust funds, and eleemosynary institutions. Those assets are managed by corporations, whose managers are more likely to look after their own interests than those of the corporate stockholders.

Corporations are, increasingly, multinational. Their power, *vis-a-vis* the governments of the political instrumentalities in which they do business, is the power to leave and produce somewhere else. Their assets, increasingly, are not tangible land, buildings, and machinery but contracts, leases, patents, organizational procedures, and market power which cannot be geographically restricted.

Private property in productive assets plays a key role in a market economy in providing incentives for efficient utilization and allocation, reducing transactions costs, and providing incentives for saving and reinvesting. Corporations now have increasing problems with their managerial agents' taking actions which may enrich and secure the agents but not the corporations. Agency theory has emerged as a means of acquiring important analytic insight into the management of contemporary economic enterprises.[30]

Adolf Berle and Gardiner C. Means (*The Modern Corporation and Private Property*, 1933) were the first to explore the legal, managerial, and economic implications of the depersonalization of property. Their insights provided the intellectual rationale for much of the regulatory reforms of the 1930s and 1940s. Joseph Schumpeter (*Capitalism, Socialism, and Democracy*, 1950) prophesied that the attenuation of ownership and control would make capitalism progressively harder to defend against socialist critiques and lead to the transmutation of capitalist into socialist managers because of the attenuated control of former owners.

The rhetoric of the modern captains of industry has certainly changed from the nineteenth century. Profit-maximization and cost-minimization to increase the net worth of the stockholders still receive primary emphasis in economics and management textbooks. They hardly occupy such a place in annual reports, where they are relegated to a list of objectives including the interests of employees, customers, and the communities where the firm carries on its business. The rhetoric also mirrors the dismal returns which stockholders have received on their investments in common stocks of the nation's largest corporations over the past half-century.

Government's Role in the Economy. It is here that philosophy and practice have changed most over the past half-century. I have already commented on the changing attitudes toward government regulation of the economy. The other area of enormous ideological shift is in the role of the government in income redistribution and the establishment of a social "safety-net."

The United States was the last major industrial country to provide a social security system for its citizens (1935).[31] Even then, it was "sold" to the public as an actuarially based insurance plan to provide supplemental old-age assistance. Progressive taxation of income and wealth was introduced as a wartime measure which lingered on after World War II.

Redistribution by progressive taxation always had an uneasy base in economic theory. On the one hand, theorists felt comfortable with the axiomatic inference of the declining marginal utility of income. On the other hand, there seemed to be no firm basis for a similar axiomatic inference about the interpersonal comparison of income or utility other than an assumption about the equality of men.

Welfare economics (the study of the relationship between market behavior and human welfare) seemed to make progress in the 1930s in expanding the limited usefulness of Pareto optimality to Hicks-Scitovsky criteria, which inferred that society would be "better off" if gainers could (theoretically) compensate the losers from a given market change.[32] However, this came to an axiomatic dead end in the 1950s with Arrow's demonstration of the impossibility of empirically deriving a "social welfare function" to be maximized by social interference with the results of exchange transactions.[33] Paul Samuelson widened the controversy to include normative judgments about social welfare functions and called attention to the large amounts of producers' and consumers' surpluses which were available for social redistribution in an advanced society.[34] Still, economic theory in the 1960s was based on the nineteenth-century utilitarianism of J. S. Mill and Jeremy Bentham which left the legislature to apply the felicific calculus to achieve the "greatest good for the greatest number."

With very little theoretical justification, the Congress, with Lyndon Johnson's presidential leadership, launched the "Great Society" during the rapid growth and renewed social consciousness which followed the J. F. Kennedy assassination and the civil rights demonstrations of the middle sixties. The Great Society featured four major areas of governmental income redistribution from the employed to the dependent population: federal aid to education, expanded Social Security coverage and benefits, federally funded Medicare for the retired population, and expanded federal transfers to the non-employed or underemployed population through food stamps, rent subsidies, aid for dependent children, and unemployment benefits.

I do not wish to comment here on the effects of those Great Society benefits. They are of importance in our consideration of ideology and the economy because they affirmed that the solutions of the market were not only unacceptable with regard to regulation but were also unacceptable with regard to the wealth and income distributions they produced. Three centuries earlier, John Locke had argued that the state could ask a citizen for his life as a part of national defense but could not tax him without his consent because that represented a non-voluntary confiscation of property to which he had a natural right. The Great Society affirmed that all citizens had a claim on national wealth and that the federal government was the appropriate agent for its redistribution. Even the philosophic right, in the person of Milton Friedman, accepted the legitimacy of transfers and argued only that a negative income tax would be a more efficient means of transfer than the overlapping and conflicting programs which accreted from legislative action.

Intellectual historians have emphasized that John Locke's *Second Treatise on Civil Government* was an *apologia* for the rejection of the social obligations of feudalism and the affirmation of economic individualism by the rising bourgeoisie of the seventeenth century. It could be argued equally that John Rawls's A *Theory of Justice* (1971)[36] was a systematic *apologia* for twentieth-century social democratic welfare states. Rawls, like Locke, systematically developed a pseudo-historical argument to explain the basis on which individual men would consent to yield their individual interests to control by a sovereign. Rawls's social contract emphasizes a "maximin" solution to the question of income distribution. Self-interested individuals, operating behind a "veil of ignorance" would agree to associate in a civil society only with the assurance that the least advantaged would receive a basic level of income security. That basic level would be the maximum which could be secured without limiting the incentives of the advantaged portion of the population to keep increasing the wealth available for redistribution. At least conceptually, the appropriate amount of income redistribution can be empirically estimated from study of saving behavior, labor force participation, and work effort by the "advantaged."[37]

Rawls's formulation of the principle of income redistribution has two differences from the utilitarian principle previously used to justify socialism: first, it establishes the right of all individuals to a safety-net; second, it (ideally) can rely on observation of productive behavior rather than subjective comparisons of utility to quantify the appropriate levels and techniques of redistribution. The 1984 presidential campaign witnessed an acceptance by both candidates of the maximin principle for the "truly needy" and a policy debate over the appropriate levels and types of taxation to provide a safety-net without damaging incentives for growth.

The ideological assent to government regulation and redistribution has been, by no means, complete. On the regulatory side, a monetarist counterattack on Keynesian demand management has sundered what was thought a decade ago to be a national consensus. Monetarism is *not* about monetary policy. It is about whether markets are naturally stable without government intervention and the wisdom of allowing changes in prices and interest rates to bring about macroeconomic stability.

The intellectual leader of the monetarist resurrection of the neoclassical arguments has been Milton Friedman, Nobel laureate in economics from the University of Chicago—a long-time center of free market and individualist solutions to questions of social organization. In his 1968 presidential address to the American Economic Association, Friedman argued that in the long run, government policy to reduce unemployment below its "natural" rate would bring not only inflation but *accelerating* inflation.[38] Further, he noted that the short-run attempt to fine-tune the economy by demand management was doomed to failure by variable lags and the inevitable tendency of politically motivated governmental leaders to pick short-run solutions with long-run costs.

One of the ironic features of Friedman's "natural rate" hypothesis is its link with classical and Marxian economic dynamics. Classical economists argued that wages could not be increased without decreasing profits, limiting saving and investment, and, thereby, choking off growth of the capital stock, which would lead to unemployment, a decline in wages, and a decline in population growth. The decline in wages would be accompanied with a rise in profits and a return, once again, to growth through capital formation. Society was self-regulating.

The Marxian version of the "natural rate" of unemployment emphasized the necessity of a "surplus army of the unemployed" to keep wages down and prevent the limitation of profits and a retardation of capital growth. The Marxian critique of free markets emphasized that their instability in a capitalist system could only be contained by the creation of a high level of unemployment. The classical argument noted that unemployment would result inevitably from the rise in wages. Friedman's version of the "natural rate" also results in the conclusion that governmental intervention to improve the natural functioning of markets is doomed to failure by inexorable laws of economic motion. In his defense it should be noted that Friedman is in favor of concerted government action to break down the rigidities in labor markets which increase the level of the "natural rate" of unemployment.

In the last decade an even more fatalistic economic theory than monetarism has attracted considerable intellectual adherence from economists (although not the general public). This school, known at the New Classical or Rational Expectations School, holds that markets are so sophisticated and informed about the effects of monetary and fiscal policy that those policies are doomed to be ineffective. If, for example, the government should announce that it was going to increase the money supply to stimulate real output in the economy, bond prices would immediately fall, reflecting inflationary expectations, and prices would rise for the same reason. Nominal income would be increased by inflation, and *nothing* would happen to increase output and employment.

Another classical ideology which has made its reappearance in the last decade is "supply-side" economics. This approach emphasizes the incentives to increased output and saving which will result from cuts in marginal tax rates on labor and capital income. The protagonists of this approach include economist Arthur Laffer, Congressman Jack Kemp, and journalist Jude Wanniski. Their ideas have been incorporated in the Kemp-Roth tax bill which reduced tax rates twenty-five percent during the 1982-1984 period. The most comprehensive ideological *apologia* for the supply-side approach to economic and social policy is to be found in George Gilder's *Wealth and Poverty*.[39] Gilder, like Locke, argues for the *moral* superiority of private property and economic individualism. He asserts that production and exchange are rooted in faith that the gift of labor or production which is offered in markets will be reciprocated. He blames the breakdown of the family on the removal of the moral responsibility of the male for family support.

It is fair to say that the consensus about government demand management has broken down in the eighties as a result of the attack by the Monetarists, New Classical Economists, and the Supply-Siders. This, of course, does not relieve the Congress and the Federal Reserve from carrying out fiscal and monetary policy in line with the Full Employment Act of 1946 or the necessities of government. It only deprives them of a short-lived intellectual consensus on how it should be done. It has produced in the last five years the irony of a supposedly economically conservative President criticizing the Federal Reserve for tight money policies designed to decelerate deflation and an economically liberal Democratic Party criticizing the size of the government deficit at a time of high unemployment.

It would not do to leave the subject of recent changes in ideology about the government's role in the economy without referring to the rising influence of the Public Choice school of economic and political theory. This group of political economists, originating with the leadership of Ronald Coase, James Buchanan, and Gordon Tullock at the University of Virginia in the early 1960s, has applied microeconomic theory to the analysis of the behavior of legislatures and government officials. Their work undermines the assumption inherent in much of the theorizing of the past century that the government could act as an impartial and benevolent trustee of the public interest in cases of "market failure."

Neoclassical economists, starting with Alfred Marshall and John Stuart Mill, had emphasized that government had three important roles in remedying the deficiencies of the market—the provision of "public goods," the control of "externalities," and the prevention or regulation of the use of market power in the absence of conditions in which perfect competition would automatically provide socially optimal outcomes.

The major intellectual contribution of the Public Choice theorists has been to create a healthy skepticism about the necessity of government intervention in cases of so-called "market failure" and the role of government officials as disinterested trustees of the "public interest." Buchanan and Tullock demonstrated that public goods were likely to be oversupplied by legislative log-rolling and bureaucratic power-seeking.[40] Coase demonstrated both the ubiquity of externality and the theoretical unimportance of the assignment of ownership and liability to the efficiency of resource allocation in conflict situations.[41] A number of the Public Choice economists have demonstrated that "rent seeking" to control the regulators of markets was likely to dissipate resources as well as leave the regulators in the clutches of the regulated.[42]

The Public Choice school has been particularly important in countering a prevailing intellectual tendency to assume that when there are problems in the world, government action is the best way to solve them.[43] Like most ideas, the examination of the motives and outcomes of government officials is not a new one. Adam Smith's arguments against mercantilism relied heavily on close examination of actual rather than supposed outcomes. The "invisible hand" was a persuasive ideological symbol to substitute for the bumbling and corruption of guild and government functionaries.

The Public Choice critique of governmental power has had some impact on reducing the power of government. Railroads, trucking, and airlines have been deregulated. Financial intermediaries have had price controls on payment of interest to depositors lifted. In California, Proposition 13 rolled back property taxes and curbed the taxing authority of the legislature and local governments. Tariffs and quotas have been held to a minimum despite great and growing pressure for a "new industrial policy." Intellectual support for a constitutional amendment to balance the budget has been growing. Exclusionary and low-density zoning is beginning to get a bad name—even with environmentalists and urban planners.

Nevertheless, Public Choice challenges to the power and wisdom of government regulations of markets have barely begun to stem a rising tide of interference by government in the organization of markets. "Equal opportunity" has been succeeded by "affirmative action" and "equal worth" intervention in employment markets. Public utilities may be charging higher prices to their consumers in the future because of regulatory delays and rulings. "Pork-barrel" appropriations for harbor, dam, and flood-control projects are approved for political rather than realistic cost-benefit reasons. Soaring medical expenditures funded by entitlement programs with incentives to increase costs rise almost as rapidly as the unfunded pension liabilities of public employees.

Science and the Natural World. Faith in science and technology probably reached its apex in the United States in the early sixties. Agricultural productivity had been greatly enhanced by hybrid seeds and chemical fertilizers and by the use of insecticides, herbicides, and fungicides to kill off man's competition for crops. Medicine had made great forward steps with the development of antibiotics and serums for the control of serious diseases. Atomic power, developed during World War II for destructive purposes, was held out as the promise of the future for cheap, clean energy. The jet engine and radar led to an enormous expansion of air travel. The computer, the laser, and semiconductor technology revolutionized control and communications technology. The development of cheap, simple contraception by "the pill" promised to women the control of their bodies and to the world the control of its population. The discovery of DNA promised to mankind the control of the biological world. People believed that if science could solve the problems of putting a man on the moon, the problems of man on earth were soluble.

By the mid-sixties, a wave of reaction against science and the use of science to promote economic growth had set in. In 1962 Rachel Carson wrote *Silent Spring* and started the environmental movement by sounding an alarm about the effect of agricultural chemicals on the environment.[44] In the late sixties, Paul Ehrlich started the Zero Population Growth movement with *The Population Bomb*.[45] Barry Commoner brought the anti-technology, anti-interventionist ethic full circle with *The Closing Circle: Nature, Man, and Technology*.[46] Commoner's message was a thoroughgoing repudiation of the intervention of man in natural processes. He was, in effect, counseling the return of civilization to a pre-industrial society without scientific agriculture or the use of fossil fuels.

The fear of nuclear war and the mysteries of fission and radiation were exploited by opponents of nuclear power. They demanded one hundred percent surety against the possibility of leaks or explosions and absolute security for the spent fuels from the nuclear production of energy.

The horrors of the Vietnam war were brought into every American living room on television for a decade. The revulsion against napalm and Agent Orange and the use of science and technology in war was converted into a widespread distrust of science and technology everywhere.

America's universities became the focal point for dissent and violence in the 1960s, beginning at Berkeley in 1964 with the Free Speech movement. Columbia University was occupied and shut down for a period in 1968 by dissidents who demanded that the University cease all classified research for the federal government. Most American campuses were closed down in 1970 in protest against American strategy in Vietnam and the killing of four students by the Ohio National Guard on the campus of Kent State University. A generation of students experienced a concerted attack on scientific research by universities which might be weapons-related or affect the environment and heard radical questioning of the role of universities in training manpower for the nation's businesses.

By the early 1970s, much of the passion of the civil rights movement of the early sixties and the anti-war activism of the late sixties had subsided or had been refocused into the environmental movement or varieties of passivity associated with Eastern religious thought. Jerry Brown was elected governor of California in 1972 on a platform which severely questioned the benefits of economic growth. He identified E. F. Schumacher's *Small is Beautiful* as his guidebook to appropriate technology.[47] In 1973 the trebling of world oil prices was widely viewed as signaling a new period of our economic history. The term GNP was ridiculed as "gross national pollution" rather than gross national product and people who advocated its increase were viewed as evil or foolish or both.

I may have exaggerated the extent of the intellectual revulsion against science and technology and the American belief in progress over the past two decades. The attack on Jimmy Carter's identification of American problems as "a national malaise" by the Republicans in the 1980s and the call for a return to traditional values, self-confidence, and economic growth may indicate that the swing of the pendulum was limited in moment and amplitude. Nevertheless, it is important to realize that the emphasis on ecology by scientists and their followers is a statement of ideology about man's place in nature which repudiates the long-standing Western belief in man's ability to control nature for his own purposes. As Kenneth Boulding noted,

> The evolutionary vision is unfriendly to romantic nature worship, the view that the human race and its artifacts are not part of nature and that nature without the human race is somehow wise and good. This is a fallacy into which many people of goodwill fall. The human race has been produced by the evolutionary process and so have its artifacts. The automobile is just as "natural" as the horse. It is just as much a species, just as much a part of the total ecological system,

and the idea that there is something called "ecology" in the absence of the human race and human artifacts at this stage of the development of the planet is romantic illusion. The human race, of course, needs to be aware of its impact on the total system, but the concept of the "environment" as removed from human endeavor is largely illusory. When we talk about the environment, we mean the evaluation of the total state of the planet according to human values, which are the only values we know very much about. If "nature," whatever that is, has values, they are unknown to us. Certainly nature is no respecter of species and all species are endangered. Nature cares no more about the whooping crane or the blue whale than she did about the dinosaur. Indeed, personification of nature is a romantic substitute for religion without the intellectual substance of a practical argument for faith in the divine as an act of will and commitment.[48]

Beliefs about the nature of the world and man's place in it are the foundation of American science and technology.

Conclusion

Ideology has had a profound effect on the development of the American economic system. In an impersonal and interdependent world in which governments and corporations exercise pervasive control of economic activity, we continue to affirm individual liberty and voluntary association as the basis of our economic organization.

I have largely ignored the problem of which came first, the eagle or the egg. Which came first, ideology or economic organization? Lockean doctrines of individual liberty and private property were obviously well-suited to an empty land. Yet, French Quebec and adjacent Mexico were also empty lands which experienced the development of very different economies.

The world shares technology, and capital is mobile. Yet, such geographically contiguous and resource-similar pairs of countries as Israel/Jordan, Switzerland/Austria, Japan/the Philippines have remarkably different ideologies and economies.

I have to conclude that economic organization is a function of ideology (with cybernetic linkage) and not the other way around. The unanswered question is, what determines ideology? I leave that to the philosophers.

NOTES

1. Karl Marx, *Das Kapital*, 1868. Republished in English as *Capital: A Critique of Political Economy* (New York: The Modern Library, 1906).

2. In Gordon C. Bjork, *Private Enterprise and Public Interest: The Development of American Capitalism* (Englewood Cliffs, N.J.: Prentice-Hall, 1969), I have developed an extended argument about the limits on private property and exchange relationships which develop over time. Another theory of institutional change, for an earlier period, argues that changes in relative factor prices lead to institutional change. See also D.C. North and R.P. Thomas, *The Rise of the Western World: A New Economic History* (Cambridge: Cambridge University Press, 1973).

3. Wayne D. Rasmussen, "The Impact of Technological Change in American Agriculture, 1862–1962," *Journal of Economic History* 22 (1962).

4. Gordon C. Bjork. "Regional Adjustment to Economic Growth: The United States, 1880–1950," *Oxford Economic Papers* (March 1968).

5. Karl Polanyi, *The Great Transformation* (Boston: Beacon Press, 1957).

6. R. L. Ransom and R. Sutch, *One Kind of Freedom* (Cambridge: Cambridge University Press, 1977).

7. Angus Maddison, *Phases of Capitalist Development* (New York: Oxford University Press, 1982).

8. Gordon C. Bjork, *Life, Liberty, and Property: The Economics and Politics of Land Use Planning and Environmental Controls* (Lexington, Mass.: D. C. Heath, 1979), Ch. 5.

9. Willard Hurst, *Law and the Conditions of Freedom in the Nineteenth Century United States* (Madison, Wisc.: University of Wisconsin Press, 1956).

10. The due process and just compensation clause did not prevent individual states from using the power of eminent domain to secure right of way for railroads and canals for transport improvements, even when carried out by state-chartered private corporations. See Harry N. Scheiber, "Property Law, Expropriation, and Resource Allocation by Government, 1789–1910," *Journal of Economic History* 33 (1973).

11. The origins of the Civil War are complex. For a compact summary of alternative explanations, see Stanley Lebergott, *The Americans: An Economic Record* (New York: W. W. Norton, 1984), Ch. 20.

12. An extended summary of the role of property rights in a market society will be found in Bjork, *Life, Liberty, and Property*, Ch. 3.

13. Victor Fuchs, *How We Live* (Cambridge, Mass.: Harvard University Press, 1983).

14. Bjork, *Life, Liberty, and Property*, Ch. 2.

15. *The Federalist Papers*, ed. Jacob E. Cooke (Middletown, Conn.: Wesleyan University Press, 1961). For example, Paper 10 by James Madison.

16. Jacob E. Cooke, ed., *The Reports of Alexander Hamilton* (New York: Harper and Row, 1964).

17. Bjork, *Life, Liberty, and Property*, Ch. 6.

18. Lebergott, Ch. 2.

19. For an extended discussion of the attitudes and skills of the American labor force in the nineteenth century in comparative terms, see H.J. Habakkuk, *American and British Technology in the 19th Century* (Cambridge: Cambridge University Press, 1962).

20. A.D. Chandler, *The Railroads: The Nation's First Big Business* (New York: Harcourt, Brace, and World, 1965).

21. The importance of the development of knowledge and of impersonal economic organization is emphasized in Simon Kuznets's Nobel Laureate Lecture, "Modern Economic Growth, Findings and Reflections," *American Economic Review* 63:1.

22. Bjork, *Private Enterprise and Public Interest*, Ch. 3.

23. F. J. Turner, *The Frontier in American History* (New York: Henry Holt, 1921).

24. G. Murphy and A. Zellner, "Sequential Growth, the Labor Safety Valve Doctrine, and the Development of American Unionism," *Journal of Economic History* 19 (1959).

25. Bjork, *Private Enterprise and Public Interest*, Ch. 8. The classic legal case which affirmed the legitimacy of state intervention also contains a brilliant statement of the classical argument against the control of private property. Munn v. Illinois, 94 U.S. 125 (1877).

26. Richard Hofstadter, *Social Darwinism in American Thought* (Boston: Beacon Press, 1955). Also, Robert McCloskey, *American Conservatism in the Age of Enterprise* (Cambridge: Cambridge University Press, 1951).

27. Thorstein Veblen, *The Theory of the Leisure Class* (New York: Macmillan, 1899). Also, *The Theory of Business Enterprise*, 1904, and *The Instinct of Workmanship*, 1914.

28. John Galbraith, *The Affluent Society* (Cambridge, Mass.: The Riverside Press, 1958).

29. The legitimation of government's active role in the economy among business leaders is surveyed perceptively by Robert Heilbroner, "The View from the Top: Reflections on a Changing Business Ideology," in *The Business Establishment*, ed. Earl F. Cheit (New York: John Wiley and Sons, 1964).

30. A useful recent survey of an accumulating literature on the exent to which modern corporate management behaves to secure social objectives may be found in Robin Marris and Dennis Mueller, "The Corporation, Competition, and the Invisible Hand," *Journal of Economic Literature* 18 (1980).

31. Gordon C. Bjork. "Welfare Policy and Economic Development," *Journal of Economic History* 26 (1966).

32. I. M. D. Little, "The Foundations of Welfare Economics," *Oxford Economic Papers* NS 1 (1949).

33. Kenneth Arrow, *Social Choice and Individual Values* (New York: John Wiley, 1951).

34. Paul A. Samuelson, "Arrow's Mathematical Politics" in *Human Values and Economic Policy*, ed. Sidney Hook (New York: New York University Press, 1964).

35. It is always dangerous to assert that Milton Friedman's policy position on a particular issue can be easily ascertained. His philosophic position in the late sixties, at least as summarized in his classic *Capitalism and Freedom* (Chicago: University of Chicago Press, 1962) was that consensus on property rights was more important than their content or origin. "The existence of a well-specified and generally accepted definition of property is far more important than what the definition is" (p. 27).

36. John Rawls, *A Theory of Justice* (Cambridge, Mass: The Belknap Press, 1971), Ch. 5.

37. This idea is elaborated in Arthur Okun, *Efficiency and Equality* (Washington, D.C.: The Brookings Institution, 1975).

38. Milton Friedman, "The Role of Monetary Policy," *American Economic Review* 58 (1968).

39. George Gilder, *Wealth and Poverty* (New York: Basic Books, 1981).

40. James Buchanan and Gordon Tullock, *The Calculus of Consent* (Ann Arbor: University of Michigan Press, 1962).

41. R. H. Coase, "The Problem of Social Cost," *Journal of Law and Economics* 3 (1960).

42. J. Buchanan, G. Tullock, R. Tollison, eds., *Toward a Theory of a Rent-Seeking Society* (College Station, Texas: Texas A. & M. University Press, 1980).

43. Public choice theorists have recognized that invalidating the intellectual rationale for market intervention by governments is an important part of the process in creating greater market freedom. See W. C. Stubblebine and R. Smith, "Obstacles to Restoring a Market Economy," unpublished manuscript presented to the Mont Pelerin Society in Cambridge, England, September, 1984.

44. Rachel Carson, *Silent Spring* (Boston: Houghton-Mifflin, 1962).

45. Paul Ehrlich, *The Population Bomb* (New York: Baltimore, 1968).

46. Barry Commoner, *The Closing Circle: Nature, Man, and Technology* (New York: Alfred Knopf, 1971).

47. E. F. Schumacher, *Small is Beautiful* (New York: Harper & Row, 1973).

48. Kenneth Boulding, *Ecodynamics: A New Theory of Societal Revolution* (Beverly Hills, CA.: Sage Publications, 1978), p. 19.

PART III

IDEOLOGY AND
AMERICA'S PLACE
IN THE WORLD

VII

Ideology and United States Foreign Policy

P. EDWARD HALEY

Brilliant achievements are as rare in diplomacy and strategy as they are in science, literature, or any other area of human endeavor. The rise of a Lincoln or Churchill is unexpected. Great leaders defy their origins and move unscathed through events that consume or paralyze their peers. Their grasp of people and events, their foresight, their ability to translate thought into accomplishment seem miraculous.

However, there is more to understanding a nation's foreign policy than recognizing the mystery that clings to greatness. One must also pay attention to the beliefs that are widely shared within a society. These beliefs shape the values, institutions, and practices of a nation which, in turn, influence the goals and conduct of foreign policy. In the case of the United States these beliefs are best understood as an "outlook."[1] The American outlook is a compound of a belief in inalienable individual rights, representative democracy, limited and decentralized government, civilian dominance of the military, and the separation of powers. This outlook, cherished by most Americans throughout the life of the Republic, favors the preservation of liberty rather than governmental efficiency.

The American outlook affects United States foreign policy in two significant ways: it shapes the institutions and practices through which contemporary American foreign policy is formulated and carried out; and it fosters a strong and widespread attitude of anti-communism among citizens and leaders of the United States. This essay considers the effects of the American outlook on the institutions and procedures of United States strategy and diplomacy. Its principal argument concerns the impact of anti-communism on American foreign policy, and particularly its influence on the decision to commit the United States to direct military support of the government of South Vietnam.

Outlook, Institutions, and Operations

At dawn on October 25, 1983, U.S. Marines and Rangers struck from air and sea against a self-styled Marxist-Leninist dictatorship on the island of Grenada. The invasion succeeded. The brutal junta led by Bernard Coard and Hudson Austin was overthrown, and hundreds of Cuban combat engineers were expelled from the island. But the Reagan Administration's undeniable success in the Caribbean could not erase the haunting images at Beirut airport of broken American bodies, tormented wreckage, and failed policy, destroyed barely two days earlier in a suicide truck-bomb attack against U.S. Marines.

The debacle at Beirut joined a long list of failures: the abortive attempt to rescue American hostages in Tehran; the embarrassment in Angola; the loss of Ethiopia; the total defeat of American policy in Vietnam; the humiliation of the Bay of Pigs. Why is the list so long? Why is it that before Grenada, the last example of a successful unilateral American intervention was the landing in Lebanon in 1958? Is there something intrinsic in the American outlook that has condemned recent United States foreign policy initiatives to failure?

The successes of United States arms and diplomacy have been too frequent and too precious to permit such a conclusion. From the defeat of Nazi Germany and militarist Japan to the Marshall Plan, the North Atlantic Treaty and the opening to China in the 1970s, American beliefs and actions have joined in valuable and effective military and diplomatic combination. However, the American outlook strongly influences the institutions and practices of United States foreign policy. This may be seen in the persistent controversies over human rights, in the divisions between President and Congress, divisions within the executive branch, and in the education of military officers.

All governments must reconcile the actions they take to achieve security and influence in the international system with their nation's vision of justice and appropriate behavior. The commitment of American citizens to due process, inherent political and legal rights, representative democracy, and limited decentralized government makes the process of reconciling external requirements and internal values exceptionally difficult and controversial. It is impossible, for example, for the United

States government to intervene in another nation without linking that intervention to the realization of self-determination and certain minimum standards of decency, or "human rights."

Some critics of United States foreign policy use these standards to attack support for authoritarian regimes in geopolitically vital areas— the Philippines, Korea, El Salvador, Chile, South Africa—where the clash between international effectiveness and domestic values is often most acute. Others apply the same high standards to United States relations with Communist regimes and revolutionary movements and conclude that principle demands an unyielding opposition to them.[2]

In theory it is possible for the two sets of critics to agree: The fundamental values are the same, after all, and human rights abuses in the Soviet Union or Poland are as extensive and reprehensible as those in Chile or the Philippines. Indeed, for two decades after the end of World War II, critics of both schools were united in anti-Communist opposition to the Soviet Union and China. This was the basis of bipartisanship in United States foreign policy. However, the national consensus was lost during the Vietnam War and has not been restored. United States policy makers now find themselves in the excruciating position of having to contend with a nation whose values pull it in opposite directions.

The distrust of government revealed in Federalist 10 was given permanent institutional form in the constitutional separation of the powers of American government. Nowhere is this separation more pronounced than in the area of international affairs. The president directs warfare, but Congress alone may change the nation from peace to war. The president is commander-in-chief, but Congress alone may raise an army. The president recognizes foreign governments and conducts relations with them, but the Senate must give its consent to all treaties. Money for all programs comes from Congress alone and may be stopped or diminished by Congress at any time. Congress can and often has set conditions which the executive must meet in order to receive funding for its programs of aid or intervention. In the best of times, in order to obtain the funds it needs to operate, the executive branch must spend literally months on Capitol Hill in lengthy and often bitter and exhausting hearings before a multitude of subcommittees. A government that is centralized, secretive, and quick in its actions is usually regarded as most likely to be effective in international affairs. Often the American government is dispersed, public, and ponderous.

In practice, the Congress regularly follows the president's lead in foreign affairs, and this mitigates the difficulties of decentralization, openness, and inertia. The worst problems arise when judgments differ between the branches about the political feasibility of a course of action the executive branch wishes to pursue. Congress is sensitive above all else to popular opinion, and if representatives and senators conclude that a policy has become deeply unpopular among their constituents, they will defeat it. This was precisely the situation in the closing months of the Vietnam War. Congress concluded that the American people wished to end the nation's role in that war. Against that conclusion the executive branch was powerless.[3] Similarly, during the 1930s, Congress legislated isolationism and obliged the executive branch to refrain from any form of intervention in the succession of wars that broke out in Asia, Africa, and Europe. With the Neutrality Acts, Congress unquestionably gave the American people what they wanted. Tragically, neutrality held the United States on the sidelines until it had lost any chance to prevent aggression by the Nazis and Japanese militarists. As isolationism and the Vietnam War suggest, when facing a Congress convinced that policy has become widely unpopular, the executive branch must yield, however unwise its compliance may be. Again, this runs counter to the requisites of effective international action.

If disputes between Congress and the president were the only legacy of the American outlook, the chances for a successful United States foreign policy would be greater than they are. However, the list of policy makers' headaches would not be complete without recognizing the importance of bureaucratic politics. In a sense, the difficulties of coming to agreement within the United States executive branch are not a result of the American outlook. All modern governments have become bureaucratized. The squabbles over jurisdiction and the push toward policies chosen to satisfy internal organizational needs rather than external security requirements are the result of a universal logic of bureaucracy rather than a specific national outlook. However, the political negotiation inside the American bureaucracy occurs in a system decisively affected by the American outlook. Determined American bureaucrats possess political options denied to their counterparts in other nations. They may "leak" information to friendly members of Congress, or to the press, which enjoys a unique degree of constitutional protection. In these ways it is possible to continue to oppose a decision long after the president would have wished to end opposition. At the very least the coherence of policy may be disrupted and other nations can be given repeated opportunities to escape the leverage the United States seeks to wield. At worst, policy can be paralyzed or defeated. At best, congressional and popular opinion may be awakened to prevent serious blunders. It is a perfect mirror of the preference in the American outlook for liberty over efficiency.

Finally, civilian dominance over the military—a fundamental part of the American outlook—exercises a decisive influence on United States foreign policy. The chief effect would appear to be a kind of remaking of the United States military in the image of a large but not terribly effective American corporation. Rather than warriors, the United States military would appear to have adopted a bland, not too effective manager as the ideal. The corporate executives and union management of Ford and U.S. Steel have been most notable in recent years for being unable to cope with their foreign competitors. The failure in Vietnam and the botched missions in Iran and Lebanon suggest that the American military has imitated this corporate attribute as well.

Some military officers have reacted to the failures by asking why they occurred. In his persuasive study of the American military in Vietnam, Harry Summers concluded that there have been serious deficiencies in military education.[4] In the broadest sense military education has two tasks: it must understand the nature of strategy and its relation to national policy; and it must communicate this understanding to successive generations of officers and men.

Summers' thesis is that American officers have neglected the study of military strategy. To an extent that would be regarded as unusual in any other society, American military thought has been dominated by civilians. Summers does not challenge this dominance, and applauds the assistance of civilians in clarifying the ends of military action and the appropriate means that should be used to achieve those ends. He faults the military for failing to provide the critical link that they alone should supply: how to fight; how to take the appropriate means and use them to achieve national objectives. Instead the officers joined the civilians and studied the material means to be used in war. They failed to grasp the difference between preparation for war and the conduct of war. The obligation of those who prepare for war is to provide trained and equipped fighting forces. Those who conduct war must use these means to achieve the purposes of the war. By following the civilian logistics specialists and systems analysts, Summers argues, American officers behaved as if the preparation for war were the conduct of war.

To approach strategy in this way ignores Clausewitz and, to Summers, is "a regression in military thought."[5] The adoption of what amounts to an eighteenth-century view of warfare contributed to the American defeat in Vietnam. Even more important, this narrow view of strategy hurt the relationship between the American people and the military. Rather than seeing the military as their instrument, the people began to see it as an instrument of the *government*.

The final harmful effect of the American neglect of strategy has been to misunderstand the centrality of victory. Summers expresses this by pointing out that the American military learned correct and incorrect lessons from the Korean War. The correct lesson was that victory does not necessarily mean total victory: it is not always possible to destroy an enemy government or annihilate enemy military formations. But a wrong lesson was also learned. Mistakenly, the American military concluded that the achievement of victory itself had become impossible, a conclusion reinforced by a perfectly rational fear of nuclear war. Instead, Summers argued, American officers ought to have realized that victory is the attainment of the objectives for which the war was fought, however limited they might be. Victory in these terms is possible, even in the nuclear age. Throughout the 1950s and 1960s, the failure to see victory as the aim of military strategy reinforced the preoccupation of American officers with preparation for war rather than its conduct.

The preceding analysis of the impact of the American outlook on United States foreign policy has emphasized only a few of the elements of that outlook and a handful of its effects. Plainly, the emphasis on human rights, the separation of powers, and the failure of American military education have influenced United States policy in important ways. However, a complete understanding of the effect of the American outlook on United States foreign policy must include an understanding of the impact of anti-communism.

Anti-Communism and United States Foreign Policy

Twice in this century, United States security has been challenged by ideological enemies: in World War II by Nazi Germany, Fascist Italy, and militarist Japan; since 1945 by Communist governments, of which the most important are the Soviet Union and the Peoples Republic of

China. In responding to these threats the United States has mobilized its diplomatic, military, economic, and human resources for what was thought to be the duration of World War II, but has become an indefinite term, the cold war. The policy served by this mobilization is anti-ideological: in World War II it was anti-Nazi; since the inception of the cold war it has been anti-Communist.

The hostility that Americans feel toward communism does not ordain a specific policy. Rather, it contributes to a widespread popular readiness to oppose Communist governments. Because communism is joined to a major military power hostile to the United States, Americans decided they must mount major diplomatic and military efforts against that nation and its allies. In short, it was the combination of Communist ideology and Soviet and, for many years, Chinese military forces that triggered a diplomatic and military response from the United States. In the absence of the marriage of communism to Soviet military power—if, for example, the chief Communist powers in the world were Albania, Zambia, and the Falkland Islands—the United States government would never have mounted the extensive programs of military preparedness and intervention, foreign aid, alliances, and diplomatic activity that have characterized its foreign policy since 1945.

During the entire period since 1945 every administration has taken the position—in public and private—that United States security is endangered by the power of the major Communist regimes. After Mao's victory in China, United States policy makers decided that the accession to power by a Communist movement in any other country anywhere in the world would endanger the United States, mainly because it would start an "unraveling" process similar to that achieved by the Nazis and by the Japanese militarists in the 1930s and 1940s. This view was challenged within the Truman administration, in particular by George Kennan, but the dissenters grew fewer over the years, and the notion that the balance of power was fragile rather than robust gained widespread acceptance among policy makers.[6]

While both the Truman and Eisenhower administrations in public and private agreed that the seizure of power by a Communist movement in any country anywhere in the world would endanger United States security, they declined to use military force unilaterally to prevent such a development. Truman used American troops to thwart the conquest of South Korea by the North, but he regarded the North Korean invasion as a Soviet probe and as an action too flagrant to ignore. Truman's most important decision on intervention came not in June 1950 over

Korea but two years earlier when he had to decide whether to prevent Mao's victory in China by force. Truman declined, because the goal, however desirable, was beyond United States means and because he put the economic and political restoration of Western Europe and Japan ahead of all other foreign initiatives. Eisenhower sent marines into Lebanon in 1958 in a show of force. But his crucial decision on intervention had come four years earlier when he declined to save the French garrison at Dien Bien Phu by massive American air strikes. He refused because he could find no support for the intervention from United States allies and disliked supporting French colonialism. For both administrations only direct invasions by China or the Soviet Union were sufficient to justify a unilateral American response. The Kennedy administration lost this restraint and sent large numbers of American troops into Vietnam without meaningful allied support. What trapped the Kennedy administration in Vietnam?

One answer often given is that the United States became a prisoner of its anti-Communist beliefs. Convinced that any Communist victory would contribute importantly to Soviet power, the United States resorted to military intervention to prevent the fall of South Vietnam. As one analysis put it: "An ideology whose very existence seemed to threaten basic American values had combined with the national force of first Russia and then China. This combination caused American leaders to see the world in 'we-they' terms and to insist that peace was indivisible. . . . Communism came to be seen as an infection to be quarantined rather than a force to be judiciously and appropriately balanced."[7] Townsend Hoopes, a cabinet member turned critic, argued that American policy makers became obsessed with opposing communism. Their obsession, according to Hoopes, blinded them to changes in the Communist movement after the death of Stalin and the Sino-Soviet split and caused profound "distortions of threat and interest" which were "progressively embedded in the unspoken suppositions of policy formulation, accepted by both political parties and sustained by American public opinion" from the time of the Korean War onward.[8]

There is truth in Hoopes's observations and those of others who emphasize the effects of anti-communism on American foreign policy. Certainly this is one of the ways in which the American outlook has strongly marked the country's foreign policy. However, there are three problems with relying on anti-communism to explain the entrapment of the Kennedy administration in Vietnam. First, both the Truman and Eisenhower administrations shared that anti-communism, and yet escaped the quagmire. Second, as George Kennan's early analyses and policy recommendations showed—and they were repeated sporadically by different analysts over the succeeding years—a principled opposition to communism and the extension of Soviet power does not automatically provide a self-evident set of international goals and measures to reach them. And third, anti-communism is an appropriate stance for American policy makers, and indeed for the leaders of any country to adopt. Communist nations pose the greatest threat to the values and security of the United States and of any nation seeking a future open to pluralism, tolerance, and limited government. Any well-meaning attempt to learn from the blunders of past or present administrations must not lose sight of this, for it is essential to the mobilization of a nation's material and spiritual resources.

A comparison of the Vietnam policies of the Eisenhower and Kennedy administrations suggests that it was not anti-communism but the inferior strategic and political understanding of the Kennedy administration that moved the United States into a direct military role in Vietnam.

The Eisenhower Administration and the Indochina Conflict

The Eisenhower administration entered office determined to reverse what it regarded as a needless surrender of the psychological and military advantage in dealing with the Communists. To recapture the initiative it announced a policy of "massive retaliation" against the instigators of aggression. There would be no more Koreas. "It is not sound military strategy," John Foster Dulles told the Council on Foreign Relations, "permanently to commit U.S. land forces to Asia to a degree that leaves us no strategic reserves." Rather, "local defenses must be reinforced by the further deterrent of massive retaliatory power. A potential aggressor must know," he warned, "that he cannot always prescribe battle conditions that suit him. . . . The way to deter aggression is for the free community to be willing and able to respond vigorously at places and with means of its own choosing."[9]

The approach that Dulles announced with such a flourish was not as reckless as it seemed. It was, above all, a deterrent strategy. Its purpose was to prevent aggression by exploiting the terrifying nuclear advantage the United States enjoyed over the Soviet Union and China. In this way distant friendly governments could be protected without military deployments and expenditures so vast as to cause bankruptcy. "We want," Dulles avowed, "for ourselves and the other free nations, a maximum deterrent at a bearable cost."[10]

While it enjoyed nuclear superiority, the United States would bring the threat to use nuclear weapons to bear in any clash with Communist governments. The nuclear weapons would not necessarily be used. The point was to prevent war, not to wage it. "That does not mean," as Dulles put it:

> turning every local war into a world war. It does not mean that, if there is a Communist attack somewhere in Asia, atom or hydrogen bombs will necessarily be dropped on the great industrial centers of China or Russia. It does mean that the free world must maintain the collective means and be willing to use them in the way which most effectively makes aggression too risky and expensive to be tempting. . . . The point is that a respective attacker is not likely to invade if he believes the probable hurt will outbalance the probable gain.[11]

In practice, the "New Look" of the Eisenhower administration produced little immediate change in its Indochina policy. The awesome weight of the United States nuclear arsenal had been brought to bear against China and the Soviet Union. Behind this deterrent screen "local defense," manned in this case by the French, would be strengthened. In principle, it would be feasible to build a strong local defense, because the American deterrent would have taken away the demographic and geographic advantages of the principal Communist powers. In keeping with its approach, the Eisenhower administration increased its monetary and material aid to the French, nearly doubling the funds and sending a number of bombers. The administration also pushed the French to develop a plan that had a chance of achieving victory against the Viet Minh.

In American eyes, the concept offered by the French general, Henri Navarre, was such a plan. The French submitted the plan to the head of an American military mission to Hanoi, General John O'Daniel, in June-July, 1953. Stripped of its meaningless repetition of such phrases as "take the offensive" and "attacking the flanks and rear of the enemy," inserted presumably for American consumption, the Navarre plan called for intensifying the French military effort and for increasing the number of non-Communist Vietnamese under arms.[12] In return the French sought a large increase in American aid. Taking the Navarre plan together with French promises to create "strong free states in Indochina," the administration decided to augment its assistance and to continue to support the French in Indochina.[13] Additional hundreds of millions of dollars were authorized for the French military effort and more heavy weapons and transport aircraft were supplied. Throughout, the French generally succeeded in relegating the Americans to a role of a "blind partner"; the administration bestowed more and more money but never achieved any significant influence over French political and military strategy. On this slender and eroding ledge, the Eisenhower administration stood and developed its own long-range plan, NSC 5405.

Approved by the president on January 16, 1954, the document stated the importance of Southeast Asia to United States security and prescribed a course of action based on a consideration of all foreseeable developments, including a decision by France to abandon the war. NSC 5405 began by reiterating the administration's commitment to prevent the "domination of Southeast Asia" by communism. However, the weight of the argument concerned the "loss" of the region as a whole and not Vietnam or even Indochina. Above all the administration regarded Malaya and Indonesia as most important.[14] The authors of NSC 5405 held that the fall of Indochina would have "serious" repercussions for the United States and "free world interests in Europe and elsewhere." It would be a development that would require immediate and effective counteraction to prevent the "submission to or an alignment with communism" by the remaining countries of Southeast Asia, Indonesia, and even the Middle East, with the possible exception of Pakistan and Turkey. A realignment on such a scale, NSC 5405 concluded, would seriously endanger European security and stability.

The French were fighting to prevent this. With the ample American military aid they had been given, the French were, according to NSC 5405, in no danger of suffering a military defeat. However, the French might give up. No French government would be strong enough to refuse negotiations with the Viet Minh. If their new military efforts failed to lead to victory, "the French might seek to negotiate simply for the best possible terms, irrespective of whether these offered any assurance of preserving a non-Communist Indochina."[15] The administration pledged to continue to try to strengthen France against such an outcome, but if it should nonetheless occur, the administration was clear about its reaction. *In the absence of Chinese Communist intervention*, the United States would not resort to force to prevent the fall of Indochina.[16] The list of what the Eisenhower administration would do for France occupied more than three typed pages. But armed intervention was not included.

Only the intervention of China would trigger an American military response, and even then the United States would act only if it were joined by the United Nations or Britain and France.

The elaboration of plans and "contingencies" ahead of time often proves to be a waste of time, because the assumptions necessary to planning never match the circumstances of the moment when action is required. However, there is a striking coincidence between the course of action laid down for the United States in NSC 5405, three months before the crisis erupted over Dien Bien Phu, and the course that the Eisenhower administration actually followed in the months and years ahead. As 1954 began, the administration had agreed to continue to stiffen the French and to pressure them to win the support of the Indochinese peoples by making genuine concessions leading to their sovereignty.

It was a plan. It was not without promise. But it did not work. As spring approached, the French political and military position began to deteriorate. The negotiations feared by the administration were set in train by a decision of the "Big Four" foreign ministers (Britain, France, the United States, the USSR) meeting in Berlin in February 1954 to place the war in Indochina on the agenda of an East-West conference to convene in Geneva in April. Maneuvering to derive maximum diplomatic advantage from military operations, the Viet Minh surrounded a French garrison—originally sent to Dien Bien Phu to bait a trap for the guerrillas—producing an immediate military emergency in Indochina and a gathering political crisis in France, pregnant with the collapse of the entire French presence in the region. A plea from the French for American air strikes to relieve the garrison brought the administration to a practical decision on armed intervention in Indochina.

In the process of reaching agreement on NSC 5405 three months earlier the National Security Council had declined to take action on an annex, which spelled out the choices for the United States if the French were defeated. There were differences between the State and Defense Departments, and within the Defense Department as well, over whether the United States should intervene with its own troops to prevent the loss of Indochina. Some of the representatives of the military services and, in particular, Army Chief of Staff General Matthew Ridgway, strongly opposed the use of force by the United States. In late 1953 the Plans Division of the Army General Staff stressed that the administration could find division-size forces for intervention in Indochina only by taking them from Europe and Asia, and that this would deny the United States the power it needed to fulfill its commitments in those two vital theaters. It made more sense to the Army to reconsider "the importance of Indochina and Southeast Asia in relation to the possible cost of saving it."[17]

Facing a crisis over Dien Bien Phu, the National Security Council turned once more to a consideration of the courses of action available to the United States in the event of a French defeat. The atmosphere was very different from what it had been three months earlier. Now a French garrison had been encircled in Laos, the French had asked the United States for air strikes to help relieve it, and a dangerously weakened French government was about to enter negotiations with the Vietnamese Communists and their Soviet and Chinese allies at Geneva.

The Army again intervened strongly in the discussions, this time by rejecting the view that air and naval action could accomplish anything permanently beneficial in Indochina, even if nuclear weapons were used. In order to maintain effective air action, the United States would have to commit ground forces to protect its air bases on the mainland of Indochina. This could lead to Chinese intervention. In any case United States planners could not assume the Chinese would stay out. If the French remained and the Chinese intervened, the United States would have to commit seven divisions (about 240,000 men) to win. If the French withdrew, the United States would need twelve divisions (410,000) to achieve victory. In addition, the United States would have to conduct five hundred fighter-bomber sorties per day, "exclusive of interdiction and counter-air operations," and provide the aircraft needed to drop one paratroop division into combat and the naval vessels required to move one for amphibious landings. Not surprisingly, the Army view was a flat "No!" Or, in the words of the Army position paper for the NSC: "U.S. intervention with combat forces in Indochina is not militarily desirable . . . ."[18]

In his memoirs, Ridgway wrote that at the time of the siege of Dien Bien Phu, he felt the United States government begin to move toward unilateral American intervention in the fighting in Vietnam. Some said it was a chance to test massive retaliation. Others maintained the United States could win with air and naval power, or perhaps nuclear weapons. Ridgway was convinced that none of those advocating United States intervention had any conception of the problems or costs of such an action. He set out to inform them:

> To provide these facts, I sent out to Indo-China an Army team of experts in every field: engineers, signal and communications specialists, medical officers, and experienced combat leaders who knew how to evaluate terrain in terms of battle

tactics. They went out to get the answers to a thousand questions that those who had so blithely recommended that we go to war there had never taken the trouble to ask. How deep was the water over the bar at Saigon? What were the harbor and dock facilities? Where could we store the tons of supplies we would need to support us there? How good was the road net—how could supplies be transported as the fighting forces moved inland, and in what tonnages? What of the climate? The rainfall? What tropical diseases would attack the combat soldier in that jungle land?[19]

The answers to these questions confirmed the doubts Ridgway had harbored from the outset. The area lacked highways, railways, and telephone lines. Ports and airfields were "totally inadequate." All of these could be built but only at tremendous cost and by great engineering efforts. The terrain was rice paddy and jungle, ideal for guerrilla operations. Every American unit, no matter how small, would have to be protected by riflemen or suffer constant ambush and attack.

In these circumstances, Ridgway understood, the costs of a successful intervention—and after Korea the United States could ill afford even a stalemate—would be tremendous. The size of United States forces in battle and their casualties would be at least as great and perhaps even greater than they had been in Korea. Air power and naval power alone could not win and neither could "inadequate ground forces."

Ridgway believed that the Army's case against intervention had helped stop, perhaps been decisive in stopping, a "tragic adventure." Ridgway was proud of his role in stopping the intervention, and he made his pleasure plain in his memoirs: "When the day comes for me to face my Maker and account for my actions, the thing I would be most humbly proud of was that fact that I fought against and perhaps contributed to preventing, the carrying out of some harebrained tactical schemes which would have cost the lives of thousands of men. To that list of tragic accidents that fortunately never happened I would add the Indo-China intervention."[20] Writing in 1956, Ridgway may be forgiven for being premature in his conclusion that the intervention in Indochina had been foreclosed. Just five years later the decision would be reconsidered, and when it was, President Eisenhower's successor would receive quite different military advice than that supplied by Ridgway.

The Army's position showed that air and naval action would not be decisive and that the use of ground forces would harm the country's ability to honor its most vital strategic commitments to Western Europe and Japan. The State Department did not disagree, and was particularly worried about Chinese intervention. However, the secretary of state was unwilling merely to stand by while the French were undone in Indochina and Geneva. An alternative was found and named "united action." The idea was to bring together a coalition of states in the region, to be joined by Britain, France, and the United States. The coalition would then fight together, if that were necessary, and, in any case, would be able to negotiate from a strong position at Geneva. Thailand and the Philippines were willing, and Dulles would try to win the agreement of Britain and France.

Because the administration was seriously considering the use of force, it brought the congressional leadership into the deliberations on April 3. Ironically, the Senate majority leader, Lyndon Johnson, (who, as president, would unilaterally send American troops into combat in South Vietnam) argued strongly, with the support of his colleagues, that the United States should intervene only if it had the support of its European allies. President Eisenhower had always been reluctant to intervene on the French side so long as Vietnamese independence of the French empire had not been truly established. Thus, while congressional consultation may be said to have laid a basis for "united action," the combination of Army opposition, congressional conditions, and presidential misgivings established three criteria which would have to be met before the United States would intervene militarily in Indochina: (1) a coalition of the United States and its allies committed to "united action"; (2) a French commitment to hasten the independence of the states of Indochina; and (3) the consent of Congress, which was dependent on the first two.[21]

The United States had not narrowed the yawning gap between the grand strategic importance it accorded Indochina and the meager claim on American combat troops it would allow. However, the moment for unilateral American military action had passed. Secretary Dulles set about obtaining the consent of the British and French to "united action" before the debut of the Geneva Conference. The French were cool because the coalition would escape exclusively French direction. The British opposed the concept because it might prevent a compromise settlement at Geneva. Little could be done, therefore, before the signature of the Geneva accords, which called for military cease-fires, regrouping of forces throughout Indochina, and elections in Vietnam within two years.

Ultimately, the United States dissociated itself from the accords, and began earnestly to strengthen the non-Communist part of Vietnam through economic and military assistance. "United action" was eventually embodied in the Manila Pact, or SEATO as it came to be called, and a form of indirect protection thrown over Vietnam, Laos, and Cambodia by use of a protocol to the basic treaty. Even from the American point of view, however, this was a deterrent alliance and not a fighting alliance. The instructions to American negotiators at Manila strictly forbade them to agree to anything that required the unilateral commitment of American troops to military action.[22]

The Kennedy Administration and the Indochina Conflict

The first weeks of the Kennedy administration were filled with international pressure, disappointment and, after the Bay of Pigs fiasco, humiliation. The new president had serious problems in Berlin, the Congo, Cuba, and Laos. The deteriorating situation in Vietnam was pushed aside temporarily. Even when scheduled for discussion at the presidential level, Vietnam often ended up being displaced by worried speculations on how to cope with Communist gains in Laos, which moved under the cover of diplomatic and material assistance from Moscow. The Kennedy administration turned to Vietnam in earnest in the late summer of its first year. When it did, its deliberations and actions were colored by a desire to make good for the setbacks in Cuba and, especially, in Laos. The administration's decisions on the best way to take a stand in Vietnam occurred in an atmosphere in which policy makers felt a need to recover something of what had been lost elsewhere.

President Kennedy's actions on Vietnam were routine. He offered South Vietnam's President Ngo Dinh Diem increased aid and an expansion of his armed forces (ARVN) and militia. At the same time, the president undertook to try to compel Diem to reorganize his military and civil institutions along more rational lines. Diem had replaced the French as the object for American pressure for reform. In general, Kennedy was no more successful with Diem than Eisenhower and Truman had been with the French.

The Kennedy administration formally made clear in May 1961 that it shared its predecessor's determination to prevent the further spread of communism in Southeast Asia. Specifically, the president approved as the United States objective in Vietnam: "To prevent Communist domination of South Vietnam; to create in that country a viable and increasingly democratic society, and to initiate, on an accelerated basis, a series of mutually supporting actions of a military, political, economic, psychological and covert character designed to achieve this objective."[23]

But beyond this shared objective the approach of the Kennedy administration differed sharply from that followed by Eisenhower and Truman. Above all, there were no readily observable conditions standing in the way of unilateral American intervention in the war in Vietnam.

By 1961 there was still a need to obtain congressional approval to use force, but that was all that remained of the Eisenhower administration's criteria for intervention. France was gone from Indochina and the countries of Vietnam, Laos, and Cambodia were sovereign, although Vietnam had suffered a *de facto* partition and there were rival claimants for the sovereignty of that country. The Kennedy administration did not regard "united action" as essential. As for the views of the United States armed forces, the president's military advisors chose to emphasize that a successful intervention could be achieved at low levels and low costs.

In some ways it is easier to understand the relative indifference to allied support than the change in the military analysis. Britain and France were far less important on the world scene by the early sixties than they had been a decade earlier. For whatever reason, the most one finds in the classified record is similar to a recommendation by Secretaries Rusk and McNamara in a memorandum for the president in the fall of 1961. Allied cooperation in case of intervention "would seem important," they told the president. The position of the United States "would be greatly strengthened." It is far different from the demand by Lyndon Johnson and his congressional colleagues for full British and French support of any intervention.

The greatest difference was in the military advice on which the Kennedy administration acted. The military counsel given to President Kennedy was inferior to that provided President Eisenhower in at least two critical areas: in the initial estimates of the numbers of American troops needed to achieve victory in Vietnam; and in the assessment of how difficult it would be for American soldiers to fight in Southeast Asia.

American military intervention in Vietnam was considered early in the Kennedy administration and a decision postponed. It was not until the late summer and early fall that the question was seriously examined, and then a series of fateful decisions were taken. In brief, the administration decided to introduce large numbers of American soldiers into Vietnam primarily to demonstrate an American commitment to Vietnam and to give the South Vietnamese army a capability to move around the countryside effectively. The primary mission of the helicopter companies and other engineering and logistics formations that were sent was not to engage in combat, although they were attacked and suffered casualties, as Ridgway had foreseen. The United States delayed introductions of large combat formations until 1965, but that action came as the logical conclusion of the steps taken four years earlier, steps from which there was no going back.

According to the Pentagon study, the Kennedy administration took up the issue of sending American troops to fight in Vietnam more or less continuously after April 1961.[24] In early May the Joint Chiefs of Staff recommended that the United States deploy combat troops to Vietnam.[25] Two battle groups, a battalion of combat engineers, and four hundred Special Forces troops (about 3600 men) was the minimum figure given, with the chief of the U.S. Military Advisory Group in Saigon, Lt. General Lionel McGarr, suggesting a force of 10,000. One rationale given for the commitment was to improve the training of the Vietnamese army, but the real purpose appears to have been twofold: to get United States troops into combat, with all that this would mean as a deterrent to the Communists; and, if the United States force were large enough, to free Vietnamese units to launch offensive operations. Initially, President Kennedy scrupulously avoided any significant change in the numbers or mission of United States troops in Vietnam. The early proposals, therefore, are best read as an indicator of the views of his advisors. However, the contrast between them and those of General Ridgway is apparent.

On October 5 a proposal by White House advisor Walt Rostow was sent to the Joint Chiefs. Rostow's plan was to introduce a United States-SEATO force of 25,000 on the Vietnam border between the Demilitarized Zone and Cambodia. The reply of the Joint Chiefs is instructive and, in retrospect, of enormous significance. The Chiefs easily brushed aside the Rostow proposal. Such a small force deployed along the border could be attacked piecemeal or bypassed. It would not stop infiltration, and it would have been placed in the hardest places to defend should North Vietnam or China invade South Vietnam. Instead, the Chiefs preferred the application of what appears to have been a pre-planned SEATO or United States operation to introduce large numbers of troops into Laos: "What is needed is not the spreading out of our forces throughout Southeast Asia but rather *a concentrated effort in Laos* where a firm stand can be taken saving all or substantially all of Laos which would, at the same time, protect Thailand and protect the borders of South Vietnam.[26]

Fatefully, the Chiefs went on. If a major intervention in Laos was considered "politically unacceptable" they were prepared to "provide" a

"possible limited interim course of action." The limited JCS plan of
1961 outlined the course followed by the United States when it intervened in strength four years later, although the later action involved
much larger numbers of American troops. The JCS suggested that a
SEATO force of about 23,000 be sent to Vietnam. About 11,000 (of
which 6,000 American) combat troops would be deployed to the highlands around Pleiku. The remaining troops would be in headquarters,
logistics, and communications units. The U.S. Seventh Fleet would
support the intervention with two attack carrier groups.

The JCS doubted that the Communist bloc would react by an overt
intervention. If North Vietnam invaded, SEATO forces would have to
be increased to twelve divisions, of which the United States share would
be three divisions (129,000) not including naval units. The United States
would be obliged to call up one division and other forces needed to maintain its strategic reserve. At most, in the event of North Vietnamese
and Chinese intervention, the Chiefs appear to have anticipated a need
to field a force of 278,000, approximately half of which would be
American.[27] In short, the Chiefs told the president that the United States
could win a war against China and North Vietnam with 140,000
American troops in combat, and by mobilizing one division to maintain
the United States strategic reserve.

The judgment by the nation's highest military officers that a Vietnam
intervention could be made relatively easily and inexpensively was not
the only factor that pushed the American government toward intervention. As observed earlier, the Kennedy administration shared its
predecessor's anti-communism, and was determined to oppose the expansion of communism anywhere in the world. However, the Chiefs' views
colored the debate that followed and weighed heavily, particularly after
President Kennedy was assassinated.

An even more persuasive military recommendation followed the Chiefs',
in the report of General Maxwell Taylor. He, too, counseled intervention, and believed that the troop commitment could be kept small. President Kennedy sent General Taylor to Vietnam in October 1961 to develop
a course of action the United States could follow to stop the deteriora-
tion in the political, economic, and military situation in South Vietnam and eventually to defeat the Communists. Taylor was accompanied
by Walt Rostow and representatives of the executive departments. General
Taylor recommended that the United States join South Vietnam in a
"massive joint effort" to save the country. As part of this effort, Taylor

recommended that the United States introduce a military task force into Vietnam to raise Vietnamese morale, provide an emergency reserve in case of sudden military reversals, and act as an "advance party" for additional American forces.

In an "Eyes Only" cable for the president, Taylor supported his recommendations. He began by admitting that the strategic reserve was "presently so weak" that the United States could not safely allow large numbers of its troops to become indefinitely engaged in Southeast Asia. He admitted, as well, that a direct intervention would tie United States prestige ever more closely to the Diem regime and, if the first American units did not turn the tide, it would be virtually impossible not to send reinforcements. And yet in Taylor's mind these problems were outweighed by the need to demonstrate an American commitment to South Vietnam.

The American force need not be large, Taylor argued. About 8,000 would do, primarily logistical units. It would not be used "to clear the jungles and forests of Viet Cong guerrillas." That was the responsibility of the South Vietnamese army. As if the differences with Ridgway were not great enough, Taylor went on to deny that Vietnam was a difficult place for American soldiers to fight in:

> As an area for the operations of U.S. troops, SVN is not an excessively difficult or unpleasant place to operate. While the border areas are rugged and heavily forested, the terrain is comparable to parts of Korea where U.S. troops learned to live and work without too much effort. However, these borders . . . are not the places to engage our forces. In the High Plateau and in the coastal plain where U.S. troops would probably be stationed, these jungle-forest conditions do not exist to any great extent. The most unpleasant feature in the coastal areas would be the heat and, in the Delta, the mud left behind by the flood. The High Plateau offers no particular obstacle to the stationing of U.S. troops.

To this extraordinarily benign appraisal of the terrain and climate of Vietnam, Taylor added a comparably optimistic assessment of the risks of war with North Vietnam and China and of the strategic handicaps of the North Vietnamese:

> The risks of backing into a major Asian war by way of SVN are present but are not impressive. NVN is extremely vulnerable to conventional bombing, a weakness which should be exploited diplomatically in convincing Hanoi to lay off SVN. Both the DRV and the Chicoms would face severe logistical difficulties in trying to maintain strong forces in the field in SEA, difficulties which we share but by no means to the same degree.[28]

Immediately after the Taylor report reached Washington, the secretary of defense strongly urged the president to send American troops into combat in Indochina. Speaking for himself, the Joint Chiefs, and Under Secretary of Defense Roswell Gilpatric, McNamara told the president that the introduction of the 8,000 troops recommended by General Taylor would not suffice. A prolonged war would result, possibly even the intervention of North Vietnam and China. Instead of proceeding in this way, the United States should make an explicit commitment to prevent the fall of South Vietnam to communism. Having made this commitment the United States should then prepare itself to commit the troops that would be necessary to achieve this goal. At most, this would require six American divisions (205,000 men) fighting on the ground. They could be provided without interfering with United States ability to honor its commitments in Western Europe.[29]

Three days later the secretaries of state and defense gave the president a slightly different memorandum. It, too, was based on a commitment to prevent the fall of South Vietnam to communism. The secretaries agreed that the United States should commit its forces to combat in Vietnam if that were necessary to achieve victory. This could mean striking at North Vietnam. The memorandum repeated the figures McNamara had used earlier: no more than 205,000 American troops would be needed. But the secretaries then offered the president a rationale for avoiding the immediate commitment of American combat forces to Vietnam. There were two kinds of troops the United States could send, they said. There were units whose mission was to help the South Vietnamese fight more effectively: reconnaissance, communications, helicopters, air transport, naval patrols. And there were larger units with a combat mission.

The first kind of unit should be sent immediately, and their dispatch should be accompanied by an imaginative diplomatic campaign designed to undercut the legitimacy of the Communists' actions against South Vietnam and, if possible, to persuade the Soviet Union to use its influence to stop the subversion. A decision on sending the combat units, the secretaries advised, could be deferred. Even so, the Department of Defense should be ordered to formulate plans for the commitment of American troops to combat in Vietnam for three different purposes: as a show of force; to assist the South Vietnamese army against the Viet Cong and North Vietnamese in guerrilla war; and to deal with an overt Communist invasion.[30]

The memorandum shows clear signs of having been written to the president's specifications, and he adopted almost all the recommendations in it. Accordingly, the United States did not send large units with a combat mission to Vietnam in 1961 but drastically increased the number of American military personnel in Vietnam in an actively supportive role. On December 11, exactly a month after the Rusk-McNamara memorandum, the *New York Times* reported the arrival in South Vietnam of two helicopter companies (33 aircraft and 400 men), in the words of the Pentagon study, "the first direct U.S. military support for the GVN."[31]

Conclusions

The Truman, Eisenhower, and Kennedy administrations shared a determination to prevent the expansion of communism in Indochina. When faced with a decision, Truman and Eisenhower declined to assign a direct military role to American troops in Vietnam. By the end of its first year the Kennedy administration had started the process of direct American military intervention. In reaching this decision, President Kennedy and his advisors repeatedly underestimated the cost of the intervention in lives and money, the size of the American forces that would be needed to achieve victory in Vietnam, and the importance of the support of the Western European allies of the United States.

The situation that Kennedy faced was significantly worse than that faced by either Eisenhower or Truman. Of the three, only the Kennedy administration had to choose between intervening directly in Vietnam or risking the exclusion of the United States from the mainland of Indochina. It is also true that the anti-communism of the three administrations prevented them from attempting to turn Ho Chi Minh into an Asian Tito. But there is some doubt that it would have worked. It is fear of China and not of the United States in the 1980s that has prompted a victorious and united Communist Vietnam to grant naval bases to the Soviet Union. For unchanging geopolitical reasons the national interests of the Soviet Union and Vietnam coincide. This is not to suggest that treating the Vietnamese Revolution as part of a monolithic, expanding communism could lead to a recognition of this. Rather, it implies that the three administrations were correct—even if, perhaps, for the wrong reasons—in concluding that the success of the Viet Minh would redound to the military advantage of the Soviet Union.

Finally, it was not a possibility in the 1960s for the United States to make common cause with China, even against the Soviet Union. When the chance arose, the United States seized it and began to play the

"China card." The anti-communism of President Nixon and his advisors was no less strong than that of their predecessors. Nor did it prevent them from assisting Mao in his role as an Asian Tito. Indeed, the withdrawal of the United States from Vietnam probably was essential to the development of a rapprochement between China and the United States. In Indochina, the question was whether the United States should intervene directly to prevent the further expansion of communism. Truman and Eisenhower said no. Kennedy said yes.

As the preceding discussion reveals, the American outlook decisively affects United States foreign policy. Anti-communism is a natural component of the American outlook, and this helps set the general orientation of policy. The beliefs, institutions, and procedures that are basic to the Republic—separation of powers, suspicion of centralized power, dominance of the military by civilian authority and role models—conflict with the centralization, secrecy, and speed that are necessary for effective international action.

Any attempt to improve American foreign policy by jettisoning anti-communism would be doubly mistaken. It would not lead to the fostering of the wisdom, skills, and procedures on which sound strategy and diplomacy depend. Moreover, because the American outlook is so fundamentally opposed to the practices and beliefs of existing Communist governments, the effort to discredit anti-communism would confuse and divide American opinion rather than unite it. In the process, much of the popular support needed to enable the United States to play an active and constructive role in world affairs would be lost in bitter internal wrangling and scapegoating, as paralysis-induced failures mounted.

It should, nonetheless, be possible to take specific concrete actions that will mitigate the effects of those elements of the American outlook that reduce the effectiveness of United States foreign policy. Two such steps would be: (1) to achieve within the executive branch the centralization of decision and action necessary for the conduct of cogent and potent foreign policy; and (2) to reward "warriors" as well as "managers" within the armed forces.

The centralization intended here is not a reduction of the constitutional powers of the Congress over foreign affairs. It would require the Congress to refrain from the foolish exercise of its ultimately dominant prerogatives in that field. Much more modest changes are needed. Within the White House, for example, presidents would do well to recall that neither Truman nor Eisenhower used a powerful national security advisor, and yet achieved an enviable record in foreign policy. In Truman's case, the achievements—Marshall Plan, democratization of Germany and Japan, Atlantic Alliance—were arguably the finest since the revolutionary diplomacy of the Founders of the nation. If Nixon relied on Henry Kissinger, it must be remembered that Nixon himself was at home with international problems, perhaps as the best-prepared president in that field in the history of Republic. Nixon also avoided problems by concentrating power within the White House. He left to the State Department only those matters he regarded as unimportant or unready for action. It is the failure to choose between the State Department and the White House that is fatal to coherence and success, as the nation observed during the Carter and first Reagan administrations, when neither president seemed able to manage the admittedly formidable personalities of the likes of Zbigniew Brzezinski and Alexander Haig. At the Pentagon, the United States must stop slighting its "warriors" and educate them better for war. Officers with proven combat ability must be cherished and promoted and allowed to lead rather than follow effective logistics managers. They must also study strategy and be rewarded for it.

These recommendations surely do not constitute a complete "cure" for what ails United States foreign policy. Even so, their virtues are not negligible. They are consistent with the American outlook. They counter problems with practices that have proven their worth in earlier periods of foreign policy success. Above all, they augment the great strengths of United States foreign policy: its basis in an outlook that is itself humane and decent; its consistency—for four decades the United States has joined the democratic nations of Japan and Western Europe in opposition to Communist expansion; its ability to seize the main chance in Europe and Asia; and its willingness to bear the burdens of leadership.

NOTES

1. Edward Shils, "Ideology: The Concept and Function of Ideology," in *International Encyclopedia of the Social Sciences,* ed. David L. Sills (New York: The Macmillan Company & The Free Press, 1968), 7:66–76.

2. Compare Jeane Kirkpatrick, "Dictatorships and Double Standards," *Commentary* (November 1979): 34–45 to Alan Tonelson, "Human Rights: The Bias We Need," *Foreign Policy* 49 (Winter 1982–83): 52–74.

3. See P. Edward Haley, *Congress and the Fall of South Vietnam and Cambodia* (East Brunswick, N.J.: Fairleigh Dickinson University Press, 1980).

4. Harry Summers, *On Strategy: A Critical Analysis of the Vietnam War* (New York: Dell, 1984); for a view of another shortcoming, see Colonel Yasotay, "Warriors: An Endangered Species," *Armed Forces Journal International* (September 1984): 117-19.

5. Summers, *On Strategy*, p. 23.

6. See especially George F. Kennan, *Memoirs, 1925-1950* (Boston: Little Brown and Company, 1967); and the studies by John Lewis Gaddis, especially his *Strategies of Containment: A Critical Appraisal of Postwar American National Security Policy* (New York: Oxford University Press, 1982).

7. Leslie H. Gelb with Richard K. Betts, *The Irony of Vietnam: The System Worked* (Washington, D.C.: The Brookings Institution, 1979), p. 22.

8. Townsend Hoopes, "Legacy of the Cold War in Indochina," *Foreign Affairs* 48 (July 1970): 607.

9. John Foster Dulles, "The Evolution of Foreign Policy," *Department of State Bulletin*, January 25, 1954, pp. 107-8.

10. Ibid.

11. John Foster Dulles, "Policy for Security and Peace," *Department of State Bulletin*, March 29, 1954, p. 462.

12. General Navarre's concept of his plan is in Secretary of State to American Consul, Hanoi, May 20, 1949, *United States-Vietnam Relations, 1945-1967* (hereafter USVR), USVR, V.B.3., Justification of the War—Internal Commitments—The Eisenhower Administration, 1953-1960, Book 1-1953, pp. 136-37. For the American military reactions to the Navarre plan and to other French military plans at this time, see ibid., pp. 11-14, 22, 24-26, 31, 34-36, 38-43, 59-100, 107-8.

13. Ibid., pp. 97-100, 107-8, 145-55, 201.

14. NSC 177 (later renumbered 5405), January 14, 1954, ibid., Book 2: 1954—The Geneva Accords, ibid., pp. 221-22.

15. Ibid., p. 225. According to NSC 5405 the U.S. had supplied $969 million in military and economic aid for Indochina for FY 1950-53. The administration proposed to give $839 million in FY 1954, $1,159 million in 1955; and $713.5 million in 1956. Ibid., p. 236.

16. Ibid., pp. 230–33.

17. Ibid., II. B. 1, p. B-4.

18. Ibid, p. B-10. Compare with the wording of the document, ibid., V.B. 3., Justification of the War—Internal Commitments, The Eisenhower Administration, 1953–1960, p. 332.

19. Matthew B. Ridgway, *Soldier: The Memoirs of Matthew B. Ridgway* (New York: Harper & Brothers, 1956), p. 276.

20. Ibid., pp. 275-78.

21. USVR, II. B.1, p. B-12.

22. Ibid., IV. A. 1., Book 1, A Comparison of NATO and SEATO, p. 2A. The "uncompromisable pre-conditions" given to U.S. negotiators were: "(a) The U.S. would refuse to commit any U.S. forces unilaterally; (b) were military action to be required, one or more of the European signatories would have to participate; (c) the U.S. intended to contribute only sea and air power, expecting that other signatories would provide ground forces; (d) The U.S. would act only against communist aggression."

23. Ibid., U.S. Involvement in the War—Internal Documents, The Kennedy Administration: January 1961–November 1963, IV.B.4, Book 11, p. 136.

24. USVR, IV.B.1., Book 2, p. 64; see also pp. 32ff.

25. Ibid., p. 42.

26. Ibid., V.B.4., Memorandum for the Secretary of Defense from the Joint Chiefs of Staff on Concept of Use of SEATO Forces in South Vietnam, JCSM-716-61, October 9, 1961, p. 298.

27. Ibid., pp. 300–12.

28. Ibid., pp. 332–42.

29. Ibid., Memorandum for the President on South Vietnam, November 8, 1961, pp. 343–44.

30. Ibid., pp. 359–66.

31. Ibid., Book 2., p. 22.

VIII

Is There an American Ideology?

MORTON A. KAPLAN

Although the ancients had world views, the concept of "ideology" is modern. And its use has a specific origin. In the seventeenth century, French materialistic philosophers, who denied the existence of innate ideas and who believed that ideas were based on sensations, developed the concept. They believed that ideas were representations of external reality. Their validity depended upon their correspondence with reality and not with essence or form. A scientific set of ideas that had a systematic correspondence with the world was an ideology, they told us. Thus, ideologies in this usage could be true world views.

These philosophical concepts had been embodied earlier in Hobbes's assertion of motion as the ultimate reality and also in Locke's well-known notion of mind as a *tabula rasa*, that is, as a blank tablet upon which sensations make impressions. That the presuppositions of this philosophical approach were false—that no mind or transceiver could receive signals in the absence of a code for interpreting them—need not concern us as we attempt briefly to explicate the development of the concept. However, these faulty presuppositions do raise serious questions about defining the concept of ideology, although many current definitions are very closely related to the one stated above.

Although Hegel did not use the term "ideology," we cannot understand the next major development in the concept, that of Karl Marx, without brief reference to those elements of Hegel's philosophy that are relevant to Marx's use of the concept. On first consideration, it might appear quite implausible that an idealistic philosophy such as Hegel's would be relevant to a materialist concept such as that of ideology. But then we must remember that Hegel's idealism was an objective idealism that placed great emphasis on development in history. History was a realm of accident in which the ideas of individual human beings developed dialectically through their transactions with their environments. However, no actual historical idea could capture essence entirely and, thus, all historical ideas contained some degree of error. It is only in the Absolute in which every thing has an inner relationship to every other thing and, thus, is identical with the Absolute, that is, in the true infinity, that error is absent.

Marx, who did use the concept of ideology, related his concept to the sociological development that was inherent in Hegel's design. In *The German Ideology*, Marx said, "The social structure and the state are continually evolving out of the life-process of definite individuals . . . as they act, produce materially, and hence as they work under definite material limits, presuppositions, and conditions independent of their will."[1]

Marx claimed that he stood Hegel on his head, that rather than being the unfolding of Idea, evolution is the unfolding of man's material transactions with his environment. But the difference is perhaps a trifle obscure, as Hegel's *Phenomenology of Mind* portrays the same unfolding process. And Marx's collective concepts—worker, capitalist, and so forth—seem uncomfortably close in character to Hegel's concrete universals, a category that Marx also employs. This follows from his adoption of Hegel's concept of internal relations, real truth emerging only in the Totality, which is Marx's equivalent of the Absolute. Furthermore, in this Totality human beings become identical with their essence; in fact every thing becomes identical with the Totality. In the Totality, Truth, and not ideology, or truth, would characterize consciousness.

The crux of Marx's position was that ideology evolves out of one's class position. This was not a matter of vulgar economic advantage, but rather referred to the superstructure of beliefs that accord with the interests of a particular class at a given stage of development of a society. Thus, all belief systems are infused with error, that is, they are ideological, according to Marx. The only potential exception was that of the worker because in communism, in which antagonistic classes would not exist, man as producer would be identical with his essence. Thus, in communism there would be a harmony of interests that would not require a state with its police functions. Unfortunately, however, Marx said, the ideas of actual workers are pervaded by a false consciousness that is imposed by the class dictatorship of the bourgeoisie.

Although Marx's philosophy had a very powerful impact on intellectuals, it suffered from a fatal intellectual flaw. Marx and Engels were members of the bourgeoisie. If ideology is determined by class position—and, again, I am not talking about economic advantage—then it should have been impossible for Marx to formulate the "true" position that his philosophy specifies, for only a worker without false consciousness could be without ideology. If, on the other hand, Marx's theory of social evolution was correct, then his concept of ideology and the philosophical base on which it was founded are incorrect. Yet the former conception was the base upon which his putative unification of theory and practice rested, for only if true man can exist only in communism was Marx's prescription for a practice unified with theory relevant. Otherwise, the motivation to achieve communism would not follow from the theoretical analysis. Of course, Marx could have retreated to the concept of evolutionary partial truths. However, his emphasis on the inevitability of communism cannot be accommodated to a materialistic dialectic in which the movement of ideas does not shadow that of Idea: the one aspect in which he did not follow Hegel.

There is one other major position to which I shall make brief reference, that of Karl Mannheim. Mannheim perceived the basic defect in Marx's position. Therefore, in *Ideology and Utopia* he developed a disjunction between ideologies and utopias. Ideologies, he said, represented the class-bound beliefs of those who had an interest in maintaining the status quo. Utopias represented the interests of those for whom the status quo was insufficient. But where did this leave truth? So Mannheim argued that intellectuals were in a sense classless and, thus, could be employed by the members of any class to represent their interests. These intellectuals would not be ideologically motivated. And hence they could discover truth.

Now the idea that individuals may become detached from their former class positions and critical of them is certainly not absurd, for there are many instances of this phenomenon. However, why should we regard the position of the intellectuals as the pivot upon which truth can be founded? Among other things, intellectuals disagree with each other. Thus, some of their positions must be false. In the second place, it is far from clear in what sense a classbound position is false. In one sense, that of representing the interests of the class, it is likely true if intelligently chosen. A safecracker who correctly understands the mechanism of the safe has surely risen to at least one level of truth. His actions are against the interests of the owners of the safe and even against the laws of society;

but in what sense are they untrue? If we retreat from the concept of truth to the concept of justice, then there is surely a sense in which the safecracker's interests are unjust. However, on what basis do we argue that this concept of justice should be binding upon the safecracker? In what sense are these higher concepts of justice true? I am not arguing that they are not true, but only that Mannheim, in addition to not raising the question in this form, did not produce any foundation for it.

One problem with all of these approaches, from those of the French philosophers to that of Mannheim, lies in their conception of objectivity. As both Hegel and Marx argued, there are phenomena that are significantly independent of human will in the sense that they occur regardless of the intentions of particular human beings or even sometimes contrary to them because of the characteristics of independent decision making. Thus, farmers may raise more wheat to make more money and succeed only in lowering the price for wheat. And where Mercury is in the sky does not depend on the intentions of the astronomer. There is, however, no such thing as a truth that is objectively independent of the transactions of humans with their environments such that it has characteristics that are entirely independent of the frame of reference of perceivers. All information involves interpretation.

This, however, does not mean that a neutral and objective standpoint for different frameworks of interpretation can never be found. For instance, to take an example from science, that of the clock paradox in Einsteinian relativity theory, two observers on independent inertial systems, if they are familiar with relativity theory, will agree on the equations that govern relativity theory and will predict that each will believe that time is moving more slowly on the other system. Thus, despite their first-order disagreement, there is a second-order agreement on the character of the phenomena at issue that is neutral with respect to their differences of position. That some believe this to be contradictory or paradoxical arises only from the reifications of ordinary thought that lead us to believe that time is a simple stream that univocally envelops all things.

We can never obtain a standpoint that is independent of position, but we can often develop standpoints that are neutral with respect to particular differences of position. Similar phenomena occur in the realm of value theory. However, whereas observers on different inertial systems are not subject to practical conflict because of their inconsistent first-order evaluations, in the moral realm first-order disagreements may be crucial.[2] Thus, tragedy, although not necessarily pervasive, is inherent in the human order, for all institutional organizations and practices within a society necessarily invoke design compromises that impact differentially on different human beings and sometimes so greatly so that tragedy is the result. And sometimes, different societies are on independent "inertial paths" that cannot be reconciled.

Having given some of the philosophical background, I find it useful now to distinguish between ideologies and other forms of conceptual patterning, for these terms ordinarily are very loosely used. The best exposition of this problem that I have found is contained in "The Concept and Function of Ideology" by Edward Shils.[3] As Shils notes, ideology is simply a variant of a comprehensive pattern of cognitive and moral beliefs about man, society, and the universe. These patterns differ from each other in their explicitness, their systematic integration, their affinity with other patterns, their closure to extraneous elements, the imperativeness of their claims upon conduct, the affect they generate, the consensus demanded of others, the authoritativeness claimed for them, and their relationship to an actual institution designed to realize them.

Shils distinguishes ideologies from outlooks, creeds, systems of thought, and programs. According to Shils, ideologies "are characterized by a high degree of explicitness of formulation." They are authoritative and are explicitly promulgated. They have high systematization and are integrated "around one or a few pre-eminent values." Outlooks on the other hand are not explicitly promulgated or authoritative; creeds do not demand as much orthodox adherence as ideologies; systems of thought are not insistent upon action; and programs are limited in their objectives.

I recognize that several of the writers represented in this book wish to define ideology as a comprehensive system of beliefs or ideas. If we did this, it would still be necessary to make the distinctions that Shils makes, for they correspond to important differences in beliefs and conduct. It would be more awkward, in my opinion, to modify the concept of ideology by adjectival means than to restrict the term to the case that is often employed in actual uses of the term as, for instance, in reference to Communist ideology in the Soviet Union. Although Soviet writers do refer to Marxism as a living system, it is authoritatively promulgated at any particular period of time, and it is integrated around a few key concepts such as the classless society and state ownership of the means of production that cannot be relinquished whatever other modest transformations occur.

If we follow Shils in usage, as I propose to do, although perhaps I should change the term "outlook" to (non-comprehensive) "belief system," for this includes the potentiality for strong moral responses in certain kinds of situations, then it follows that there is no such thing as an American ideology. It is true that some small subgroups in the United States may have a comprehensive pattern of cognitive and moral beliefs that constitutes an ideology, for instance, American Communists or Scientologists. But the beliefs of even the extreme conservatives in the Republican party or leftists in the Democratic party come closer to being creeds or even belief systems than to being ideologies. The worst one can say of them is that they come closer to being ideologies than does mainstream American thought.

But, of course, the interesting thing about the United States is that there is no systematic belief system that can be definitively labeled American. There are occasional programs that for periods of time might be regarded as definitively American, for instance, the civil rights movement of the early 1960s or the anti-war movement of the late 1960s and early 1970s. The New Deal program of the middle 1930s also would come under the rubric of a program. But even with respect to these phenomena, there were important dissenting programs, which occasionally became manifest in policy. Therefore, almost anything one says about an American belief system, except in the sense of distinguishing it from an ideology or a creed, is bound to be misleading. With that caveat in mind, and with considerable trepidation, I shall attempt to outline what I regard as the mainstream American belief system, at least for particular periods of time.

One core of the American belief system lies in Federalist Paper Number 10, in which Madison pointed out that if men were angels they would not need government and if angels were men they would not need the separation or division of powers. If one combines this with Jefferson's skepticism concerning the role of government, one comes close, I believe, to a basic American belief system. With the possible exception of a thirty-year period beginning with Franklin Roosevelt, Americans have always been suspicious of bigness in government and of a state apparatus. In Jefferson's terms, Americans have believed that that government is best which governs least. Despite the vast contributions that such great entrepreneurial figures as John D. Rockefeller, Andrew Carnegie, and Henry Ford made to American economic progress, Americans have always been suspicious of bigness in business and more lately also of bigness in labor unions. More than other nations, but, in the end unsuccessfully, Americans have fought, or at least tried to delay, the bureaucratization of government, business, education, and society.

Americans have believed strongly in self-government; but, with the exception of the occasional New England town meeting or occasional populist campaigns for referenda or recall, they have preferred a representative rather than a direct democracy, a form of government that insulates the political process from momentary or passing passions. Although the Constitution embodies a federal system in replacement of the ineffective Confederation of the Articles, it still represented a decisive rejection of the unitary systems characteristic of Europe and a belief in the individuality of the participating states.

This conception of government was republican in its essential characteristics. Here, I am in firm agreement with Andrew Reck. The early restrictions on the franchise had their intellectual origins in James Harrington's *The Commonwealth of Oceana*, wherein the stability of good government was seen in a relationship between political power and a concrete interest in the protection of the commonwealth. Harrington found this concrete interest in landed property and the Founding Fathers saw it in generic property. Furthermore, they were good students of Roman history and recognized how that republic was first corrupted and then overthrown when the relationship between property and power was broken.

Contemporary evidence for the continued validity of this relationship was provided by the virtual bankruptcy of the city of New York in 1975, a condition imposed by the political power of unions and welfare clients who benefited from a governmental largesse—a modern equivalent of *pane et circenses*—that they imposed on the city. Only federal and state legislative impositions on a non-independent governmental unit were able to prevent actual bankruptcy and to restore fiscally prudent government.

However, such an austere republicanism was at least partly inconsistent with the democratic aspirations enunciated in the Declaration of Independence—a document that is also deeply imbedded in the American outlook—that legitimated successive additions to the franchise that are too well known to be recounted here. Few would wish to reverse this development. Yet, along with the advancement of the democratic franchise, there also occurred a decline in the republican virtue of prudence, a virtue that once was highly characteristic of the political leadership of the nation. Thus, Harry Truman refused to remove Dean Acheson as secretary of state, although he was so unpopular among senators that he no longer could be effective, as if justice to Acheson rather than the effective conduct of the nation's business was the good to be achieved.

The concept of a republic included the idea of a commonwealth and at least some of the individual states were called commonwealths, as in the case of the Commonwealth of Pennsylvania. Although there was a firm separation between state and society and a strong emphasis on individuality and human autonomy, a concept of public duty in support of the common weal definitely characterized the American people despite momentary outbursts of rebelliousness.

That the public good might be achieved even by self-centered individual behavior, as was argued in the cases of Adam Smith's hidden hand and de Mandeville's *Fable of the Bees*, was certainly not foreign to this system of beliefs. But the American belief system did not entirely exclude either planned coercion or cultural suasion. Instances of such included the mandating of an army, public support for national railroads, cultural suasion through moral beliefs that carried imperative status, the institutionalization of public behavior as in the salute to the flag, or even draft laws.

The inherent tension between individual interests and the common good, although weighted heavily on the side of individual interests, always has been recognized in the American tradition. And we have been aware that the proper mix cannot always be determined by autonomous calculation. For instance, during the water shortage in New York City in the 1960s, when the mayor asked citizens to take baths rather than showers that wasted water, no individual shower in the privacy of an apartment would have deprived anyone else of more than a fraction of a drop. Nor, since it was secret, would it have led to imitation. Yet, in the absence of a moral rule generally, even if not universally, adhered to, the water supply would have been exhausted, for even altruism would not have weighed heavily against a shower for those who preferred it inasmuch as the damage they would have done to others would have been negligible. It is true that the individual decides to obey moral rules. On the other hand, acculturation is at least one element in their acceptance, as moral differences among societies attest; and acculturation is partly coercive, although subtly so.

Furthermore, when it comes to a draft during a war, although the right of principled conscientious objection to wars is sanctioned, the right to object to a particular war is not; for this would impose on the good behavior of the average citizen while permitting the slick and the selfish to take a free ride at everyone else's expense. A system that institutionalized this type of choice likely would produce cynicism and neglect of the public good and, therefore, would be immoral. Similarly, although it would be a mistake to adopt tax laws that many citizens regarded as unjust, it would also be a mistake to allow individuals to decide the rate at which they should be taxed and the purposes for which the money should be spent. Such extreme individualism eventually would dissolve society.

Decisions concerning these matters necessarily are responsive to the facts of the case. Consider the issue of the draft even during peacetime. More than half of the Defense Department's budget goes to personnel costs. The rate of pay for skilled career soldiers cannot be cut unless we wish to sabotage the effectiveness of the forces. But a two-year draft period combined with several additional years in the reserves for ordinary soldiers would permit both reductions in the military budget and improvements in the readiness of the forces.

If the United States were to go to war today, fewer than one-tenth of the physicians needed would be available. Thus, those in the service would be deprived of necessary medical assistance. This obviously would be an immoral state of affairs. The requisite number of physicians could not quickly be processed in a wartime draft. To obtain the needed number of physicians voluntarily would require unconscionably high payments that would interfere with morale elsewhere in the services and that likely would attract those types of physicians who could not be depended upon to perform honorably.

However, I do not wish to rest my case on the accuracy of the estimates I have made. The important point is that if they are correct a draft at least of physicians should be made and likely already would have been made, except for current public attitudes. This is but one illustration of the fact that moral conclusions can no more be reached on the basis of rules and principles alone than on the basis of consequences alone.[4]

Although no one would wish most important matters to be decided politically or at either the local or the national level, there are other important public interests that override individual decisions. For instance, a nation has an interest in the aesthetic quality of its capital city or of its leading city. The Times Square area in New York is an instance where economic decision making on an individual basis has been allowed to override any reasonable conception of the public good. And surely education is not a matter merely of individual decision making. Regardless of how much I detest the present educational system in the United States, certainly, as a collective entity, we have an interest in what kinds of human beings are produced by the educational system. Will they be educated sufficiently well to live productively in a highly complex, computerized age in which robotics takes care of most of what is now manual labor? Has the educational system turned out the kinds of inquiring minds that are consistent with the maintenance of a democratic polity?

During a period in which the public school system has failed, I surely favor greater individual effort in setting up schools to train children, although even here there is a national and state interest in certain minimal requirements. But if we lacked a system of public schools and if the private schools set up individually were failing in these tasks, surely I would support a system of compulsory public education designed to do what is necessary. Although I agree that individual initiative and responsibility are important ingredients of good societies, I believe that it is destructive to emphasize them beyond the limits that are appropriate in any period or set of circumstances.

Although I am a strong proponent of private capitalism, which by means of its independent decision making (parallel processing) is both extraordinarily efficient, thus producing the means for a good life, and receptive to that type of individual responsibility that is important to the development of good and autonomous human beings, I see no need to apotheosize it. Like all other human institutions, it represents a design compromise. The costs of its side effects upon the individuals who are ground under by the process—for instance, those who lose their jobs in their forties or fifties when an entire industry becomes obsolete—and whose sense of individual worth may be damaged beyond repair are not negligible. It is quite possible that if computerization and robotics solve the problems of production, we may want to turn individualism in different directions and treat industry in a more planned fashion, particularly if its importance has so diminished that this does not make the state too powerful.

The confusion over the role of acculturation, planning, and coercion arises from an abstract concept of freedom and of human nature, the grounds on which Marx, in good Hegelian style, criticized Feuerbach, although his own approach left much to be desired. Freedom has meaning only in terms of appropriate constraints. The freedom of a ball to roll depends both on its roundness and the flatness of its environment. It would make no sense to argue that a person under the influence of LSD is free to choose intellectually or morally although he is physically free. The moral and intellectual constraints placed on children are conditions for their human freedom in society, although particular constraints may be destructive. Furthermore, the institutions, expectations, and moral rules that characterize a society condition adult freedom. Where either set of conditions does this poorly, it gives use to the ontological dysfunctions of mind I discuss in *Alienation and Identification*.[5] But where they do it well, this makes for a good society and good people.

I recognize that good societies provide a wide orbit for individual choice that responds to differences among individuals and conditions and that this helps to reinforce the sense of individual worth. I also recognize that, in less than optimal conditions, constraints that would otherwise be desirable may be unwise because they would produce cynical evasion, for example, compulsory Bible reading when the students are not religious.

There is much to be said for leaving room in society even for bad or socially harmful choices, but the example of Hitler reminds us that this must not be carried too far. But some constraints, even though resisted by some, may help to reinforce the sense of worth among the rest of us and, thereby, to reinforce our freedom to choose. Although I do not wish entirely to condone the recent shooting of four thugs in a New York subway, the widespread public applause for this emphasizes the extent to which some types of choices undermine the sense of worth of the rest of us. Although I chose a case of criminal behavior because of its clarity, not all choices that have similar consequences need be criminal. In some cases, widespread evasions of national service during emergencies also might have dysfunctional consequences, for instance, cynicism concerning the worth of virtue. Who can forget Falstaff's question concerning the worth of honor to those who have lost precious things or even their lives? We may have to coerce some to retain a society in which free individual choice retains important moral meaning.

In any event, some degree of coercion is inevitable in society. Putting a murderer in jail also is involuntary servitude. This troubled Hegel so much that he made the jury the substitute for the accused's conscience. Taxation and the garnishing of the pay of a delinquent father are also involuntary. In the last two cases, no direct injury was done to another. No society that wishes to survive can avoid coercion. The real questions concern the justification for particular coercions and, thus, involve moral inquiry into obligations that the moral person will assume voluntarily and obligations that will be imposed even on those who do not accept them. Thus, I believe that the objection to any planning or coercion is not merely foreign to the American tradition but also is philosophically and practically unsound. Community is part of that tradition.

However, there is a sense in which the role of community in America is qualified. The conception of duration through time that characterizes Oriental society has never been characteristic of American society. Americans would never desire the degree of subordination of the individual to society that characterizes Japan, for instance. Yet Abraham Lincoln's Emancipation Proclamation does begin with rhetoric that recognizes the presence of some traditional and enduring elements in American society. We are members of a common enterprise that has endured. We build on the efforts of those who preceded us—even in those cases when they did not consciously sacrifice for us—and we are participating in a process that continues into the future. This is a process in which rights and duties are correlatives and in which transactions between the members of society with each other and with society are reciprocal.

This is not a matter of a contract, even if only hypothetical, but of an ongoing relationship that establishes our status as Americans. We often have the opportunity to opt out, but not the right to assert membership while deciding which obligations to assume and which to reject. There is nothing in the enterprise that requires us to agree with majority decisions or to refrain from attempting to change them. But there is no obligation for society to accept an individual's rejection of the consequences of just procedures because the individual disagrees with the substantive result. The individual then may have a moral duty to rebel; but in this case the first-order identification of the individual and society has been shattered and they are at war, at least in this respect.[6]

The early American belief system or ethos was that of an individualism closely related to community obligations. For instance, the pioneers who took off westward in wagon trains had a firm sense of obligation to each other. The early American individual had a sense of community, if not always of locality. Unlike the Englishman, who would find it difficult to choose an occupation different in class from that of his father, or the Frenchman who would find it difficult to leave his locality, the American knew how to combine his sense of civic virtue and membership in a community with high mobility in occupation or location.

Unlike the Oriental outlook, however, this American outlook was largely contemporary and without a strong sense of structure through time. The emphasis eventually shifted to newness and change for their own sakes; the past was merely to be overcome and discarded.

In this phase of the American nation's history, the latter aspects of individualism were retained while the earlier concepts that gave rise to duty, civic virtue, and relatedness to place or institution sharply declined. The new American became highly mobile. He became atomized without a sense of past or a framework of moral structure. The key concepts became happiness and advantage. The sense that one should receive what he earned was almost replaced by a sense that people should receive what they wanted. This was a set of values against which happily a strong reaction is now developing in favor of civic virtue and patriotism.

The early republic saw itself as exceptional. It wanted no part of the corruption, the wars, and the power politics of Europe. Later on, when America became strong, there was a powerful feeling of mission in the American outlook, whether this was a matter of making the world safe for democracy or bringing Christianity to the heathen. This was overbearing and parochial at times. But it also represented a sense of commitment to making both the nation and the world a better place in which to live. There was also a deep sense of optimism in this position. Americans believed that it was possible to make the world a better place and that the United States could play a role in doing this.

In the early days of the republic, there was no wall between religion and government. Beginning with the Declaration of Independence that recognized that all men are created equal, the Founding Fathers established a government dedicated not against religion but against the establishment of a religion. This position was institutionalized in the first ten amendments, the Bill of Rights, which ensured widespread support for the Constitution. Many of the Founders were at least deists, if not Christians, and even those who were not recognized the importance of religion to good government.

Until the Civil War, this American outlook did permit the outrage of an institution of slavery that was inconsistent with the Declaration and also with any universalistic religion. However, until shortly before World War II, the basic religious outlook that characterized the United States held sway. At that time it began to be overshadowed by a form of secular humanism that had many good aspects. Secular humanism did not discriminate against non-Christian religions. It made it easier to accept blacks, Orientals, and Jews as full participants in American society. However, it also began to foster a cultural relativism that made it difficult to adhere to even relatively absolute values[7] that transcended the particular wants of particular individuals. Although usefully relaxing some of the rigid rules governing the activities of consenting adults, secular humanism began to generate a type of hedonism that was supportive of abortion on demand, the flaunting (and not merely the practice) of homosexuality, theft, violence, and even child pornography; in short, the replacement of duties by rights, a view that was not entirely without merit but that was carried much too far. The excesses of secular humanism have led to the revival of religious movements in the United States.

These two elements became mixed in the post-World War II world. Although the ultimate decisions in postwar politics were made by a mainstream American like President Harry Truman, the intellectual analysis that produced the American posture was led by such eastern establishment figures as Dean Acheson, who tended to apply nineteenth-century *Realpolitik* beliefs to the third world. Thus, in the early post-World War II period, American foreign policy did have its idealistic aspects. These included the Marshall Plan and Point Four. Democracy and recovery in Europe were supposed to take the rest of the world in their wake. However, at a time when the Soviet Union was extremely weak, a direct reformist mission in the Third World that might have produced beneficial change at minor risk was not pursued. The revolutionary pulse that at times had characterized Franklin Roosevelt's foreign policy, thus, was dampened.

In a country such as the United States, strictly instrumental foreign policies can retain support only while they succeed and are cheap. Although American idealism was waning, the latent idealism that might have been fanned to flame by policies with a positive mission was never really tapped, except rhetorically for a short period of time by John Kennedy. The conditions, therefore, were ripe for the domestic disaster of Vietnam. Even Ronald Reagan, who has tapped the American longing for positive values in terms of domestic policy, has made insufficient effort to tap the American sense of missionary idealism in foreign policy.

The children of the eastern establishment, that is, those who became the new eastern establishment, reacted to Vietnam with deep feelings of guilt, self-flagellation, and pessimism. These are the people who see resources running out and doomsday approaching. Although they are dominant in the media, they have never been part of the American mainstream, which is now reacting against these values as well. These are the people who wished to apologize to Hanoi, who would attempt to flatter the Marxist-Leninists of Nicaragua, and who are unable to see evil, except in American policy.

Certainly the United States has made mistakes, and we have at times followed policies of which we cannot be proud; but on the whole this has been a good and generous nation. And the naysayers and doomsday specialists have never been representative of it.

The main questions concerning the American belief system involve the directions that it will take in the future and the institutional means that will implement its objectives. Our industrial leaders tend more to be financial and legal manipulators than productive managers. Few of our political leaders inspire any confidence. Yet, like periods of disintegration, periods of regeneration also often appear highly chaotic at the time. So perhaps this is such a period.

In addition to everything else that I have mentioned, the American belief system and temperament always have been pragmatic. We do not like to impose rigid ideological or theoretical views on a complex reality. We have seen the failures of the recent past; and the reactions—sometimes too unqualified—against the values and policies that produced those failures are quickening.

Do we have resources and intelligence to take what is best from our religious past, to combine it with those aspects of secular humanism that did at least for a time enrich our national experience, and to find in the Oriental world an approach to time that, without denigrating the American concept of individuality, still places important value both on the past and future and not merely on the always vanishing present? The question is not "What is the American belief system?" but "What will be the American belief system?"

NOTES

1. Karl Marx, *The German Ideology* (Moscow: Progress Publishers, 1975), p. 41.

2. Readers who are interested in the philosophical foundations of this position will find its exposition in Morton A. Kaplan, *Science, Language, and the Human Condition* (New York: Paragon House Publishers, 1984).

3. Edward Shils, "Ideology: The Concept and Function of Ideology," in *International Encyclopedia of the Social Sciences*, ed. David L. Sills (New York: The Macmillan Company & The Free Press, 1968), 7:66–76.

4. For a discussion of the rules-consequence problem in ethics, see Kaplan, *Science, Language, and the Human Condition*, pp. 228–48. The same conclusion is reached from a similar perspective in my discussion of John Rawls's *Theory of Justice*. See my *Justice, Human Nature, and Political Obligation* (New York: Free Press, 1976), pp. 107–81.

5. See Morton A. Kaplan, *Alienation and Identification* (New York: Free Press, 1976), pp. 131–42.

6. See Kaplan, *Justice, Human Nature, and Political Obligation*, pp. 183–245 for a discussion of his issue.

7. For a discussion of relative absolutes, see Morton A. Kaplan, *On Human Freedom and Human Dignity: The Importance of the Sacred in Politics* (Morristown, N. J.: General Learning Corporation, 1973), pp. 53–55.

IX

─────

Ideology and The American Future: Reflections Toward Public Philosophy

────

John K. Roth

The analysis of thought and ideas in terms of ideologies is much too wide in its application and much too important a weapon to become the permanent monopoly of any one party.

Karl Mannheim, Ideology and Utopia

George Orwell's *1984* provides a grim image of the future. Nowhere is its focus sharper than in an exchange between Winston Smith, the novel's protagonist, and O'Brien, his interrogator. Although Smith lacks belief in God, he does profess faith in "the spirit of Man." Soon he will be broken, however, for O'Brien intends that Winston shall love Big Brother. Earlier, Winston thought O'Brien was his friend, a hope shattered when the "friend" revealed himself to be among the most cunning members of the Thought Police. O'Brien specializes in the subtleties of betrayal and human domination; his disdain for God exceeds Winston's. As for the latter's trust that "the spirit of Man" will prevail, O'Brien gives this blunt rebuttal: "If you want a picture of the future, imagine a boot stamping on a human face—forever."[1]

Moving beyond the year 1984, we should concede that even O'Brien's prognosis may be too optimistic in assuming the continuation of a future that contains human faces. Nuclear realities now render that supposition less than self-evident. But if the future can no longer be taken for granted in any sense, it is all the more important to contemplate how Winston's faith might be vindicated against O'Brien's stamping boot and against forces that could prove even more crushing.

However the human future unfolds, the character and opinion of Americans will be decisive in it. That description fits ideology as well, a fact the German social theorist, Karl Mannheim (1883–1947), clarified in his seminal study, *Ideology and Utopia* (1936). There he argued that ideology offers something for everyone. Thanks mainly to Karl Marx

231

and his followers, ideology does so, first, because the term functions pejoratively. In such usages, an "ideology" is a set of ideas belonging not to me but to someone else. Despite a systematically coherent structure that creates appearances to the contrary, those ideas mask reality. Such masking serves "interests" that the critics of "ideology" deplore. As Mannheim pointed out, however, utilizing "ideology" as an indictment is a strategy nobody can monopolize. Instead, as political beliefs and economic theories collide in practice, they all tend to become "ideologized." That process "exposes" every claim to absolute truth as the servant of someone's self-serving motive. The result is a world where—functionally and therefore increasingly—might makes right.

Such an account seems far removed from the prior understanding of ideology pioneered by Antoine Destutt de Tracy (1754–1836) and other French *philosophes*. To them, ideology simply meant a scientific study of ideas. What Hegel would later call "the cunning of reason" was at work in their project, however, for one of its parts involved investigation of the *derivation* of ideas. That aim opened a door wider than intended. As Marx would help to show, the scientific study of the derivation of ideas is not one thing methodologically. Nor do such inquiries yield a single set of objective results to which all rational persons will assent. Indeed, objectivity itself may succumb to reason's cunning. At the least, it suffers the fate of becoming only one value among many.

Destutt de Tracy's interests in ideology inadvertently changed the world. They did so by intensifying the awareness that no thinking person can be certain that he or she possesses absolute truth concerning what is just, right, or good. Bereft of such assurance, people inhabit an anxious world. For human beings—not to mention political regimes—fail to master ambiguity. Ironically, that assessment holds partly because people *feel* very strongly about matters of value. We *believe* because we do not know. We *judge* even if we are not wise. We *love* more than we understand. Creatures of passion and will, it is hard to imagine us otherwise in an age of ideology that seems unlikely to end until human life disappears.

Ideology makes ours less than the best of all possible worlds. But a world of ideology need not be the worst one either. If absolute truth eludes us, we can still have reasons—good ones—for choosing to live as we do and for wanting those basic forms to continue without fear that they will be stamped out. A world of ideology, however, cannot help but be a dangerous place. For in an arena where the possibility of political agreement on absolute truth has dissolved—if it ever existed at all—human philosophies transcend their finitude and fallibility to attain a dangerous, idolatrous, functional ultimacy. Even recognizing their differences, they can tolerate each other only so far before their own lives are at stake. In principle, of course, we might hope for a world in which all ideological commitments are complementary if not friendly. History, unfortunately, hardly affords the luxury of contemplating that kind of a future. "Ideologized" as it is, ours will be a world at risk.

Certainly the globe would not be a "danger-free zone" if all tensions between the Soviet Union and the United States magically disappeared. Nevertheless, nothing puts our world more at risk than the continuing confrontation between a Soviet way of life that finds its philosophical underpinnings in the thought of Karl Marx and an American tradition that stems from very different roots. Founded on diverse premises, these ways of life are understandably prone to see *the other* as ideological. Perhaps neither side can overcome the blindness that hides its own self-deceptive pretensions to know the truth. But steps in that direction would signify wisdom because they would help everyone to understand better why we differ. Consider in greater detail, then, how a critical facet of that proposition pertains to the American future.

Arguably the greatest American poet, Walt Whitman (1819–1892) is best known as a celebrant of democracy. In fact, as his *Democratic Vistas* (1871) states, he liked to think of "the words America and democracy as convertible terms."[2] That same work, however, displays Whitman's uneasiness about the validity of his hopes. Specifically, he worried that there were too few persons with "some definite instinct why and for what [America] has arisen."[3] Lacking that instinct, the United States might "prove the most tremendous failure of time."[4] In any case, he contended, America would have to count "for her justification and success . . . almost entirely on the future."[5]

More than a hundred years have passed since Whitman expressed his ambivalence. Yet he would be unlikely to sing a different song in our ideologized world. Indeed, his insistence that Americans find out "why and for what [America] has arisen" would probably be all the greater. Speaking honestly, the answers to those questions never were "self-evident." Even Thomas Jefferson may have sensed as much when he wrote that we *hold* certain claims in the latter light. Nor can Americans assume that we grasp them better today. Therefore, if the United States is to enjoy vitality in the future, it is critical to reflect on ideology and the American future as Century 21 approaches.

To think of an ideology for the United States jars American sensibility. Equating ideology with doctrinaire politics that is systematic, all-embracing, aimed at enlisting every citizen in a fundamental mission whose inevitable success is proclaimed, and steeled against the possibility of disconfirmation, ideology and America seem poles apart. Such an understanding of ideology, however, is not the only one applicable. Nor is America so divorced from ideology as this sensibility supposes. A set of beliefs does govern American life. If it is not systematic and all-embracing, that qualification is one of degree. For not only do Americans explain existence in terms of those beliefs; even if we acknowledge that our beliefs may not be in the category of absolute truth, we would die before admitting that our basic political commitments have been falsified. That fact suggests that Americans—however dimly they may realize it—have a fundamental mission, too: namely, to insist that democracy and capitalism are indeed the best ways for us if not for everyone.

Still, the argument might continue, ideology pertains to political belief systems that are obviously more rigid and programmatically specific, more explicitly promulgated and demanding of orthodox adherence, than any creed found in the United States. That conviction has merit. Its strength, moreover, is sufficient to render it unlikely that Americans will want to speak about, let alone embrace, anything called an American ideology. Thus, even if we have and need some ideological elements in our society, it is best to designate them differently.

For much of the post-World War II era, American life has been split, even splintered, by the emergence of powerful special interests and a loss of national consensus. We therefore need to refashion a collective sense of social and political commitment. This task should include conscious identification and evaluation of those beliefs and values that are, in fact, matters of life and death. In short, if Americans have good reasons for keeping ideology at a distance, we do need something that approximates a functional equivalent. Let us call it American public philosophy. To clarify that idea, note that the concept *public philosophy* encompasses at least three important perspectives.[6] First, society is not simply derived from bargains struck by individuals. Instead society is real in itself; in shared life sustaining meaning is found. Next, the task of public philosophy is to provide a mirror for society to reflect on its history and tradition. Third, public philosophy invites open, critical, communal debate about the public good and its future.

Unfortunately, if it cuts against our grain to think about American ideology, we may not easily develop sound public philosophy either. To illustrate, consider that outside observers often understand Americans better than we do ourselves. A salient example is provided by the French statesman and philosopher, Alexis de Tocqueville, whose tour of the country resulted in the classic called *Democracy in America*. The sesquicentennial of the publication of its first volume was observed in 1985. Volume II did not appear until 1840, but following up on his early impression that nothing characterized Americans so much as their emphasis on *equality*, Tocqueville began the second half of his book with a chapter entitled "Concerning the Philosophical Approach of the Americans." "Less attention," he there observed, "is paid to philosophy in the United States than in any other country of the civilized world."[7] Nevertheless, continued Tocqueville, "of all the countries in the world, America is the one in which the precepts of Descartes are . . . best followed."[8] Prizing individualism so much, he explained, Americans are Cartesians in their propensity to display "a general distaste for accepting any man's word as proof of anything."[9] Instead they rely on "individual effort and judgment" to determine what they believe.[10]

As with most of the American qualities he discussed, Tocqueville found "the philosophical approach of the Americans" possessing both assets and liabilities. Skepticism might nurture a praiseworthy critical attitude; self-reliance could produce desirable innovation. But a cunning consequence of that asset was the undermining of authority and tradition. That result, in turn, could lead to other mischief. For where reliance on authority and tradition is severely undermined people seek confirmation of their views in the judgments of others. The despotism of unthinking conformity, which is a long way from the public spirit that ensures real freedom, is not far behind.

Tocqueville's uneasiness about American individualism was justified, and the consequences for our national well-being are enormous. In sum, while American individualism honed the ingenuity and industry that took us to positions of economic and political world leadership, the same spirit drew us apart even as we lived closer together in outward conformity. Now giving self-fulfillment precedence over civic virtue and a publicly responsible patriotism, we care more for individual wealth than for our commonwealth.

Abundant evidence for these contentions can be found in the sociological survey conducted recently by Robert N. Bellah and his associates. Borrowing one of Tocqueville's phrases to title the study, they assayed "habits of the heart" in the powerful American middle class of the 1980s. Bellah found that "individualism may have grown cancerous—that it may be destroying those social integuments that Tocqueville saw as moderating its more destructive potentialities, that it may be threatening the survival of freedom itself."[11] In brief, many Americans tend to be so obsessed with personal self-fulfillment that our capacity for commitment to the basic institutions of marriage, family, politics, and religion is dangerously impaired. Tocqueville, of course, would have found none of this surprising. His ambivalence toward democracy was considerable just because he feared it would unleash a sense of self-interest so badly understood as to starve our sense of civic obligation and wither our concern to seek first what is best for the community as a whole.

On the other hand, Robert Bellah and his colleagues observed that contemporary Americans do not always practice the radical individualism we preach. Functionally, our lives are given meaning by familial, communal, public ties that transcend the individual calculus of self-fulfillment and cost-benefit analysis at which we have become so verbally adept. If we express yearnings for autonomy and self-reliance better than we acknowledge needs for and experiences of social commitments to sustain us, nevertheless we do sense that those relationships of memory and hope are the substance of our lives. They become us well, moreover, just to the extent that we think of them less as the means to our personal self-satisfaction and more as essential elements of our personhood.[12]

Our individualistic rhetoric to the contrary notwithstanding, Bellah rightly contends, "we have never been, and still are not, a collection of private individuals who, except for a conscious contract to create a minimal government, have nothing in common."[13] But we do need to bring these elements to new levels of self-awareness because for too long we have been living with "a thin political consensus, limited largely to procedural matters."[14] Fearful that the effort might exacerbate domestic conflict, we have been too shy about articulating the more substantial consensus that awaits rediscovery.

Tocqueville wrote that "the Americans have no school of philosophy peculiar to themselves, and they pay very little attention to the rival European schools. Indeed they hardly know their names."[15] Like many of his judgments, that one was not infallible then, and even less would it stand now. For American thinkers have developed a variety of distinctive philosophical perspectives. In one way or another, issues about individualism and community have often been their focal point. Together these views do not comprise ideology, but they do point toward the public philosophy we need.

When Walt Whitman spoke about a "definite instinct why and for what [America] has arisen," he did not describe all that it involved.[16] But he clearly understood that unless Americans sense why and for what the United States exists, the courage of conviction will be undermined. Conversely, if we are confident that we can and do have convictions worthy of courage, then we can live in a world of ideology not with equanimity but with poise. Among other things, that poise would enable us to respond to Marxist thought and practice more intelligently than we have often done in the past. We would be better able to state what we are for and not just what we are against. We would have a conviction equipping us to see that the critical theory introduced by Karl Marx contains valuable insights we can use without becoming Marxists, let alone "soft on communism." The net gain of such exploration would be the strengthening of a desirable patriotism.

Contributions toward an American future of that kind must be many and various. They reach far beyond the scope of one essay. In the remaining pages, however, a start can be made by identifying some ingredients of a sound instinct about "why and for what" the United States exists. To identify, to sort out and sift the components that deserve a place in American public philosophy for the future, we can do little better than to reflect on what the historian James Truslow Adams aptly called "the epic of America." That epic—past, present, and future—depends on individualism to a large degree, but what we must revise is how individualism in America is now best to be understood.

One part of the saga that Americans share began at 7:52 on Friday morning, May 20, 1927. Opening the throttle on the *Spirit of St. Louis*, Charles A. Lindberg taxied down a Long Island runway to begin his solo flight across the Atlantic. Nearly thirty-four hours later—it was 10:24 P.M. Paris time on Saturday—"Lucky Lindy" and his plane emerged from the darkness to touch ground again. A world had journeyed with the "Lone Eagle," and his flight's significance was not lost on American ministers who preached to their Christian congregations the next day. A typical example of the sermonic rhetoric that Sunday would be found in the words of the Reverend Dr. Russell Bowie of Grace Episcopal Church in New York City. Within his topic, "The Lure of the 'Impossible,' " Bowie remarked that Lindberg "manifested that indomitable heroism which, whether . . . in victory or defeat, has made possible the progress of the human race toward the mastery of its world." The preacher then went on to say: "There is a fund of moral heroism as well as a fund of physical heroism among men, which thrills to the challenge of the impossible."[17]

That same Sunday morning, far to the west of Paris and New York, another Christian pastor spoke to his congregation. If the record does not show what Reinhold Niebuhr (1892–1927) told those predominantly blue-collar workers in Detroit, it is doubtful that his sermon was as effusive and glowing as Russell Bowie's. For during this period, one of the entries in Niebuhr's diary included these words:

> I wish that some of our romanticists and sentimentalists could sit through a series of meetings where the real social problems of a city are discussed. They would be cured of their optimism. A city which is built around a productive process and which gives only casual thought and incidental attention to human problems is really a kind of hell. Thousands in this town are really living in torment while the rest of us eat, drink and make merry. What a civilization![18]

The world Reinhold Niebuhr saw was certainly "this side of paradise," to borrow the title of one of F. Scott Fitzgerald's novels. Moreover, Niebuhr struggled within it quite differently from Fitzgerald's Amory Blaine, an American who honestly admitted, "I detest poor people."[19] As a young pastor in Detroit, and later as one of the most perceptive theologians America has yet produced, Niebuhr worked to develop a religious perspective relevant to the broad social and political questions that faced the United States and the world in the twentieth century. During the period 1930–1960, he was to theology in America what John Dewey (1859–1952) was to philosophy. Together with George Santayana (1863–1952), a third observer of American life who addresses the concerns of this essay, they can contribute much to sound responses about "why and for what" America exists.

One gray March day, while trying to fathom the horror of the Nazi concentration camp at Dachau, I read the inscription, "Those who cannot remember the past are condemned to repeat it." So frequently quoted, that warning comes from *The Life of Reason*, a book beautifully written by George Santayana. Born in Madrid, he remained a Spanish citizen throughout his life. His university training, however, was at Harvard, where his teachers included William James and Josiah Royce. Between 1889 and 1912, he taught philosophy there and wrote many books, but upon his resignation, Santayana left the United States never to return. England was home for a while, then Rome, where he died with a long list of literary credits. Describing himself as an American only "by long association," Santayana nevertheless acknowledged the influence of

American thought, culture, and friends. Indeed, he affirmed, "it is as an American writer that I must be counted, if I am counted at all."[20]

Fitzgerald's *This Side of Paradise* appeared in 1920. That same year, Santayana published a volume of his own, a series of essays entitled *Character and Opinion in the United States*. For its motto, he might have taken one of Fitzgerald's comments about Amory Blaine—"It was always the becoming he dreamed of, never the being"—for Santayana would have thought that such a trait was not only "quite characteristic of Amory" but of Americans in general.[21]

In *Character and Opinion in the United States*, Santayana warned that his way of speaking would be "mythical." For he reflected on "the American in the singular, as if there were not millions of them, north and south, east and west, of both sexes, of all ages, and of various races, professions, and religions."[22] At the same time, he argued, his assessment of the American in the singular would be "largely adequate to the facts."[23] As Santayana proceeded, then, he found, first of all, that every American is an exile—either voluntary or involuntary. Pilgrim voyages, pioneer treks, the violence of forced relocations, or just changed jobs—these things make us a nation of people who live together in being pulled apart. But exile status is more complicated than that. American uprootedness, combined with a spirit of youth which Santayana underscored repeatedly, leads Americans to think very little about the past. Ignoring or forgetting it—putting things behind them; out of sight, out of mind—is a quality matched only by the romantic nostalgia when Americans do choose to recollect.

As a people, Santayana believed, the Americans' greatest fascination is for the future. He also detected overwhelming optimism about what lies ahead, often supported by religion or by industrious trust in nature's bounty. Blend and clash of idealism and materialism though it may be, Americans have a tendency to think that all things do and shall work together for good—at least in the United States. According to Santayana, these attitudes in turn support a rough-and-ready individualism. He emphasized, for example, that Americans expect "every man to stand on his own legs." Possible harshness in that outlook he found tempered by the feeling that there is also a responsibility to help one another. But, Santayana observed, when an American "has given his neighbor a chance he thinks he has done enough for him." Humanitarian concern, yes; "coddling socialism," no.[24]

American character revealed still other qualities as Santayana described it in 1920. It was imaginative and inventive, conservative generally but quick to act in emergencies. Santayana held, moreover, that these qualities are linked to another peculiar trait. That trait includes but is not exhausted by open space; the Americans' perpetual motion as a people is involved as well. Together, said Santayana, they produce "the moral emptiness of a settlement where men and even houses are easily moved about, and no one, almost, lives where he was born or believes what he has been taught."[25] As a result, experimentation and novelty are American bywords. To compensate for instability, there is a driving spirit to get down to business: "For the American the urgency of his novel attack upon matter, his zeal in gathering its fruits, precludes meanderings in primrose paths; devices must be short cuts, and symbols must be mere symbols."[26] Americans look to the future, but it is also a very *immediate* future because they may not be here tomorrow. "Gone west"— or just gone—is the destination set by the pace of American life as Santayana noted it.

All the while, though, Americans sense fulfillment close at hand. Indeed, Santayana contended that the American "is not a revolutionist; he believes he is already on the right track and moving towards an excellent destiny."[27] Americans have youthful enthusiasm: Others may not have the gumption or the spirit to succeed, but that will not be America's fate. Thus, if Santayana thought that Americans take too lightly the long record of human failure and self-delusion, he could assert that "the American is wonderfully alive."[28]

Not so differently from Whitman, however, Santayana also wondered how the epic of America would continue. For, he noted, the American "has never yet had to face the trials of Job."[29] Neither the Civil War nor World War I, he believed, had seriously undermined an optimistic and "apparently complete absorption in material enterprise and prosperity."[30] If Santayana saw this materialism less as love of wealth and more as "preoccupation with quantity,"[31] he also recognized how complex an American fate might be because our materialistic values existed side by side with expansive moral and spiritual ideals: Liberty and opportunity for all; equal justice under the law; one nation, under God, indivisible; America, the beautiful.

Santayana called the American "an idealist working on matter."[32] That provocative description, however, made Santayana pause: If "serious and irremediable tribulation" ever overtook the land, would Americans' concern for the material or for the ideal be more at the heart of our national character? For at least two reasons, Santayana could not be sure. First, he took the ideal and the material to be inseparable in American life. Our ideals depend on the existence of places and things; the relationship works the other way as well. Second, he understood that the becoming would do much to determine the being. He therefore concluded with Whitman that to think of the being without placing a premium on the ideal would incline America toward becoming one of the most tragic wrecks of time.

More than six decades later, perhaps not all of Santayana's American profile tells us accurately who we are. One feature that remains valid, however, is our expecting people "to stand on [their] own legs and to be helpful in [their] turn."[33] We divide over what the nature of the help should be, but Americans are not mean-spirited; and the reason is that they have a fundamentally shared commitment to the individual's pursuit of happiness. Probably more than anything else, that commitment accounts for American suspicion of Marxist analysis and for our antipathy toward communism. Though promising liberation and happiness together, Marxism's appeal here is muted because the meanings it gives those words are not ours.

Such disagreement is not confined to ideological conflict on an international scale. It exists domestically as well. For as Abraham Lincoln once stated, Americans "all declare for liberty, but in using the same *word* we do not all mean the same *thing*."[34] That American fact may preclude any single answer to Whitman's question about "why and for what" America exists. But if irreducible differences of opinion about fundamentals are in some sense a feature of American character, that reality enjoins us to think further about the *individualism* that Santayana saw as fundamental to America's way of life. So consider next a contemporary of Santayana's who had much of importance to say on that issue.

Born in Vermont, that bastion of Yankee individualism, John Dewey spent most of his life in the collective hustle of Chicago and New York. His experience led him to *Individualism Old and New* (1929–30). Writing in the depression, Dewey saw that the long-standing American emphasis on "individualism" provided a pivotal issue for the nation and the world. In the United States, argued Dewey, individualism has a natural history. If the outcome of that history has been problematic, the ideal neither can nor should be excised. American identity depends on it. Therefore, Dewey's effort was to reinterpret individualism so that it would be not a hindrance but a help.

Always somewhat mythological, old-style American individualism, contended Dewey, had been modeled after the image of self-reliant, self-made pioneers. They saw opportunities for personal fortunes and set out to win them on their own. Dewey believed that circumstances were threatening that ideal. A basic reason was that America was increasingly organized in huge corporations. Ironically, that had occurred because the old individualism was once an effective dream. It spurred people to build amazing businesses and industrial plants, but this very success had burst the bubble. Though individuals remained, more and more they were becoming cogs in wheels that turned out products collectively. People were becoming incorporated; most lacked the opportunity needed to "make it" on their own.

According to Dewey, a dangerous exception to this analysis did exist. Old individualism could still take the form of measuring success in terms of money. Even within the corporate structure, such individualism could yet find expression in grabs for all-that-one-can-get. Dewey believed, too, that Americans had learned new ways to argue collectively so that management and labor, even government and people, seated themselves repeatedly at a table of hard bargains. In most cases, though, Dewey sensed that the individual remained the loser. As the old individualism persisted, alienation and frustration rose. Even if the old ideal dissolved in one person, its presence in others took a toll as the rounds of competition spiraled on—right into a crash.

Dewey advocated no return to a pre-industrial, pre-corporate America. Assuming such a reversal had been possible, he would not have favored it. Even in the midst of an economic slump, he saw vast increases in knowledge and technological power as vindicating the potential for good that use of scientific method can bring to life. His point was rather that human intelligence must be used more extensively and rigorously than ever to harness that potential and to channel it so that humanizing benefits accrue. Instead of encouraging the practical rationality of cost-effectiveness to become the tail that wags the dog, Dewey thought that Americans must rally ingenuity to discern a revised and renewed understanding of what the initiatives of individualism ought to entail.

The individualism advocated by Dewey supplements Santayana's profile of American character. For example, Dewey's "new" individual would be scientifically oriented, at least in terms of an education that would equip him or her with critical methods for tackling life's problems. In addition, this individual's concern would focus on the social utility of action and planning, on the broad range of effects that policies have on national and international life. While recognizing that Americans must build upon and beyond—rather than tear down—their existing industrial, scientific, and technological base, Dewey's individual would have an awareness tempered by understanding that economic concerns are appropriate just to the degree that they serve civic quality. That concern, Dewey believed, argued in favor of a strong role for government in guiding social and economic development. It also suggested that the individual's pursuit of happiness would best find its fulfillment in working for the well-being of society. If those efforts sometimes required persons to oppose established policies, Dewey hoped their attitudes would nonetheless seek to overcome alienation between individuals and society, labor and management, government and people.

Viewing this sketch today, Americans would not be likely to agree on its content. But we might concur with Dewey when he argued that "the problem of constructing a new individuality consonant with the objective conditions under which we live is the deepest problem of our times."[35] The reason for that concurrence, moreover, would not be simply that "the United States has steadily moved from an earlier pioneer individualism to a condition of dominant corporateness."[36] Even if the 1980s have witnessed more small business starts than any comparable period in our history, the fact remains that Americans also live in the shadows of transnational corporations and of unprecedented economic competition from other countries, most notably those of Asia. National destiny, and thus the American's sense of individualism, is influenced and threatened by a web of economic and political forces that move beyond American control.

John Dewey thought "the publicity agent is perhaps the most significant symbol of our present life."[37] That observation still has merit. The only change is that the publicity may be controlled by Arab oil or Japanese productivity. Far from being a nation of the self-employed, Americans find it increasingly difficult to know their real employers face to face. Companies own companies as much as individuals do. Too many Americans live "in a situation which is so incomplete that it cannot be admitted into the affections and yet is so pervasive that it cannot be escaped: a situation which defines an individual divided within himself."[38] Dewey's appraisal still fits us.

The basic problem facing Americans, contended Dewey, was that "of forming a new psychological and moral type."[39] Probably that order is more than we can handle. Fortunately, it may also be true that such an order is unnecessary to reclaim and act upon the purposes for which America has arisen. For what Dewey talked about was essentially something quite close to the core of an already existing American sensitivity. Granted, that sensitivity may not be as keen as could be wished; and even if it is intensified, Americans will achieve no easy consensus about its policy implications. Still, it can be agreed that Dewey was on target in urging us to renew what we recognize, however dimly, to be the best element of American individualism, namely, what Walt Whitman would have called its "*personalism.*"[40]

To clarify how that quality is indispensable if we are to understand "why and for what" America exists, the point can be put this way: Democracy American-style insists that there is an equality of individuals. That equality means nothing, however, unless it entails a two-fold recognition: first, that whatever our differences, we are one in being persons; and, second, that being persons enjoins us to respect others and entitles us to dignity as well. In short, if America and democracy deserve to be convertible terms, then one fundamental reason for America's existence is to encourage esteem for persons.

That such convictions are shared among us is evidenced by the fact that Marxist programs exert relatively little appeal in the United States. For in practice, those programs too frequently kill people in order to "save" humankind. Our instincts about "why and for what" America exists rightly make us skeptical about such activities. Yet they may not do so in a foolproof way, which is why instinct must be reinforced by reasoned willing to reaffirm and defend our commitment to what we find undeniably good. As that process goes forward, we may need to admit that, as the critical dimensions of Marxist theory can help us to see, we do not always practice well what we most deeply believe. To illustrate that point, consider again Reinhold Niebuhr, a scholar who knew his Marx but was no Marxist precisely because he affirmed the personalism of democratic individualism as a creed that justified America's existence.[41]

Reinhold Niebuhr shared Dewey's ethical and pragmatic concerns, but his appreciation for tragedy in human life was more profound, thus giving him affinities with Santayana. The difference between Santayana and Niebuhr was also significant, however, for Santayana saw religion mainly as an aesthetic phenomenon, while Niebuhr was fundamentally committed to the notion that history is not simply a drama involving

244

men and women but also one that includes God. Yet the focus of Niebuhr's theology was not so much on God as on history itself, or, as one of his most influential books would call it, on *The Nature and Destiny of Man*.

Niebuhr's previously mentioned diary ended in 1928 when he was about to begin his career as a professor and a writer. But it contains many of the notes that Niebuhr would sound repeatedly in the decades ahead as he explored the relations between love, power, and justice. In one of its last entries, for example, he wrote:

> I persevere in the effort to combine the ethic of Jesus with what might be called Greek caution because I see no great gain in ascetic experiments. I might claim for such a strategy the full authority of the gospel except that it seems to me more likely to avoid dishonesty if one admits that the principle of love is not qualified in the gospel and that it must be qualified in other than the most intimate human associations. When one deals with the affairs of a civilization, one is trying to make the principle of love effective as far as possible, but one cannot escape the conclusion that society as such is brutal, and that the Christian principle may never be more than a leaven in it.[42]

Following up on those observations, *Moral Man and Immoral Society* (1932) remains one of Niebuhr's most significant books. The study owes that status to its investigation of the hypothesis that individuals can be —and even are likely to be—far more moral than human groups, especially as those groups are organized today into modern political states. Thus, if F. Scott Fitzgerald correctly called Amory Blaine a "romantic egotist," Niebuhr argued that the dangers of such individualism were pale by contrast with what emerged when *collective egoism* came to the fore.[43] It could consume the individual, bring good intentions to naught, and unleash global power struggles that endanger every person. Standing beside such might, the contributions of morally or religiously motivated men and women seemed fragile and weak, and yet Niebuhr also believed they can work like leaven and make all the difference. "Realities are always defeating ideals," Niebuhr had written as early as 1919, "but ideals have a way of taking vengeance upon the facts which momentarily imprison them."[44] Perhaps "vengeance" was overly strong, however, for later Niebuhr would note that all too often moral and religious ideals "can be victorious only by snatching victory out of defeat."[45]

As well as any American ever has, Niebuhr understood the nature of human power and aspiration. He discerned the cunning within reason and the irony within history. He recognized that love untempered by justice becomes sentimental and impotent, just as justice without mercy retains a harsh edge that will leave people unreconciled in hatred. He was, as Santayana thought "the American" to be, an idealist working on matter—the matter of history, power politics, and a modernized, industrial, economic order. His realism about human beings was somber enough to suit the most dour of Puritans, but if he was correct in saying that there is "enough original sin in human nature to create opposition" to the substance of the gospel, Niebuhr also found that "there is enough natural grace in the human heart" to respond to that message as well.[46] As Fitzgerald described Amory Blaine, there was "no God in his heart, . . . his ideas were still in riot . . . ."[47] That description might fit many Americans, then and now, but not Niebuhr. He kept confidence in "a Divine Power, whose resources are greater than those of men, and whose suffering love can overcome the corruptions of man's achievements, without negating the significance of our striving."[48]

Niebuhr never counted on religion to be the unifying element in American life. Not only did he recognize that the varieties of our religious and non-religious experience were too extensive for that outcome to occur, he also harbored skepticism about so-called "civil religion," suspecting that it typically legitimated established ways undeserving of the favor. In that respect, Niebuhr had learned from Karl Marx. But he also drew the line where Marx's influence was concerned. Though Niebuhr agreed that religion could be the opium of the people, he stressed that its role could and must be very different. Religion, he believed, was properly a critic of culture. Within America, he affirmed, one of its tasks was to keep attention focused on the personalism that lies at the core of democratic individualism.

The best insights of Western religious and democratic political theory, attested Niebuhr, converge to affirm the sanctity of individual personhood. The religious sensitivity of Americans could provide a much needed leaven, he added, to make that belief a "resource for the highest forms of social realization."[49] For to the extent that any individual or group takes seriously the individual personhood of another, the recognition that respect is owed them receives a boost. Niebuhr helps us to see that religion, though it cannot unify us, remains a vital ingredient in any sound understanding of "why and for what" America exists.

Niebuhr's instinct about America suggested to him a creed that combined competition and cooperation. The energies of individual freedom, he thought, could issue common purposes. Our quarrelsome differences as brothers and sisters might keep driving home the fact that we are one people, if not a family. By communally ensuring each other basic rights to go our own ways, we could stay together on the same way.

Still seeking the covenant so rarely found, Americans need to use the irony within our history as a prod to discover the twists of biblical paradox that Niebuhr also loved to employ: The ones who try to secure their own ways alone are far more likely to lose themselves than those who do their best individually in order to take on the risks of giving their lives for others. Just as coherent individualism requires caring relations that reach far and wide, interdependence is a condition that makes independence possible. Personal initiative that does not serve others impoverishes the communal spirit that gives it birth and vitality.

Each in his own way, Santayana, Dewey, and Niebuhr all hoped that, through our ability and effort, individual Americans could achieve success and thereby reveal the depth of our potential for creating and sharing a true commonwealth, one that would extend even well beyond the borders of American ground. Yet, hopeful though they were about the American future, their optimism also remained rightly guarded by critical—even skeptical—questions. Santayana wondered what the mix of idealism and materialism in American life would be. Dewey pondered whether Americans would use their vast scientific and technological skill for rational moral ends. Niebuhr tried to find the needed ways to make relevant the messages contained in the ancient traditions of Passover and Easter. They all might have affirmed, not only for themselves but also for the nation, what Walt Whitman and F. Scott Fitzgerald would also have found convincing in the words of their American sister, the poet Emily Dickinson (1830–1886), when she wrote, "I dwell in Possibility."[50]

Emily Dickinson knew possibility to be a fickle friend. It guarantees no fortunes; it may spell disaster. If possibility permits glimpses of paradise, only rarely does it tend that way. Yet to dwell in possibility is the ambiguous gift bestowed upon America. If this complex fate means, as Walt Whitman said, "that the fruition of democracy . . . resides altogether in the future,"[51] then American public philosophy can be at least partly derived from the *individualism* discerned by Santayana, the *personalism* Dewey added to it, and from the leavening role of Niebuhr's religious vision, which reminds us that the highest forms of social realization depend not only on the *sanctity* of the individual person's life but also on the *cooperative interdependence* of pluralistic selves.

From this ore, and from other veins that we can mine as well, Americans will not extract utopia, but we can refine public philosophy that revisions "why and for what" America exists. Thereby we will be better prepared to deal with the weapon that Karl Mannheim showed ideology has become. Probing our American ways of life by moving toward public philosophy, we can take steps to ensure both that a human future will remain and that it will not be one of boots stamping on human faces forever. That process entails that more than the becoming should occupy us. The being, the substance of what America has been and is, must grip us equally. For the being informs and even determines what the becoming can possibly be.

NOTES

1. George Orwell, *1984* (New York: New American Library, 1983), p. 220.
2. Walt Whitman, *Democratic Vistas* (New York: The Liberal Arts Press, 1949), p. 2.
3. Ibid., p. 36.
4. Ibid., p. 2.
5. Ibid., p. 1.
6. For insights about *public philosophy*, I am indebted to Robert N. Bellah et al., *Habits of the Heart: Individualism and Commitment in American Life* (Berkeley: University of California Press, 1985), pp. 297–307.
7. Alexis de Tocqueville, *Democracy in America*, ed. J. P. Mayer and trans. George Lawrence (Garden City, N.Y.: Doubleday Anchor, 1969), p. 429.
8. Ibid., p. 429.
9. Ibid., p. 430.
10. Ibid., p. 429.
11. Bellah et al., p. vii.
12. Ibid., especially pp. 20–22, 50–51, 81–84, 138–41, 150–55, 146–47, 277, 281–96.
13. Ibid., p. 282.
14. Ibid., p. 287.
15. Tocqueville, p. 429.
16. Whitman, p. 2.
17. Quoted from Kenneth S. Davis, *The Hero: Charles A. Lindbergh and the American Dream* (Garden City, N.Y.: Doubleday & Company, 1959), pp. 213–14.
18. Reinhold Niebuhr, *Leaves from the Notebook of a Tamed Cynic* (San Francisco: Harper & Row, 1980), p. 143.
19. F. Scott Fitzgerald, *This Side of Paradise* (New York: Charles Scribner's Sons, 1970), p. 256.
20. Quoted from Santayana's "Apologia Pro Mente Sua" (1940). See *The Philosophy of George Santayana*, ed. Paul Arthur Schilpp (New York: Tudor Publishing Company, 1951), p. 603.
21. Fitzgerald, pp. 17–18.
22. George Santayana, *Character and Opinion in the United States* (New York: W. W. Norton, 1967), p. 167.
23. Ibid., p. 168.
24. Ibid., p. 171.
25. Ibid., p. 172.
26. Ibid., p. 174.
27. Ibid., p. 176.
28. Ibid., p. 178.
29. Ibid., p. 187.
30. Ibid., pp. 187–88.

31. Ibid., p. 185.

32. Ibid., p. 175.

33. Ibid., p. 171.

34. Quoted from an address given at Baltimore, Maryland, dated April 18, 1864. See *The Political Thought of Abraham Lincoln*, ed. Richard N. Current (Indianapolis: Bobbs-Merrill, 1967), p. 329. Lincoln's italics.

35. John Dewey, *Individualism Old and New* (New York: Capricorn Books, 1962), p. 32.

36. Ibid., p. 36.

37. Ibid., p. 43.

38. Ibid., p. 50.

39. Ibid., p. 83.

40. Whitman, p. 32. The italics are mine.

41. Reinhold Niebuhr's writings are filled with references to Karl Marx's philosophy and its subsequent Soviet interpretations. He finds merit in Marx's critical insights about the development of capitalism in the nineteenth century, but there is little sympathy for the versions of Marx's theory and practice that Soviet policy from Lenin onward has carried out.

It is worth noting, too, that in 1963 Niebuhr wrote the introduction for a standard collection of Marx's writings on religion. Acknowledging an "original humanistic passion" in Marx's critiques of nineteenth-century religion, Niebuhr nevertheless concluded that "it was from the very beginning too indiscriminate, too lacking in empirical precision, too much the weapon of the 'class struggle' and the instrument of the revolutionary prophet who had transmuted atheism into a new religion. The priests of this religion are now the priest-kings of an empire based on utopian illusions, of a culture in which materialism has become the canonized philosophy. The vaunted affinity between empiricism and materialism has been transmuted into a new dogma." (See Reinhold Niebuhr, Introd., *On Religion* by Karl Marx and Friedrich Engels (New York: Schocken Books, 1971), p. xiv.). Niebuhr spent much of his life disputing Marxist dogma. But doing so, he urged, required continuous self-critical analysis of American democracy as well.

42. Niebuhr, *Leaves*, pp. 196-97.

43. See Fitzgerald, p. 1. See also Reinhold Niebuhr, *Moral Man and Immoral Society* (New York: Charles Scribner's Sons, 1960), p. xii.

44. Niebuhr, *Leaves*, p. 23.

45. Ibid., p. 39.

46. Ibid., p. 41.

47. Fitzgerald, p. 282.

48. Reinhold Niebuhr, *The Children of Light and the Children of Darkness* (New York: Charles Schribner's Sons, 1972), p. 190.

49. Ibid., p. 81.

50. Emily Dickinson, *Further Poems of Emily Dickinson*, ed. Martha Dickinson Bianchi and Alfred Leete Hampton (Boston: Little, Brown, and Company, 1929), p. 30.

51. Whitman, p. 30.

Notes On
The Contributors

GORDON C. BJORK is the Jonathon B. Lovelace professor of economics at Claremont McKenna College. A consultant to government and private corporations, he is also the author of *Private Enterprise and Public Interest: The Development of American Capitalism* and *Life, Liberty, and Property: The Economics and Politics of Land Use Planning and Environmental Controls.*

DOUGLAS J. DEN UYL is associate professor of philosophy at Bellarmine College. Especially interested in ethics and political philosophy, he has published extensively on these topics in numerous journals and books.

P. EDWARD HALEY is director of the Keck Center for International Strategic Studies, chairman of the International Relations Committee, and professor of political science at Claremont McKenna College. His books on United States foreign policy and international affairs include *Revolution and Intervention; Congress and the Fall of South Vietnam and Cambodia; Qaddaffi and the United States Since 1969;* and *Nuclear Strategy, Arms Control, and the Future.*

MORTON A. KAPLAN is professor of political science and director of the Center for Strategic and Foreign Policy Studies at the University of Chicago. Frequent consultant to government on foreign policy questions, he is also the author of more than twenty books. Two significant examples are *Strategic Thinking and Its Moral Implications* and *Science, Language and the Human Condition.*

TIBOR R. MACHAN, senior fellow of the Reason Foundation, has taught philosophy in the New York and California state university systems, at Franklin College, Lugano, Switzerland, and the University of San Diego. In addition to the many articles he writes for scholarly journals and popular periodicals, Machan has authored numerous books, among them *Human Rights and Human Liberties* and *The Main Debate: Marxism Versus Capitalism.*

DOUGLAS B. RASMUSSEN is associate professor of philosophy at St. John's University. He is co-editor of *The Philosophic Thought of Ayn Rand,* and his articles have appeared in *The Personalist, Modern Age,* and other important journals. Currently he is writing *Towards a Philosophy of Freedom,* a work in social and political ethics.

ANDREW J. RECK is professor and chairman, Department of Philosophy, and director of the Master of Liberal Arts program at Tulane University. Internationally recognized as an expert on American thought, he is the author of *Recent American Philosophy; Introduction to William James;* and *Speculative Philosophy.* His edition of George Herbert Mead's *Selected Writings* was reissued by the University of Chicago Press in 1981.

JOHN K. ROTH is the Russell K. Pitzer professor of philosophy at Claremont McKenna College. A specialist in American philosophy and religion, he has been Fulbright lecturer in American Studies at the University of Innsbruck, Austria. He has also served as visiting professor of philosophy at Doshisha University, Kyoto, Japan. Among his publications on life in the United States are *The American Religious Experience* (with Frederick Sontag); *The American Dream* (with Robert H. Fossum); and *American Dreams*.

ROBERT C. WHITTEMORE is professor of philosophy and director of American studies at Tulane University. His prolific writings on various topics in metaphysics, philosophical theology, and intellectual history include books entitled *Makers of the American Mind* and *American Puritan Calvinism*.

Index

Index

Acheson, Dean 219, 226
Ackerman, Bruce A. 112
Adams, James Truslow 237
Adams, John 90-92, 95 (18), 96 (31)
Aiken, Henry D. 50, 58, 59, 67 (2),
    68 (33)
Alexander 75
Alger, Horatio 163
America
    economy and 99-179
    philosophy and 13-96
    the world and 183-251
    developments, early 20-23
    future 229-251
    ideology in 99-119, 211-228
    origins of ideology in 159-166
    rejection of ideology in 111-113
anti-communism. See communism
Apter, David E. 43, 95 (5)
Aquinas. See Thomas Aquinas
Aristotle 15, 22, 62, 65, 77, 79, 90-92,
    95 (8), 96 (38), 118 (31), 131, 141 (16)
Arrow, Kenneth 168, 179 (33)
Arthur, C.J. 41 (37)
Augustine 15
Austin, Hudson 186
Austin, J.L. 70 (43), 71 (43, 45)
authority 129-133

Bacon, Francis 16-17, 38 (3), 135
Bailyn, Bernard 39 (17), 67 (1)
Bambrough, Renford 141 (13)
Baudelaire, Charles 142 (18)
Bauer, Bruno 41 (35)
Bauer, Edgar 41 (35)
belief system 48, 55-59, 76, 102, 147,
    158, 185, 214, 217, 218, 220, 224,
    227, 234
Bell, Daniel 34, 35, 43 (69)
Bellah, Robert N. 235, 236, 249 (6, 11)
Bentham, Jeremy 25, 169
Bergson, Henri 32
Berkeley, George 39 (19)
Berle, Adolf 167
Betts, Richard K. 209 (7)
Beum, Robert 142 (18)
Bianchi, Martha Dickinson 251 (60)
Billet, L. 117 (13)
biology 26, 31

Bjork, Gordon 143 (30), 145-179, 177
    (2, 4, 8, 12, 14), 178 (17, 22, 25, 31)
Bondy, François 122
Bonnet, Charles 39 (23)
Boulding, Kenneth 175, 179 (48)
Bowie, Russell 237, 238
Bradley, Francis Herbert 32
Brenkert, George G. 141 (2)
Brown, Gerry 175
Brzezinski, Zbigniew 208
Buchanan, James 112, 172, 173,
    179 (40, 42)
Burke, Edmund 25

Caesar 75
Calhoun, John C. 21-23, 33, 40 (30-31)
Campbell, R.H. 116 (5)
capitalism 26-28, 104, 116 (1), 125, 126,
    134, 148, 157, 159, 163, 164, 168,
    222, 257
Carey, Henry 161
Carlsnaes, Walter 43
Carnegie, Andrew 161, 163, 218
Carson, Rachel 174, 179 (44)
Carter, Jimmy 175, 208
Cerf, Walter 41 (43)
Chamberlin, Edward H. 165
Chandler, A.D. 178 (20)
Chandler, H.W. 69 (40)
change, economic growth and 150-159
change, view of 148-150
Cheit, Earl F. 178 (29)
Chugerman, Samuel 43 (63)
Churchill, Winston 185
Cicero 77, 78, 81, 83, 84, 90, 92,
    95 (9, 16), 96 (28)
Ciesckowski, August von 41 (35)
Clausewitz, Karl von 190
Coard, Bernard 186
Coase, Ronald H. 172, 179 (41)
cognition 61-65
collectivism 133-135, 142 (18)
colonialism 7, 80-83, 85, 87, 93, 153,
    161, 192, 199
commitment 36, 49, 54, 56, 186, 225,
    234, 236, 241
Commoner, Barry 174, 179 (46)
Commons, John R. 161
commonwealth 81-84

communism, U.S. foreign policy and 190-193, 207
Communist party. See political parties
community 26, 220-224, 234, 236, 239, 243, 246, 247
Condillac, Etienne Bonnot de 19, 39 (19)
conceptual scheme 51, 53-63, 68, 217
concurrent majority. See majority
conscience 24, 25, 34, 36
conservatism 24, 28, 29, 33, 75
Cooke, Jacob E. 177 (15), 178 (16)
corporations 83, 84, 153, 154, 161, 162, 167, 168, 176-178, 189, 242, 243
Cralle, Richard K. 40 (29)
Crèvecoeur, Hector St. John de 100, 116 (7)
Cromwell, Oliver 63
Cunningham, R.L. 142 (25)
Current, Richard N. 250 (34)

Darwin, Charles 26, 27, 163
Darwinism, social 25-34
Das Adam Smith Problem 102-119
Davie, Maurice 42 (49)
Davis, Kenneth S. 249 (17)
De George, R.T. 142 (18)
Declaration of Independence, The 47, 48, 161, 219, 225
democracy 7, 33, 35, 84, 87, 89, 90, 185, 186, 219, 233, 244
Democratic party. See political parties
Den Uyl, Douglas L. 7, 99-119, 255
Descartes, René 16, 61, 69 (35), 134
Destutt, Antoine Louis 40 (25). See also Tracy, Antoine Destutt de
Dewey, John 32, 79, 95 (11), 238, 241-243, 247, 250 (35)
Dickinson, Emily 247, 251 (50)
Diderot, Denis 19, 39 (22)
Diem, Ngo Dinh 200
Drucker, H.M. 44
Duane 21
Dulles, John Foster 193, 194, 199, 209 (9-11)
duty 220, 221, 224-226
Dwight, Timothy 21

economics
    Public Choice 172, 173, 179
    welfare 168-170, 219
economy
    government and 155-159, 168-174
    ideology and 99-179

education 150-152; labor force and 166-167
Edwards, Jonathan 21
Ehrlich, Paul 174, 179 (45)
Eidelberg, Paul 96 (30)
Eisenhower Administration 193-200
Eisenhower, Dwight D. 191-201, 206, 207
Ellison, Ralph 5, 8-9 (1-2)
Elster, Jon 116 (4)
Ely, Richard T. 161
Emancipation Proclamation 224
empiricism 15-19, 62, 63, 69, 159, 250
Engels, Friedrich 41 (35, 37), 49, 215, 250 (41)
ethics, business 118 (34)
evolution 26, 30-33, 125, 161-164

fascism 6, 48, 75, 190
Feuer, Lewis S. 44
Feuerbach, Ludwig 24, 41 (35), 222
Feyerabend, Paul 53, 54, 68 (19-21)
Fichte, Johann Gottlieb 41 (43), 50
Fiske, John 26
Fitzgerald, F. Scott 238, 239, 245, 247, 249 (19), 250 (47)
Ford, Henry 218
foreign policy, United States 183-210; communism and 190-193, 207, 217, 218
Franklin, Benjamin 158
Frazer, Aleander Campdell 39 (13)
freedom 26, 80, 81, 93, 147, 222, 223
Freud, Sigmund 171
Friedman, Milton 170, 171, 179 (35, 38)
Fuchs, Victor 177 (13)
future, American 229-251

Gaddis, John Lewis 209 (6)
Galbraith, John Kenneth 164, 178 (28)
Geertz, Clifford 76, 95 (5)
Gelb, Leslie H. 209 (7)
George, Henry 161
Gibson, Roger F. 67 (15)
Gilder, George 103-107, 116 (9), 117 (11, 12), 118 (30), 171, 179 (39)
Gilpatric, Roswell 205
Gilson, Etienne 62
God 15, 18, 78, 79, 231, 245, 246
government
    economy and 155-159, 168-174
    mixed 89-92
    of laws 77-81
    popular 84-88

Griffin, David Ray 38 (9)
Guegen, John A. 116 (3)
Gumplowicz, Ludwig 29

Haack, Susan 71 (43)
Habakkuk, H.J. 178 (19)
Haig, Alexander 208
Haldane 69 (35)
Haley, P. Edward 7, *183-210*, 209 (3), *255*
Hamilton, Alexander 33, 155
Hampton, Alfred Leete 251 (50)
Harrington, James 19 (17, 18), 83, 219
Harrington, Michael 142 (18)
Harris, H.S. 41 (43)
Hayek, F.A. 134-138, 142 (20, 25, 27)
Heath, Douglas Denon 38 (8)
Hegel, George Wilhelm Friedrich
    23-25, 40 (33, 35, 43, 45), 50,
    213-216, 222, 232
Heidegger, Martin 55
Heilbroner, Robert 178 (29)
Helvétius, Claude Adrien 39 (23)
Hess, Moses 41 (35)
Hitler, Adolf 223
Hobbes, Thomas 135, 138, 141 (9)
Ho Chi Minh 206
Hofstadter, Richard 178 (26)
Holbach, Paul von 39 (23)
Hollis, M. 116 (4)
Hook, Sidney 179 (34)
Hoopes, Townsend 192, 209 (8)
Hospers, John 141 (11)
human nature 57, 58, 102-114, 126, 137,
    138, 147, 152, 246
human rights. *See* rights
Hume, David 108, 110, 117 (24, 26)
Hurst, Willard 177 (9)

idealism 213, 214, 226, 239, 240
ideology
    America's place in the world and
        183-251
    American 99-119; origins of 159-166
    American economy and 99-179
    American philosophy and 13-96
    contemporary 166-176
    denotation of 35
    evolution of 161-164
    new 164-166
    objectivity and 45-71
    philosophy and 48-50
    political theory and 45-71
    rejection of 111-113

republican 73-96
    utopia and 34-35
idols 16, 17
inalienable rights. *See* rights
individualism 124-127, 138-139, 150-152
Indochina conflict 193-206
intervention 186-208, 210, 226

James, William 238
Jefferson, Thomas 21, 76, 79, 91, 158,
    218, 233
Johnson, Harry M. 95 (4)
Johnson, Lyndon 169, 201
Johnson, M. Bruce 119 (37)
Jowett, Benjamin 95 (8)
Julliard, Jacques 80, 95 (13)
justice 105-107, 139, 216, 240, 245

Kant, Immanuel 49, 50, 52, 61-65,
    67 (5), 110
Kaplan, Morton A. 7, 44, 76, 118 (36),
    211-228, 228 (2, 4-7), *255*
Keller, Albert 42 (49)
Kemp, Jack 171
Kennan, George F. 191, 193, 209 (6)
Kennedy Administration 200-206
Kennedy, Emmet 20, 40 (25, 27)
Kennedy, J.F. 169, 192, 193, 200-207,
    226
Keyes, Clinton Walker 95 (9)
Keynes, John Maynard 164
Kierkegaard, Søren 25
Kirk, Russell 142 (18)
Kirkpatrick, Jeane 209 (2)
Kissinger, Henry 208
knowledge
    contemporary view of 51-55
    sociology of 55-57
Knox, T.M. 40 (33)
Kroner, Richard 25, 41 (45)
Kuznets, Simon 178 (21)

La Mettrie, Julien Offray de 39 (23)
labor force
    education and 166
    mobility of 150-153
    values and 166-167
Lafayette, Marquis de 21
Laffer, Arthur 171
Lawrence, George 249 (7)
laws, government of 77-81
Lebergott, Stanley 177 (11), 178 (18)
Leden, W. von 142 (22)

Lenin, V.I. 250 (41)
liberty 7, 22, 26, 80, 81, 84, 93, 102,
    104, 106, 107, 150, 160-162, 176,
    185, 240, 241
Lichtheim, George 44
Lincoln, Abraham 185, 241, 250 (34)
Lindberg, Charles A. 237
Little, I.M.D. 178 (32)
Locke, John 17-21, 38 (11), 39 (13, 19),
    127, 141 (10), 142 (22), 160, 169,
    170, 171, 176
Lukas, S. 116 (4)

Machan, Tibor R. 7, 71 (49), 119 (37),
    121-143, 141 (10, 12), 142 (17, 21),
    255
Machiavelli, Niccolo 90
MacIntyre, Alasdair 44, 86, 96 (22), 141
    (6)
Maddison, Angus 177 (7)
Madison, James 177 (15), 218
majority, concurrent 21-23
majority rule 224
Malthus, Thomas Robert 25
Mandeville, Bernard de 220
Mannheim, Karl 34, 43 (68), 76, 95 (6),
    215, 230, 231, 232, 248
Mansel, Henry 63, 69 (40)
Mao Zedong 191
Marcuse, Herbert 164
Marris, Robin 178 (30)
Marshall, Alfred 172
Marx, Karl 24, 25, 34, 41 (35-38), 49,
    50, 57, 66, 76, 137, 141 (1-5, 7), 142
    (18), 154, 163, 177 (1), 213, 222, 228
    (1), 231, 233, 237, 250 (41)
Marxism 68 (30, 31), 92, 102, 116 (1, 3),
    124-128, 147, 177, 213-217, 237,
    244, 246
materialism 30, 36, 239, 240, 257
matter 30, 31
McCloskey, Robert 178 (26)
McGarr, Lionel 202
McKeon, Richard 95 (8)
McLellan, D. 141 (1, 3)
McNamara, James 201, 205
Means, Gardiner C. 167
Mellos, Koula 116 (3)
Mill, John Stuart 54, 169, 172
Mitchell, Basil 57, 68 (32)
mobility of labor force 150-153, 166-167
monetary theory. See theory
Montague, Basil 38 (4)

Montesquieu, Michel Eyquem de 80,
    85, 95 (12, 19)
"moral dualism" 107-111
morality 129-133
Moravi, Sergio 40 (24)
Morgan, J.P. 161
Mueller, Dennis 178 (30)
Munitz, Milton K. 52, 67 (6, 16)
Munn v. Illinois 178 (25)
Murphy, G. 178 (24)
Mussolini, Benito 46, 47

Napoleon Bonaparte 20, 40 (27)
National Socialism 75, 138
natural world, science and 174-176
Navarre, Henri 194, 209 (12)
Newton, Isaac 157
Niebuhr, Reinhold 244-247, 249 (18),
    238, 250 (41-46, 48-49)
Nietzsche, Friedrich 50
Nixon, Richard M. 78, 207, 208
North, D.C. 177 (2)
Norton, David L. 142 (28)
Novak, Michael 116 (7), cover
Nozick, Robert 142 (26)

O'Meara, Dominic J. 118 (27)
objectivity
    ideology and 45-71
    political theory and 57-65
Ockham, William of 128
O'Daniel, John 194
Okun, Arthur 179 (37)
optimism 148, 225, 231, 237-240, 247
Orwell, George 231, 249 (1)
Owens, Joseph 69 (35)

Paine, Thomas 95 (10)
Palmer, Elihu 21, 40 (28)
Palmer, R.R. 96 (25)
Parekh, Bhikhu 142 (19)
Parson, Talcott 77, 95 (7)
patriotism 85, 86, 225, 237
perception 49-51
persons 59, 123-140, 142, 147, 151, 166,
    167, 214, 222, 223, 244
personalism 244, 247
Phelps, William Lyon 42 (58)
philosophy
    antecedents of, ideology and 13-44
    ideology and 13-96
    public 229-251
Picavet, François 40 (24)

Pichler, J.A. 142 (18)
Plato 15, 38 (1), 76, 80, 82, 89, 111, 137
Plotinus 15
pluralism 5-8, 36, 123, 135, 193, 247
Pocock, J.G.A. 95 (17), 96 (36)
Polanyi, Michael 69 (37), 177 (5)
political parties
  Communist 190-195, 200, 203-208, 217, 218
  Democratic 172, 218
  Republican 34, 166, 175, 218
political theory 47, 67-90
  ideology and 45-71
  objectivity and 57-65
"pollution" 119 (37)
Polybius 79, 89, 90-92, 96 (27)
Poole, Robert W. 119 (37)
Popper, Karl R. 51
pragmatic attitude 7, 111-113, 118 (33), 227
Price, Richard 95 (14)
Priestley, Joseph 81, 95 (15)
privacy 7, 127-133, 152, 153, 159, 160, 167, 176-178
property 7, 81-84, 93, 112, 122, 124-140, 147, 152-155, 159, 160, 166, 167, 176-179
  nature of 127-128
  rights 121-143, 152-155, 167-168
Public Choice. See economics
public philosophy 229-251

Quine, Willard Van Orman 51-53, 67 (7-14, 17)

Ramsey, Paul 42 (46)
Rand, Ayn 69 (37, 41), 141 (11)
Ransom, R.L. 177 (6)
Rasmussen, Douglas B. 6, 45-71, 69 (38), 70 (43), 71 (49), 255
Rasmussen, Wayne D. 177 (3)
rationality 102, 104, 106-110, 113, 124, 129, 130, 134-147, 140, 168, 232, 242
Rawls, John 112, 169, 170, 179 (36), 228 (4)
Reagan, Ronald 101, 112, 158, 208, 226
realism 6, 16, 23, 30, 34-36, 51-53, 60-65, 68, 69, 213, 246
Reck, Andrew J. 6, 96 (25), 73-96, 118 (36), 219, 255
relativism 46, 226
religion 19, 24, 41, 150, 151, 159, 160, 163, 225, 246, 257
republic 33, 77-80, 84-93, 220

republican ideology 73-96
Republican party. See political parties
republicanism 21, 22, 75-94, 219
Ricardo, David 161
Ridgeway, Matthew B. 196-198, 202, 210 (19)
rights
  human 27, 47, 48, 128, 186, 187
  inalienable 7, 27, 47, 48, 58, 59, 63, 185
  natural 128-129
  property 152-155; 167-168
Rockefeller, John D. 161, 218
Rohden, Peter Richard 95 (1)
Rommen, Heinrich A. 128, 141 (8)
Roosevelt, Franklin Delano 28, 34, 101, 112, 218, 226
Rorty, Richard 54, 55, 68 (25, 27)
Ross 69 (35)
Rostow, Walt 202, 203
Roth, John K. 3-9, 118 (36), 229-251, 255
Rousseau, Jean-Jacques 19, 86, 39 (21)
Royce, Josiah 238
Rubenstein, Richard L. 5
Ruge, Arnold 41 (35)
Rusk, Dean 201
Russman, Thomas S. 69 (38)

Samuelson, Paul A. 169, 179 (34)
Santayana, George 238-241, 247, 249 (20, 22)
Scheiber, Harry N. 177 (10)
Schelling, Friedrich Wilhelm Joseph von 41 (43)
Schilpp, Paul Arthur 249 (20)
Schmidt, Karl 41 (35)
Schumacher, E.F. 175, 179 (47)
Schumpeter, Joseph 168
science 29-34, 48, 49, 51-54, 151, 158, 159, 174-176, 242, 243
  natural world and 174-176
Seigen, B. 118 (33)
self-determination 80, 81
self-interest
  Adam Smith and 102-105
  American ideology and 99-119
Seliger, Martin 44
Sherburne, Donald W. 38 (9)
Shils, Edward 15, 22, 23, 36, 38 (2), 40 (32), 95 (3, 6), 209 (1), 217, 228 (3)
Sidney, Algernon 88, 96 (26)
Sills, David L. 38 (2), 76, 95 (2), 229 (3)
Skinner, A.S. 116 (5)
slavery 22, 123, 153, 225

Smith, Adam 102-115, 116 (1, 2, 5, 6, 9, 10), 117 (12, 14, 18), 118 (28), 125, 156, 157, 160-162, 173, 220
Smith, R. 179 (43)
social theory, Lester Frank Ward's 29-34
socialism 27, 32, 33, 134, 138, 159, 168, 170
society, decent 121-143
sociology of knowledge, ideology and 55-57
Socrates 15, 16
sovereignty 78, 84-88, 170
Spain, August O. 40 (31)
Spedding, James 38 (3, 8)
Spencer, Herbert 26, 30, 31, 163
Sperry, Roger W. 141 (15)
Stalin, Joseph 192
Stein, Jay W. 40 (24)
Stepelevich, Lawrence S. 41 (36)
Stiner, Max 41 (35, 38)
Strauss, David Friedrich 41 (35, 38)
Strauss, Leo 140, 142 (29)
Stubblebine, W.C. 179 (43)
Summers, Harry 198, 209 (4)
Sumner, William Graham 25-28, 42 (52, 58), 163
"supply side" 116 (8)
Sutch, R. 177 (6)

Taylor, Maxwell 203, 204
technology 7, 154, 174-176, 222
Teich, M. 68 (28)
Teichgraeder, R. 117 (13)
theory
  monetary 170-173, 179
  political 47, 87-90
Thomas Aquinas 61, 62, 69 (36, 39)
Thomas, R.P. 177 (2)
Tocqueville, Alexis de 249 (7, 15), 235, 236
Toland, John 95 (18)
Tollison, R. 179 (42)
Tonelson, Alan 209 (2)
Tracy, Antoine Destutt de 20, 21, 23, 24, 40 (25-27), 48, 49, 56, 60, 67 (14), 116 (3), 232. See also Destutt, Antoine Louis
transcendental turn 34, 35, 49, 50, 61-64
Trigg, Roger 52, 64, 65, 67 (18), 68 (28), 71 (44, 48)
Truman, Harry S. 191, 192, 201, 206-208, 219, 226

truth 16, 48, 85, 86, 88, 91, 103-105, 219
Tullock, Gordon 172, 173, 179 (40, 42)
Turner, Frederick Jackson 160, 178 (23)

Ullian, J.S. 67 (13)
United States foreign policy 183-210
Utopia, ideology and 34-35

Valone, James 118 (36)
values, labor force and 166-167
Veatch, Henry B. 68 (23), 109, 118 (27)
Veblen, Thorstein 164, 178 (27)
Voltaire, François Marie Arouet de 19, 39 (20)

Walker, Leslie J. 96 (29)
Wanniski, Jude 172
Ward, Justus 42 (59)
Ward, Lester Frank 29-34, 42 (59), 43 (60-65)
Ward, Silence Rolph 42 (59)
Washington Institute for Values in Public Policy, The 5
welfare. See economics
Whitehead, Alfred North 15, 16, 38 (9), 32, 39 (12)
Whitman, Walt 249 (2, 16), 250 (40), 233, 237, 240, 244, 251 (51)
Whittemore, Robert C. 3-9, 13-44, 41 (44), 256
Will, George 142 (18)
Wirth, Louis 43 (68), 95 (6)
Wittgenstein 50, 53, 71 (43)
Wood, Gordon S. 91, 96 (37)
world, ideology and the 183-251

Young, R. 56, 57, 68 (28)

Zellner, A. 178 (24)